W.H. Davenport Adams

Egypt Past and Present

Described and illustrated: with a narrative of its occupation by the British, and of

recent events in the Soudan

W.H. Davenport Adams

Egypt Past and Present
Described and illustrated: with a narrative of its occupation by the British, and of recent events in the Soudan

ISBN/EAN: 9783337231705

Printed in Europe, USA, Canada, Australia, Japan

Cover: Foto ©ninafisch / pixelio.de

More available books at **www.hansebooks.com**

EGYPT
PAST AND PRESENT.

KHARTOUM. *Page 83.*

THOMAS NELSON AND SONS,
London, Edinburgh, and New York.

EGYPT

PAST AND PRESENT

Described and Illustrated.

WITH A NARRATIVE OF ITS OCCUPATION BY THE
BRITISH, AND OF RECENT EVENTS IN
THE SOUDAN.

By

W. H. DAVENPORT ADAMS.

With 100 Illustrations.

London:
T. NELSON AND SONS, PATERNOSTER ROW.
EDINBURGH; AND NEW YORK.

1894

Preface.

F Egypt presents no other attractions, the certainty, says Sir Gardner Wilkinson, that it is the oldest State of which we have any positive and tangible records, must awaken feelings of interest to which no contemplative mind can remain indifferent. The most remote point in its annals to which its extant monuments refer us, opens with a nation possessing all the arts of civilized life already matured; but though stretching so far back into the early history of the world, we still find the infancy of the Egyptian State is placed far beyond our reach. All we know is, that it was far advanced in all those arts and sciences which contribute so greatly to the comfort and adornment of social life—that it had a profound creed, a consummate polity, a fixed government, and immense material resources at an epoch when Jacob and his sons were pasturing their flocks in the land of Canaan.

But not only is the history of Egypt a theme of the highest interest in itself, and in its relations to the general history of the world, the remains which exist of its tombs, temples, palaces, and monuments are neither less valuable nor less important. The architectural memorials of Greece and Rome may exhibit a more aesthetic feeling, but they can never claim the consideration from the philosopher or the student which he will always pay to those of Ancient Egypt. Our knowledge of Greek and Roman life is chiefly obtained from other sources; our knowledge of Egyptian life can be derived only from the Egyptian sculpture or painting on the walls of the tomb, palace, and temple. From this sculpture, from this painting it is that we learn how high a standard of civilization had been attained by at least *one* great nation in those ages of the world which seem to the ignorant to belong to its very infancy. And we know that to this strange and mysterious nation Greece owed much of her highest philosophy as well as of her scientific resources; that Rome borrowed from Greece; and that through both Rome and Greece the West has been permeated with the influence originally springing from the "Land of the Nile."

But besides her history and her antiquities, Egypt offers us for study her abundant animal life, her sad and solemn scenery. Above all, she offers to us whatever of romance, and mystery, and beauty—of grandeur and sublimity—is associated with the great river of the Old World, the ever-famous Nile.

It is not a matter of wonder, then, that Egypt has attracted the attention of so many travellers, or that so copious a literature has sprung up in reference to its history, religion, art, science, and industry. It is scarcely a matter of wonder, that, bewitched and beguiled by the romance of their subject, so many writers have wandered into a region of dreams and visions, and evolved out of their own consciousness an Ancient Egypt which never existed—a grand historical panorama based on no solid foundations. And it is not a matter of wonder that every year adds to the host of travellers, historians, and philosophical speculators, who concern themselves with a land which never wearies the fancy, and with antiquities which offer—now as always—an inexhaustible field for the most ingenious conjectures.

To the literature of which we speak the present volume, however, is a very modest contribution; and whatever value it possesses, we cheerfully acknowledge, will be due to the works of our predecessors. It has not been our object to draw up a record of personal experiences—of books of this kind surely the world has had enough—but to bring together, within the compass of a moderate number of pages, the principal *facts* on which the great majority of critics seem to have agreed in connection with the history and monuments of Egypt. We have endeavoured to look coldly on the sanguine speculations of enthusiastic Egyptologists, and, so far as our design allowed, to keep within the most precise limits of actual and positive knowledge. How easy it is to err in dealing, however slightly, with Egyptian history, civilization, or religion, the critic will not fail to be aware; and this circumstance will probably induce him to judge with some indulgence a manual which, in so small a compass, presumes to deal with such extended subjects. At all events, we have not made a single statement except on what has seemed to us good authority; and we venture to believe that in no other volume of equally humble pretensions has there been brought together so much exact information on the past and present of the "Land of the Nile." So that the reader who has neither leisure nor inclination to consult the weighty volumes of English, French, and German Egyptologists, may be glad to turn for reference to the following pages; while to the young student it is hoped they will be found useful, as an introduction to a wide, an important, and a specially interesting study.

It remains only to be added, that the Illustrations are from authentic sources, and, in the main, are executed, not only with fidelity, but with artistic feeling; that we have prefixed a copious list of authorities on Egyptian subjects; and that a brief account of the Suez Canal is furnished in an Appendix.

> " Go, little booke; God send thee good passage,
> And specially let this be thy prayere,
> Unto them all that thee will read or heare,
> When thou art wrong, after their help to call,
> Thee to correct in any part, or all."

W. H. D. A.

List of Illustrations.

General Gordon,	*Frontispiece*
Khartûm,	*Vignette*
Map of the Nile Valley,	15
A Landscape in the Delta,	21
A Sacred Dance,	28
Scene on the Nile,	31
Date Palms,	34
The Sacred Ibis,	35
The Egyptian Vulture,	36
Group of Rosy Flamingoes,	37
Caravan assailed by the Khamsin,	39
Mount Sinai,	45
Tirhakah, King of Egypt (from the Monuments),	54
Herodotus (from an ancient bust),	57
Alexander the Great (from Canini's Iconografia),	61
Ptolemy Soter (Visconti's Iconographie Grecque),	62
Ptolemy Philopater (from Visconti),	63
Ptolemy Euergetes (from Visconti),	63
Julius Caesar (from Visconti),	65
Marcus Antonius (from Visconti),	66
Cleopatra (from Visconti),	66
Germanicus (from a Medal in the Florentine Museum),	68
Zenobia (from a Medal in the Florentine Museum),	69
The Emperor Aurelian (from a Medal in the Florentine Museum),	70
Massacre of the Mamelukes,	73
View of St. Jean d'Acre,	77
Khartûm,	81
Korosko,	85
Suakim,	101
Berber (from the Desert),	109
A Landscape on the Nile,	115
The Murchison Falls on the Nile,	121
Statue of the Nile (in the Vatican Museum),	128
A Papyrus Shallop,	128
Crocodiles of the Nile,	131
The Mystic Ferry-Boat,	133
Ancient Pharos at Alexandria,	135
Alexandria (before the Bombardment),	137
Arab Women in the Streets of Alexandria,	140
Pompey's Pillar,	147
Cairo,	153
Tombs of Khalifs, and Citadel of Cairo,	158
Mosque of the Sultan Hassan at Cairo,	159

Muezzin announcing the Hour of Prayer,	161
A Street in Cairo,	163
A Dancing Dervish,	164
The Ass-Drivers of Cairo,	165
The Pyramids,	170
Diagram,	173
Ancient Egyptian Mode of Conveying Stones,	173
Section of the Great Pyramid of Ghizeh,	175
Cartouche of Shufu,	177
The Pyramid of Chephren, and the Sphinx,	179
The Serapéion, Memphis,	193
Bronzes of the Egyptian god Apis,	195
Balm of Gilead,	199
The Obelisk,	200
Cartouche of Thothmes III.,	201
Dahabeeyah, or Nile-Boat,	203
The Sakia, or Egyptian Water-Wheel,	207
A View of Minyeh,	211
Beni-Hassan: Neoothph's Tomb (Exterior),	213
Beni-Hassan: Neoothph's Tomb (Interior),	214
Egyptian Spinning; Egyptians Weaving,	215
Egyptian Potter,	215
Brick-Makers (from a Tomb at Beni-Hassan),	217
Scene at Siout,	219
Propylon of the Temple at Dendera,	221
Temple at Dendera,	223
Isis or Athor, with the infant Horus,	225
Amun-Ra, the Sun-God,	229
The Rameseion of Thebes, and Colossal Statue of Rameses,	237
Operations of a Siege,	241
The Colossi, or Ramessids,	243
The Colossi during an Inundation,	245
The Thothmeseion at Medinet-Aboo, Thebes,	247
Bab-el Melook, or Valley of the Tombs of the King, Thebes,	249
Egyptian Masons,	257
Ruins at Karnak,	259
Propylon at Karnak,	261
Great Court and Obelisk of Karnak,	262
River-View of Luxor,	265
The Ramessids at Luxor,	269
The Trochilus, or Crocodile Bird,	275
Judgment of Souls, and their Future Destiny (from the Sarcophagus of Alexander),	282
Temple of Noum and Athor, at Edfoo,	284
Temple of Arveris, at Koum Ombos,	289
Distant View of the Island of Philae,	297
Temple of Isis, Island of Philae,	301
Horus, Isis, and Osiris,	303
Temple of Osiris at Philae,	304
Temple Court at Philae,	305
First Cataract of the Nile,	315
Portrait of Mehemet Ali,	321
Romano-Egyptian Temple at Dendour	326
Sacred Scarabaeus of the Egyptians,	327
Temple of Osiris, Ipsambûl,	336
Interior of Temple of Osiris, Ipsambûl,	337
A Ramessid at Ipsambûl,	338
Temple of Isis at Ipsambûl,	340
View of the Second Cataract from the Rock of Abou-Seir,	345
Temple of Amun-Ra, Soleb,	347
Temple at Meroë,	350
Chart of the Suez Canal,	366

Contents.

BOOK FIRST.

CHAPTER I.
INTRODUCTORY:—THE BOUNDARIES, SOIL, DIVISIONS, AND CHIEF TOWNS OF EGYPT, ... 17

CHAPTER II.
A SKETCH OF EGYPTIAN HISTORY, ANCIENT AND MODERN, 41

CHAPTER III.
THE RISE AND COURSE OF THE RIVER NILE, ... 114

BOOK SECOND.

CHAPTER I.
ALEXANDRIA—POMPEY'S PILLAR—CLEOPATRA'S NEEDLES, .. 134

CHAPTER II.
CAIRO: ITS MOSQUES—THE CITADEL—THE PYRAMIDS—THE SPHINX—HELIOPOLIS, AND ITS OBELISKS, ... 152

CHAPTER III.
BENI-HASSAN, AND THE TOMBS—ANTINOOPOLIS—SIOUT—GIRGEH—DENDERA, AND ITS TEMPLE, ... 205

CHAPTER IV.
THEBES: ITS HISTORY—THE RAMESEION—THE AMUNOPHEION—THE COLOSSI—THE THOTHMESEION—THE PALACE OF RAMESES—THE TOMBS OF THE KINGS—MEDINET-ABOO—LUXOR—KARNAK—THE THEBAID, ... 227

BOOK THIRD.

CHAPTER I.

ESNEH—THE ALMEHS, OR DANCING GIRLS—'EILYTHIA: THE ROCK TOMBS—EDFOO, AND ITS TEMPLE—SILSILEH, AND ITS QUARRIES—KOUM OMBOS, ... 273

CHAPTER II.

ASSOUAN, OR SYENE—ITS ANCIENT CELEBRITY—ITS QUARRIES—ISLAND OF ELEPHANTINE—TEMPLE OF KNEPH—ISLAND OF PHILAE—TEMPLE OF ISIS—OTHER MEMORIALS—SACRED CHARACTER OF PHILAE—ITS TRIAD: OSIRIS, ISIS, AND HORUS, ... 291

CHAPTER III.

THE FIRST CATARACT—HOW ITS ASCENT IS ACCOMPLISHED—THE SHEIKH AND HIS MEN, ... 312

BOOK FOURTH.

CHAPTER I.

NUBIA: ITS BOUNDARIES AND EXTENT—ITS ANNALS—CHARACTER OF ITS INHABITANTS—NATURAL RESOURCES—PRINCIPAL TOWNS, .. 317

CHAPTER II.

KALABSCHÉ—DENDOUR—GHIRSCHÉ HOUSSEYN—ITS TEMPLE—DAKKEH—VALLEY OF THE LIONS—IPSAMBÛL, ... 322

CHAPTER III.

GEBEL-ADHA—WADY HALFÂ—THE SECOND CATARACT—THE TEMPLE OF SOLEB—MEROË, AND ITS ANTIQUITIES—RUINS AT NAJA AND EL-MESAOURAT—THE SACRED BOAT, ... 343

CHAPTER IV.

THE LIBYAN OASES—THEIR EXPLORERS—THE GREAT OASIS—THE LITTLE OASIS—SIWAH, THE NORTHERN OASIS—THEIR ANTIQUITIES, AND ORACLES, ... 356

APPENDIX.

THE SUEZ CANAL, ... 365
ON THE EGYPTIAN HIEROGLYPHICS, ... 370
THE RAMESSIDS, ... 374

INDEX, ... 375

MAP OF THE NILE VALLEY.

EGYPT PAST AND PRESENT.

Book First.

CHAPTER I.

INTRODUCTORY :—THE BOUNDARIES, SOIL, DIVISIONS, AND CHIEF TOWNS OF EGYPT.

A land where all things always seem the same.
TENNYSON.

F all the countries of the old Roman Empire, Egypt is perhaps the most attractive both for the student and the traveller. Time has clothed it with a strange and solemn charm; has spread over it, so to speak, an atmosphere of mysterious romance; and the mind cannot but be impressed with awe and wonder which contemplates its sphinxes and its pyramids, its colossal statues and huge obelisks, its monuments of a remote antiquity to which the antiquity of Greece and Rome is but a thing of yesterday. Long before Cecrops founded Athens—long, long before an Etruscan colony sowed at Alba Longa the first seeds

of imperial Rome—long even before Abraham walked with angels in the plains of Mamre—Egypt was studded with great cities, and had developed a complete system of civilization. Long before "the Samian sage" taught the Athenian youth, or "the blind old bard of Scio's rocky isle" narrated in immortal verse the heroic deeds of Achilles and the devotion of Andromache, Egypt was the home of a consistent religious creed, of a recondite philosophy, of a complete literature. You may trace back its annals for some four thousand years before the birth of Christ, and many of its monuments are undoubtedly the most ancient memorials of human skill and labour existing in the world. We are accustomed to think and speak of the Hebrew patriarchs as the "world's gray forefathers;" but, in truth, Egypt was a powerful and opulent empire even in the days of Joseph, and while Jacob and his sons still tended sheep in the grassy solitudes of the Asiatic plains. It was in the Egyptian schools Moses was trained to become the lawgiver of the Jewish people. Its pyramids were rising on the bank of the Nile at an epoch coeval with that of Abraham and Isaac. We see, then, that Egypt was the cradle of the world's civilization. Thence Greece derived her art, her science, her literature; and, improving them in the light and fulness of her own exquisite imagination, handed them down to imperial Rome, whose mission it was to diffuse them over Western Europe.

And such as Egypt was in the dawn of human history, such is it now. In many important respects, no land on the face of the globe has undergone so little change. True it is that its palaces are masses of ruin, half buried in sand; that of Memphis, and Thebes, and Karnak only the shadow of their former glory survives; that in the seat of the Pharaohs and the Ptolemys sits the descendant of an alien race. But then consider that its pyramids survive almost uninjured; that its language remains; that the Nile still rises and swells with annual regularity; that the animal life teeming on its banks is the animal life worshipped, loved, or dreaded three thousand years ago by the subjects of Rameses; that the *khamsin* still scorches the meadow-land with hot fierce breath; that beyond the narrow belt of verdure which the bright river traverses still spreads the boundless yellow expanse of the dreary desert; that the husbandman still finds his sustenance and support in the palm, and cultivates his little garden of leeks and other vegetables; that the creaking water-wheel is plied now as it was plied in the days of Nectanebus;—consider these things, and own that Monotony is written everywhere on the face of the land.

But a change is coming. The grasp of Western civilization is on the throat of this weird antiquity, and the Egypt of the past will soon be as a dream that once has been. As the waters of the Mediterranean pour through the Canal of Suez, to mingle with those of the Red Sea, so will the powerful influences of the West blend with the thoughts and passions, the ways and customs of the East, until the Valley of the Nile will preserve nothing of the Past but its ruins.

Egypt occupies the north-eastern corner of the African continent, where it is linked to that of Asia by the Isthmus of Suez, and separated from that of Europe by the narrow waters of the Mediterranean. It stretches inland from that old historic sea, which for ages has been one of the principal channels of the world's commerce, to the first cataract of the Nile, that of Assouan, the ancient *Syene;* or from the parallel of latitude 31° 37', to that of 24° 3' N. Its eastern boundary is formed by the Red Sea; on the west it is bordered by the ever-shifting sands of the Libyan Desert. Following the track of the Nile, we may compute its length at about 530 miles; its breadth may be measured by that of the river valley, for the cultivated territory does not extend beyond the limits marked by the river's yearly inundations. Three-fourths of the "Egypt" shown upon our maps are a rocky, sterile waste, and except the narrow valley already spoken of, the only cultivated and inhabitable portion is found in Lower Egypt, or the Delta, an area of between 4000 and 5000 square miles.

The average breadth of the Nile valley, which is simply a strip of alluvial deposit annually fertilized by the riverine sediment, is, up to the 30th parallel, about seven miles; while that of the cultivable land does not exceed five miles and a half. Between Cairo in Lower, and Edfou in Upper Egypt, the maximum breadth may be taken at eleven miles, the minimum at two. Further south, between Edfou and Assouan, so great is the contraction of the valley—it may more justly be called a ravine—that scarcely any soil exists on either bank; but from the waters of the Nile the rocks spring up like cliffs from the sea, bold, abrupt, and precipitous. To this circumstance is largely owing the pleasure derived by the traveller from a voyage up the Nile. The landscape is

A LANDSCAPE IN THE DELTA

everywhere brought within his ken. It is set like a picture in a framework of hills and mountains, and all its details are at once comprehended by the eye.

Etymologists are unable to inform us why the Greeks called this remarkable region—Egypt, ἡ Αἴγυπτος. But the name is as old as the days of Homer, who, indeed, bestows it also on the river Nile.* In the language of its aboriginal inhabitants it was expressively termed *Chemi*, or the "Black Earth," in allusion to the colour of its rich soil; the Hebrews named it *Mizraim;* the Arabians *Mesr;* and the Copts *El-Kebit*, or the "Inundated Land."

It was anciently divided into *nomes* (νόμοι) or districts, each of which had its civil governor (in Greek, the nomarch, or νόμαρχος), its distinct priesthood, its temple, its greater and lesser towns, its magistrates, ceremonies, customs, and separate political and civil economy. The number of these nomes is uncertain; but it was never less than forty-five, and sometimes seems to have risen to fifty-five. The following were, at all events, the most important:—

I.—IN THE DELTA.

1. The *Menelaite:* chief town, Canobus, where existed a famous temple and oracle of Serapis.
2. The *Andropolite:* chief town, Andropolis.
3. The *Sebennytic:* chief town, Pachnamunis, where Latona was worshipped.
4. The *Chemmite:* chief town, Buto.
5. The *Onuphite:* chief town, Onuphis.
6. The *Phthemphuthite:* chief town, Tava.

* Homer, "Odyssey," book iv., line 477.

7. The *Saite*: chief town, Sais, which possessed a peculiar sanctity as the burial-place and sanctuary of Osiris.

8. The *Busirite*: chief town, Busiris. Here Isis was worshipped, and at one time "the red-coloured men from over the sea"—that is, Syrian and Arabian wanderers—were offered up as sacrifices on her altar.

9. The *Thmuite*: chief town, Thmuis.

10. The *Mendesian*: chief town, Mendes, where the goat Mendes (the origin of the Greek god Pan) had a temple.

11. The *Tanite*: chief town, Tanis. Here, it is said, Moses was born and educated.

12. The *Bubastite*: chief town, Bubastis, containing, according to Herodotus, a magnificent temple to Artemis.

13. The *Athribite*: chief town, Athribis, where the shrew-mouse and the crocodile were elevated into objects of reverence.

14. The *Heliopolite*: chief town, Heliopolis (*On*), the principal seat of the worship of the sun.

15. The *Heroöpolite*: chief town, Heroöpolis, where the great god of the people was Typhon, the personified principle of Evil.

There were also the *Nitriote*, the *Letopolite*, the *Prosopite*, the *Leontopolite*, the *Mentelite*, the *Pharbaethite*, and the *Sethraite*.

II.—IN THE HEPTANOMIS.

1. The *Memphite*: chief town Memphis, which was at one time the capital of Egypt, and the royal seat of the Pharaohs (after Psammetichus, B.C. 616). It rose into importance when Thebes decayed, and, in its turn, declined after the rise of Alexandria.

2. The *Aphroditopolite*: chief town, Aphroditopolis, the sanctuary of Athor or Aphrodite, whose worship was adopted by the Greeks.

3. The *Arsinoite* (or the *Faioum*): chief town, Crocodilopolis; so named from the worship paid to the crocodile. It was afterwards called Arsinoë.

4. The *Heracleote*: chief town, Heracleopolis Magna, with a temple to the ichneumon.

5. The *Hermopolite* (between Upper and Middle Egypt): chief town, Hermopolis, situated "a little to the north of the castle and

toll-house where the portage or customs-duty was levied on all craft ascending the river."

6. The *Cynopolite*: chief town, Cynopolis. Here the dog-headed god Anubis was reverenced.

7. The *Greater and Lesser Oases* were reckoned as one nome among the Heptanomites.

III.—IN UPPER EGYPT.

1. The *Lycopolite*: chief town, Lycopolis. Here the wolf was worshipped.

2. The *Antaeopolite*: chief town, Antaeopolis. The god of this nome or canton would seem to have been Typhon.

3. The *Aphroditopolite*. In cases where a northern and a southern canton possessed similar objects of worship, the former was probably a colony or an offset of the latter. The Thebaid was the birth-place of Egyptian civilization, whence, in the course of years, it gradually moved northward.*

4. The *Panopolite* (afterwards called the *Chemmite*): chief town, Panopolis or Chemmis. Here hero-worship was dedicated to an apotheosized man, whom the Greeks compared to their Perseus. The population was principally composed of stone-masons and linen-weavers.

5. The *Thinite*: chief town, This; afterwards called Abydus. There is reason to believe that this nome was the most ancient as well as the principal nome of the kingdom of Menes of This. Osiris was its principal divinity.

6. The *Tentyrite*: chief town, Tentyra. Here Athor, Isis, and Typhon were worshipped.

7. The *Coptite*: chief town, Coptos. Its inhabitants were chiefly engaged in the caravan trade between Berenice and the interior of Arabia and Libya.

8. The *Hermonthite*: chief town, Hermonthis. Here Osiris and his son Orus were worshipped.

---

* W. B. Donne, art. "Aegyptus," in Dr. Smith's "Dictionary of Greek and Roman Geography," i., pp. 36-48. To this elaborately-compiled paper we have been greatly indebted.

9. The *Apollonite:* chief town, Apollinopolis Magna. Its inhabitants reverenced the sun, and, like those of the Tentyrite, hunted the crocodile. Hence they were at constant variance with the people of—

10. The *Ombite:* chief town, Ombos, who worshipped the great saurian of the Nile.

The frequent references made in the foregoing enumeration to animal-worship will probably perplex our younger readers. They will wonder that so polished and learned a people as the Egyptians should dedicate altars and temples, and offer homage, to the shrew-mouse or the crocodile, the dog or the wolf. Unquestionably, this is one of the most perplexing subjects with which the historian of Egypt has to deal. Not its least difficulty is, that the same animals were not worshipped by the whole nation; that while some were the objects of general, many were the objects only of local adoration. Thus, throughout the entire Valley of the Nile, the sacred beetle (*scarabaeus sacer*), the ibis, the ox, the hawk, the dog, the cat, and the fishes *lepidotus* and *oxyrrynchus*, were worshipped; while the wolf was regarded with divine honours only at Lycopolis, the shrew-mouse at Athribis, the eagle at Thebes, the lion at Leontopolis, the goat at Mendes, and the sheep in the Saitic and Thebaid nomes. The god reverenced in one canton was hunted in another; the thing regarded as clean in Upper, was stigmatized as *un*clean in Middle Egypt. It seems impossible, therefore, with our present light, to determine upon what principles animal-worship was based. We know that it was in all ages "the opprobrium of Egypt;" that it was condemned by the Hebrew prophets; that it was ridiculed by the Greeks, who, nevertheless, could erect their temples to lustful gods and shameless goddesses. And, certainly, at the first glance, it appears a fair target for the shafts of the satirist. Fancy a wise and civilized people bowing down before a cat or a crocodile! But would a wise and civilized people do so, unless the cat or the crocodile was something more—that is, unless it was the symbol of some great truth, the typical representation of some moral or religious axiom? Mr. Donne suggests as probable, that among a contemplative and serious race, as the Egyptians were, animal-worship arose out of the detection of certain analogies between instinct and reason; and that, to the initiated, the reverence paid to beasts was a recognition of the Creator in every type of his work. But the suggestion will not meet the difficulty to which we have already alluded.

However this may be, it is evident that from the earliest times the Egyptians adopted certain animals as representatives of their gods; in other words, that they worshipped their symbolical deities under symbolical animal forms. The meaning of the symbols we do not know—we cannot even guess; in all probability it was lost by the Egyptians themselves at a comparatively early period of their history; and hence a religion which, in its original development, was mystical, but pure and elevated, degenerated into a mean and debased superstition.

The animal most sacred in the later age of Egypt was the bull, or Apis; and his worship eventually assumed a bacchanalian character, attended by the wildest and most extravagant revels. On the feast day of the god, says Herodotus,* all the Egyptians arrayed themselves as

* Herodotus, iii. 27.

soon as the beast left his gilded asylum, and gave way to feasting and jollity. Hilarious processions formed an important feature of the Egyptian ritual; as might have been expected in a country where the cloudless sky and the elastic air predispose men to mirth and indolence. Drumann, a German writer, remarks that they were like orgies; that even the women appeared in them; that they were followed by indecent songs and dances, by clamor-

SACRED DANCE.

ous music and drunken feasts, and by mimes and mummeries (like the Roman Saturnalia), in which the actors painted their faces, and ridiculed or struck the bystanders. At the great annual festival in honour of the goddess Pasht, held at Bubastis, these processions were conducted on a colossal scale, and more grape wine was consumed while it lasted than throughout the rest of the year.

Before quitting the subject we may add, that besides the bull Apis, the Egyptians honoured the sacred ox of Heliopolis—Mnevis, or Mne—from which, and not from Apis, according to Sir Gardner Wilkinson,* the Israelites

---

* Sir G. Wilkinson, " Manners and Customs of Ancient Egypt," ii. 07

borrowed their notion of the golden calf (Ex. xxxii. 1-7). The offerings, dancing, and rejoicings practised in its honour were doubtlessly imitated from the feasts of Mnevis, which they had witnessed during their sojourn in Egypt.

One beneficial effect of animal-worship is worth noticing; the humane feeling towards the brute creation which it caused to prevail. In no country were animals so tenderly treated as in the Land of the Nile.

Returning to our description of the divisions of Egypt, we find them reduced by the Romans, after their conquest of the land, to three: *Augusta Prima, Augusta Secunda*, and *Ægyptiaca*. A similar arrangement was adopted by the Arabs, and still exists, under the following designations :—

REGIONS.	CHIEF TOWNS.
Musr-el-Bahri, or the Delta (Lower Egypt)	Alexandria, Rosetta, Damietta, Aboukir.
El-Bastani, or the Faioum (Middle Egypt)	Cairo, Suez, Ismaila, Medinet-el-Faioum, Beni-souef, Minyeh, Manfalut.
Es Saïd (Upper Egypt)	Siout, Girgeh, El-Karnak, El-Luxor, El-Assouan.

These three regions, which are marked by distinct geographical features, are subdivided into thirteen provinced.

Let us now glance at the *general aspect* of the country.* Lower and Middle Egypt are deficient in wood; in those groves of patrician trees or fresh young plantations which

---

* Compare the works of Kinglake, Harriet Martineau, Lord Lindsay, Bartlett, Melly, Lady Duff Gordon, Eliot Warburton, and Rev. A. C. Smith.

make up the beauty and richness of an English landscape. Still the country is not utterly bare; its scenes are adorned with the tamarisk and the palm, and on the border land of the Desert, bloom bright sweet gardens of jessamine and orange. Wherever the soil is fairly cultivated, and properly watered, it amply repays the toil of the husbandman, yielding luxuriant crops of tobacco, cotton, the sugar-cane, and indigo. Among the shallows of Lake Menzaleh lingers the once-prized papyrus. In the beautiful valley of Faioum myriads of roses burden the air with fragrance; and every peasant's tiny nook of ground affords a supply of leeks, garlic, melons, and cucumbers.

Nature, however, is much more genial in Upper Egypt, and bestows a greater variety and a richer colouring on the picture. A recent traveller* declares it impossible to paint a pleasanter ideal of a summer-land than the Egypt above Thebes. The purple desert mountains press it more closely in, as if to infold a loved and lovely thing in their sheltering embrace. Their forms are wilder and more fantastic, and they revel in ruddier hues than below. Even to the Desert's edge, in these summer regions, all is growth. You wander through fields of millet and maize, and between bright flanking patches of yellow-blossoming cotton. You rove amid thickets of ricin, and meadows of poppy in bloom. Your heart is gladdened by clustering palm-groves, which whisper of peace and plenty, where every bright leaflet is tipped with an autumn gold, and mellowed by the tropic sun; and, from the midst of that lustrous gloom,

* Howard Hopley, "Under Egyptian Palms," pp. 221, 222.

SCENE ON THE NILE.

your eye may range over acres of sunny corn-fields, whose rich wealth of produce waves contiguous to eternal barrenness. And, mirroring the cloudless heavens, hither and thither, to fertilize and bless, intertwine

> "Transparent streams, whose waters go
> Through the palm-wood, serene and silent in their flow."

The *soil* of Egypt is remarkable for its fertility, and is fertile because it consists of nothing more or less than the deposits of its river-waters. These have been graphically described by St. Hilaire.

Nile mud is a sort of brown earth, he says, emphatically called *terre d'Egypte;* of the consistence of rather stiff clay, but with an extremely fine grain. It is very soft and unctuous to the touch, dissolves readily in water, and possesses scarcely any odour. When dried it becomes very hard, as may be seen in the deep cracks which furrow the ground some time after the waters have retired.

In this peculiar alluvial soil vegetation thrives with equal strength and rapidity.

We have spoken of the scarcity of timber. But the trees in Egypt are not only few in number, but of few species. First and foremost must be ranked the date-palm, which is for the Egyptian what the bread-fruit tree is for the Polynesian, or rice for the Hindu. It supplies him with food, and clothing, and house, and furniture; it is his all-in-all, his stay, his wealth, his very life. Scarcely inferior in importance is its congener, the doum or dôm palm. The acacia, or *sont* tree of the Arabs, is also common; it furnishes the *shittim*-wood of the Bible;

is the *Mimosa Nilotica* of botanists, and extensively adopted for ship-building and for similar purposes. Add to these the sycamore and the tamarisk, and our enumeration of the principal trees of Egypt is complete.*

Its *animal life* is far more varied and abundant. There are fine breeds of the horse, the ass, and the camel; the last-named being the favourite beast of burden. The giraffe has been driven into the wilder districts by the unresting advance of civilization; the hippopotamus is only found in the far reaches of the upper Nile; but the hyena, the wild

DATE PALMS.

* Rev. A.C. Smith, "The Nile and its Banks," i. 278.

THE SACRED IBIS.

dog, and the jackal, still prowl at night through the streets of the large towns; the ichneumon, the stork, the heron, the purple goose, and the sacred ibis are almost as common now as in the "olden time," though the unreasoning passion of English travellers for making large "bags of game," threatens to extirpate them from the land.

Egypt, as Mr. Hopley remarks, is wonderfully populous with the feathered tribes; their division and subdivision are infinite. From the smaller birdlings that

THE EGYPTIAN VULTURE.

dwell in the mimosa, whose plumage, gorgeous with all rainbow hues, absolutely bewilders you with its beauty, up through the ranks of wild and water fowl, to those big vultures and august eagles which perch solemnly on desert peak or crag, or skim lazily aloft in mid-air, there are endless gradations.

Their tameness appears to be extraordinary. You may almost walk into a flock of pigeons on a stubble-field, which, when it rises around you, is so dense as to cast a thick shadow over acres of land. Water-wagtails and fly-catchers on your deck will fearlessly trot up, and

ROSY FLAMINGOES.

pick a fly off your boot. A crow will parade its carrion under your very nose.*

A curious feathered denizen of the Nile Valley is the crocodile bird (the *Trochilus* of Herodotus),† which acts as a kind of parasite to that hideous reptile, and warns it of the approach of any intruder. Worthy of note, too, is "Pharaoh's hen," or the Egyptian vulture (*Neophron percnopterus*), which, with trailing wings and drooping tail, sits brooding, like an evil genius, over the ruined monu-

---

* This is the *Charadrius spinosus*, or spur-winged plover.
† Hopley, "Under Egyptian Palms," p. 206.

ments of bygone splendour. And every grove abounds with Senegal doves and blue pigeons, jaunty hoopoes, bright green bee-eaters, Sardinian warblers, great spotted cuckoos; while the corn-fields are peopled with quails, the river-banks with martins, and the Desert borders with noisy chats. Rarer, but still not uncommon, are the rosy flamingo, the common heron, the little egret, the pelican, the curlew, the spoonbill, the snipe, the shoveller, and the cormorant.

Hot and dry is the *climate* of Egypt; a climate scarcely favourable to the highest manifestations of man's intellectual and physical energy, yet, from its elasticity, promoting a singular feeling of gaiety and freshness. Its extreme dryness eminently conduces to the preservation of natural substances from decay; and in the rock-tombs and temples, the traveller looks astonished upon human bodies which, buried two or three thousand years ago, have defied corruption. The clearness of the atmosphere lends a curious distinctness—a remarkable sharpness—to every object in the landscape, so that the outline of architrave and column seems traced against the azure of the sky as with a pencil. The effects of colour produced by the after-glow of sunset would have enraptured a Titian or a Tintoretto.

The reader, however, must remember that a great climatic difference exists between the broad deltoid plain of Lower, and the narrow romantic valley of Upper Egypt. The former in its leading features resembles the African littoral, Barbary and Marocco; the latter, both in climate, fauna, and flora, is sub-tropical. In fact, rain rarely falls in the Thebaid, and the solar heat is almost intolerable to the European.

CARAVAN ASSAILED BY THE KHAMSIN.

The curse of Egypt is the *khamsin*. That fierce southern wind which, in April and May, blows as its name indicates, for fifty days; hot as the blast of a furnace, shrivelling the skin, parching the lips, blinding the eyes with minute particles of sand, and depressing the spirit as with the omen of some unutterable evil.*

The population of Egypt has increased very little since

* Rear-Admiral Smyth, "The Mediterranean."

the days of antiquity, if we may accept the statement of Germanicus, as recorded by Tacitus. At present it amounts to 6,806,381. According to the Roman historian, in the reign of Rameses it contained 700,000 men of the military age. At this rate the entire population would be about 3,500,000; allow 500,000 for error; add one-third for slaves and strangers; and the total will amount to nearly 5,500,000.

The Money, Weights, and Measures of Egypt, and their British equivalents are :—*

Money.

The Sequin.................... = Average rate of exchange, 5s. 4d.
The Piastre, of forty paras..... =   ,,   ,,   ·   ,,   2½d.

Weights and Measures.

The Killow............................ = 0.9120 imperial bushel.
The Almud............................ = 1.151 imperial gallon.
The Oke (of 400 drams)................ = 2.8326 lbs. avoirdupois.

* F. Martin, "Statesman's Year-Book."

CHAPTER II.

A SKETCH OF EGYPTIAN HISTORY, ANCIENT AND MODERN.

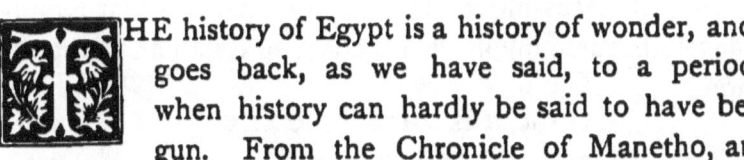

THE history of Egypt is a history of wonder, and goes back, as we have said, to a period when history can hardly be said to have begun. From the Chronicle of Manetho, an Egyptian sage, compiled about 300 B.C. and founded upon documents probably then in existence; from the evidence of hieroglyphical inscriptions abounding on the Nilotic monuments, and the papyri discovered among their ruins; and from passages in the Hebrew Scriptures, our knowledge of its course of events down to the Persian Conquest is chiefly obtained. This knowledge is, on many points, very vague and imperfect; much is hopelessly involved in obscurity; much depends upon acute conjecture; and for centuries we possess nothing more valuable than the names of kings who reigned, died, were buried, and are forgotten. Under such circumstances it is obvious that the disagreement between modern authorities is likely to be considerable, and the following summary pretends to no other merit than being the result of a very careful comparison between conflicting statements.

Egyptian history divides itself into five eras :—

α. The *Pharaonic*, which closed with the conquest of Egypt by Cambyses in B.C. 525.

β. The *Persian*, from B.C. 525 to B.C. 332.

γ. The *Greek*, from B.C. 332, when Alexandria was founded, to the death of Cleopatra in B.C. 30.

δ. The *Roman*, from B.C. 30 to the capture of Alexandria by the Arabs in A.D. 640.

ε. The *Modern*, or *Mohammedan*, from A.D. 640 to the present time.

It is in discussing the first of these periods that Egyptologers become involved in a chaos of doubt and supposition.

α. THE PHARAONIC ERA.

If we may credit Manetho, Egypt was governed by thirty dynasties of native rulers, extending, according to the Syncellus, over a period of 3553 years. Adding this total to B.C. 339, the date of the downfall of the thirtieth dynasty, we may trace back the annals of Egypt to their hypothetical commencement in B.C. 3892,* when the monarchy was founded by a shadowy and uncertain personage, named MENES or MEN.† But then it must be remembered that some of the dynasties men-

---

* This is the date fixed upon by Lepsius; but Boëkh says 5702 B.C.; Poole, 2717 B.C.; Sharpe, 2000 B.C.; and Nolan, 2673 B.C. Who shall decide when chronologists disagree?

† There is good reason to doubt whether such a personage ever existed. His name seems connected with the root *Man*, "to think and speak," which we also meet with in the *Menu* of the Hindus, the *Minos* of the Greeks, and the *Menerfa* of the Etruscans.—See *Quarterly Review*, vol. lxxviii., p. 149.

tioned by Manetho may possibly have been contemporaneous; some reigning at Memphis, others at Thebes, others at Sais,—as Dukes of Burgundy ruled at the same time as Kings of France, or Kings of Aragon, Leon, and Castile divided Spain between them. Nor is it known how many sovereigns were included in the thirty dynasties; the lowest computation says 300, the highest 500.

Herodotus, Eratosthenes, and Manetho, however, all agree in making Menes the founder of the monarchy and the creator of the city of Memphis. As we are in no position to give them an absolute contradiction, let us take this as our starting-point.

At some date between 3000 and 4000 B.C. lived Menes, the first lawgiver of Egypt, B.C. 3892.

His successor, it is said, was named Athothis, and built the great palace of Memphis. Other sovereigns of this dynasty were Kenkenes; Knephes, who raised the Pyramids at Ko or Kochome; Miebis; Semempses; and Bieneches; but their names have not been identified upon any of the monuments. This dynasty lasted for 253 years.

The 2nd, or *Thinite* dynasty, which introduced animal-worship,* ruled Egypt for about 300 years; the 3rd, or

---

* In reference to the animal-worship of Egypt, the following remarks seem worthy of consideration :—If we are forced to allow that they (the Egyptians) were so mad as to offer divine honours to various members of the animal kingdom, we shall still see some method in their madness, and can account for their seeming frenzy. Did the inhabitants of towns distant from the river worship the crocodile ? it was in order that the canals, on which their prosperity depended, might be religiously kept in repair under the nominal plea for the convenience of the sacred reptile. Was the fish oxyrrynchus worshipped at the inland towns of Behnesa, or the River Nile at Nilopolis, nine miles from the great stream? it

Memphite, for 200. Here Egyptian history begins, so far as it is told on the Egyptian monuments; and we learn from their indisputable records that Senefern,

> was for a similar reason; while Sir Samuel Baker has pointed out that the scarabaeus was so highly honoured as the harbinger of the high Nile, because it regularly makes its appearance at the season of the flood. Even the extraordinary veneration shown for the bull Apis, wherein their reverence for an animal was carried to an extreme, is explained by their belief that under this form the soul of Osiris occasionally condescended to come upon Earth, and so they deified the living shrine in which their great god was tabernacled for a time. For the reason why the sacred ibis was so highly regarded we have not far to seek, inasmuch as the services that bird rendered in destroying the armies of locusts (which were the winged serpents of Herodotus) and other noxious insects are palpable; and flights of locusts still occasionally visit Egypt and the neighbouring country of Syria in incredible numbers, to the utter destruction of the crops, as I have myself witnessed in the latter country.
>
> Then, again, the doctrine of transmigration of souls, which was undoubtedly entertained as a powerful weapon in the hands of Osiris for chastising those who lived wicked lives, in causing them to expiate their crimes under the form of various animals, was another strong motive for the reverence they showed to the creatures they held sacred, and for the pains they took to embalm their bodies after death.
>
> Then, again, with regard to the animal heads, the hawk, the ibis, crocodile, cat, jackal, and others, with which the human figures of the deities are frequently surmounted; though no one can positively assert their meaning, some very plausible explanations have been proposed. Thus, it has been thought by some that this strange practice originated in the intense reverence that was felt for the gods they worshipped, and a consequent disinclination, which English Christians can appreciate, to attempt to portray the awful face of the Deity; and therefore they put a mask before the divine countenance, or substituted the head of some member of the animal kingdom held sacred in Egypt, for that which they dared not represent in its real form. Possibly such animal's head likewise betokened the attribute for which the particular deity was notorious; but, at all events, we are not driven to believe that so wise a nation as the ancient Egyptians showed themselves to have been, really worshipped the beasts, birds, reptiles, and fishes, which are popularly represented as their gods. These were the tales in which Herodotus revelled, and yet he could scarcely believe such gross superstition, but leads the way to an explanation of their customs, in his story of the ram's head attached to the statue of Jupiter Ammon; while Cicero declares that the Egyptian custom of representing the gods with the heads of oxen, birds, and other creatures, was introduced in order that people might restrain from eating them, or from some other mysterious reason; one object doubtless being to insure the preservation of some animals which were valuable for food, and of others which were useful in destroying noxious reptiles, or for some similar purpose.—Rev. A. C. SMITH, *The Nile and its Banks*, vol. i., pp. 240–243.

one of the kings of this dynasty, opened up the copper mines of the Wady Magura, and conquered the pen-

MOUNT SINAI.

insula of Sinai. How strange a reflection is it that the armies of Egypt thus penetrated into the defiles, and wound over the rocky passes, of that mighty maze of mountains, which afterwards witnessed the revelation of the Divine Power on

"the secret top
Of Oreb or of Sinai,"

and the long procession of the Israelites as they slowly toiled towards the Promised Land !

To the 4th dynasty chronologists ascribe an aggregate duration of 284 years, and some particulars concerning its more prominent members are contained in the hieratic papyrus known as the "Canon of Turin." Of Soris there are also monumental records. The two Shufus or Chufus erected the mighty Pyramids of El-Ghizeh, and subdued Arabia. The elder Shufu is the Cheops of Herodotus—who, however, represents him as living at a later period : he raised the greater of those massive enigmas by forced labour. His brother, Num-Shufu, who reigned conjointly with him for several years, laid, perhaps, the foundation of the second pyramid; and it was completed by Sha-fre, or Chephren, of the 5th dynasty. King Men-ka-ré, or Mencheres, the Mycerinus of Herodotus and Diodorus, built the third, in which a mummy case, inscribed with the royal founder's name, has been discovered.* The most conflicting theories have been put forward in reference to the dates of these great works, and they are placed by different writers between B.C. 3229 and B.C. 2352.†

---

* Yet Manetho asserts that the third pyramid was erected by a queen of the sixth dynasty, named Nitocris.

† Compare Sharpe, "History of Egypt" (London, 1846); Lepsius, "Königsbuch der Alten Ægyptie" (Berlin, 1848); Bunsen, "Egypt's Place in the World's History;" Poole, "Horae Ægyptiacae;" and Kenrick, "Ancient Egypt."

According to Poole, the 4th dynasty began in B.C. 2352; and the 5th, which came from the island of Elephantine, about B.C. 2150. The latter terminated with Annos or Ormos, who founded the Pyramid of the Mastabat-el-Faroun, near Sakkara, and was killed by his household guards. To this dynasty, which seems to have ruled over both Upper and Lower Egypt, belong the Pyramids at Aboo-Seir. The Memphite kings recovered the throne on the death of Annos; and the 6th dynasty, of which numerous memorials are extant, contributed to Egyptian history Othoes; Phiops, or Apappus (B.C. 1920), who reigned, it is said, one hundred years, and whose court, according to Sir Gardner Wilkinson, was visited by Abraham;* and Queen Nitocris or Neetakar-tee, with whom the dynasty closed.

Of the next four dynasties we know but little. The 7th seems to have been a period of anarchy, and seventy kings (or vice-kings, *inter-reges*) reigned, it is said, in seventy days—a suspicious coincidence of numbers, which involves the whole statement in doubt. The 7th and 8th dynasties were Memphite; the 9th and 10th, Heracleopolitan; and the 11th, Diospolite,—each dynasty deriving its name from the birth-place of its founder. Their rule, if Manetho may be credited, extended over five centuries; and their list includes eighty-six (unnamed) kings.

The founder of the 12th dynasty was Amenemha I., who built, or rebuilt, Heliopolis (the *On* of the Old Testament), and reigned for nine years with undivided glory,—afterwards, conjointly with Osirtesen I. (B.C. 1715). The latter succeeded him on the throne, and

---

* Sir G. Wilkinson, "Manners and Customs of Ancient Egyptians," i. 19.

appointed the Hebrew Joseph his prime-minister or viceroy. His monuments may be seen both at Heliopolis and at Beni-hassan. He subdued forty Ethiopian tribes, and in the thirtieth year of his reign, shared the burden of his empire with Amenemha II. Then came Osirtesen II., who finally subjugated Ethiopia; and, in due succession, Osirtesen III., who carried the frontiers of the empire further south, and won so great a renown that, after his death, he was apotheosized; Amenemha III.; Amenemha IV.; and Queen Sebeknefru.

To Amenemha III. are ascribed the great works of the excavation of the Moeris Lake; the erection of the Pyramid at Crocodilopolis; of the Temple of Athor at Sarabout-el-Khadem; and of the world-famous *Labyrinth*. This curious and mysterious structure was built wholly of polished stone. It contained three thousand chambers, half above ground, and half below. The Temples of Ephesus and Samos, says Herodotus,* may justly claim admiration, and the Pyramids may be individually compared to many of the magnificent structures of Greece, but even these are inferior to the Labyrinth. It is composed of twelve courts, all of which are covered; their entrances stand opposite to each other, six to the north and six to the south; one wall encloses the whole. Of the apartments above the ground I can speak, continues Herodotus, from my own knowledge and observation; of those below, from the information I received. The Egyptians who had charge of the latter would not suffer me to see them; and their reason was, that in them were preserved

---

* Herodotus, book ii. ("Euterpe"), § 148. Compare with Bunsen. "Ægyptens-Stelle," ii. 324, 325.

the sacred crocodiles, and the bodies of the kings who constructed the Labyrinth. Of these, therefore, I do not presume to speak; but the upper apartments I myself visited, and I pronounce them among the grandest efforts of human industry and art. The almost infinite number of winding passages through the different courts excited my highest admiration: from spacious halls I passed through smaller chambers, and from them again to large and magnificent saloons, almost without end. The walls and ceilings are of marble, the latter embellished with the most exquisite sculpture; around each court pillars of the richest and most polished marble are arranged; and at the termination of the Labyrinth stands a pyramid one hundred and sixty cubits high, approached by a subterranean passage, and with its exterior enriched by huge figures of animals.

The object of the Egyptian kings in constructing this gigantic work cannot even be conjectured. It is ascribed to various monarchs, and its site cannot be accurately determined; but, in reference to the first point, the truth would seem to be that its erection occupied a long period of years, and that it was enlarged at successive periods; on the second, we may observe that though the ruins visited and identified by modern travellers do not exactly agree with the accounts of Herodotus and Pliny, yet there is good reason to believe they formed a portion of the outer buildings, though injured by time, and mutilated by barbarism.

The 13th dynasty numbered sixty Diospolite kings, who reigned, it is said, 453 years; and the 14th, seventy-six Xoite kings, extending over 184 years.

THE SHEPHERD KINGS.

The 15th, 16th, and 17th dynasties belonged to the Hyksos, or Shepherd kings, who were invaders, apparently of Arab race;* who, during a period of intestine convulsion, made themselves masters of Egypt; fixed their capital at Memphis; constructed in the Sethroite nome a colossal fortification or earth-camp, called Abaris; and eventually divided the conquered country into two independent kingdoms, one in the Thebaid, and another at Xois. No monuments perpetuate the name and fame of these invaders, having probably been destroyed by the Egyptians when they regained their independence. So proud a people would be unwilling to hand down to posterity any permanent record of their subjection to a foreign and inferior race.

According to Manetho, they ruled over Egypt for 511 years. About B.C. 1525, they were expelled by Aah-mes I. of the 18th dynasty, who reunited Upper and Lower Egypt. Thothmes I. (Thutmosis) conquered Nubia, and extended the renown of his arms as far as Mesopotamia. Then came Thothmes II.; and after him, Thothmes III., who won a great victory at Megiddo, subjugated Syria and Mesopotamia, and exacted tribute from Phœnicia, Babylon, Assyria, and the fair islands of the Archipelago. From an extant astronomical record it is believed that the year B.C. 1444 fell in the reign of this able and successful monarch,—the " Edward the First " of Egypt, —a great administrator and a famous warrior.

The glory of the dynasty was well maintained by Amunophis II., who captured Nineveh; and by Thothmes IV., who is reputed to have erected that singular

* Heeren, "Historical Researches," ii. 114.

but majestic type of Egyptian beauty, the colossal Sphinx. Amunophis IV. introduced the worship of a god named Aten, and the "heresy" continued to flourish under three of his successors, until "the fair humanities of the old religion" were restored by Hor-em-heb, or Horus.

Under the 18th and 19th dynasties the Land of the Nile waxed prosperous, powerful, and wealthy; attaining, perhaps, its highest point of civilization, and the most majestic development of its art. With the 19th dynasty began the era of the Ramessids; Rameses I. extending the boundary of his kingdom to the Wady Halfa, in Nubia. Seethee I., or Sethos, was a renowned warrior an Egyptian Tullus Hostilius, bred in the camp, and rejoicing in the "fierce delight" of battle. He invaded Syria and Mesopotamia, and chastised the insolence of the Phœnicians. In Asia he learned the worship of the deities Baal and Astarte, and introduced it into his own kingdom.

It is said that his son, Rameses II., succeeded to the crown in his childhood. A notable fact of this monarch's reign is his capture of *Saluma* or *Salem*, the precursor of Jerusalem. By his successes in the battle-field he compelled Syria to sue for peace, and a princess of that nation became his queen. His attention appears to have been largely devoted to maritime affairs, and it is recorded that his fleet—manned, I suppose, by Asiatics—swept up and down the Mediterranean. Did any Egyptian vessels, I wonder, pass the Straits of Gibraltar, and navigate our western waters? All the exploits which are attributed to him could hardly have been crowded into the life of one man, however able and energetic, and he appears, in the course of time, to have gathered to himself no small portion of the renown properly belonging to his successors; a process which takes place in all ancient and legendary history. The people love to invest their favourite hero with every grand achievement whose tradition lingers in the national memory; and thus he becomes, as it were, the focus which draws to, and concentrates in, itself the scattered rays of light.

Seventeen centuries after he had been interred in the superb temple which his genius and power erected at Thebes, Germanicus visited that once-famous capital; and the Egyptian priests, as Tacitus relates,* read to him from the monumental records the deeds and victories, the treasures and the tributes, the resources and subject-realms of this great king. His empire stretched northward to the shores of the Caspian Sea; southward, beyond the second cataract; westward, to the interior of the Desert; and eastward, it included Arabia.

He was succeeded by his thirteenth son, Merien-ptah, or Ptah-men, who made Memphis his capital, and is now generally identified with the Pharaoh of the Exodus.† He introduced the heretical worship of Typhon, or Seth —Satan—the Principle of Evil.

Of his successors, Sethos II., Amenmes, Sipthah, Tausri, and Setinekt, few particulars are recorded. We gather their names from two important and authentic monuments, the "Tablet of Abydus," and the "Tablet of Karnak."

---

* Tacitus, "Annals," ii. 60.

† This identity was first suggested by Lord Prudhoe (the late Duke of Northumberland). See Rawlinson's "Herodotus," ii. 366. Wilkinson places the Exodus in the reign of Thothmes III. ("Ancient Egyptians," i. 47)

We next arrive at the epoch of the 20th dynasty, which was wholly composed of kings of the name of Rameses, and illustrated by the genius of Rameses III.,* who subdued a revolt in Ethiopia, and gained several sea-battles in the Mediterranean. It fell from its "high estate" through some religious convulsion, and the priests of Amun Ra at Thebes were elevated to the throne under the name of the Tanite kings, ruling Egypt for about 130, or, according to some authorities, 150 years. Next followed the Bubastite, or 22nd dynasty, supposed to have descended from foreign settlers in Bubastis,† and to have been of Shemitic origin.

We now come upon a reliable synchronism with Hebrew history; Sheshonk—the Sesonchosis of the Greeks—being the Shishak of the Old Testament, who captured Jerusalem about B.C. 972.‡ His name is inscribed, with a record of his achievements, on the propylon of the great temple of Karnak.

His successor, Osorthen or Osorcho, is probably the Zerah of the Bible, who was defeated at Mareshah by Asa, king of Judah. §

Under the 23rd (another Tanite) dynasty Egypt greatly declined in power, and at the close of the 24th, was subjugated by Ethiopia, its last monarch, Bocchoris, being captured in battle, and burned alive. Sabaco, or Sebichos, who founded the 25th or Ethiopian dynasty,

---

* Some Egyptologists make the dynasty to have begun with Rameses IV., and ascribe to him the military achievements related in the text.

† Now called Tel-Bustak, on the Pelusiac Nile, about 70 miles from its mouth.

‡ 2 Chronicles xii. 1-10. See also Josephus, "Antiquities of the Jews," viii. 10, 3.

§ 2 Kings xvii. 4; 2 Chronicles xiv. 8, 9.

flourished about B.C. 730–720. He is the *So* of the Hebrew records, with whom Hoshea, king of Israel, entered into an alliance; while his successor, Tarkus, is identified with the *Tirhakah*, king of Ethiopia, the enemy of Assyria and Sennacherib* (Isa. xxxvii. 9). He reigned from about B.C. 720 to B.C. 710.

TIRHAKAH, KING OF EGYPT.

A period of intestine trouble followed his death, fermented apparently by foreign interference, and significant of the rapid decay of the empire. Sethos, a priest of Phtah, is said to have seized the sovereign power, and to have ruled despotically, degrading the military caste, and confiscating their lands. After him came the Dodekarchy, or Twelve Kings, who probably reigned contemporaneously, and each over a semi-independent province, united only for resistance to foreign aggression (B.C. 700–670). They were overthrown, however, with the aid of Greek and Phœnician mercenaries, by Psammetichus I., of the 26th dynasty, who reigned fifty-four years,

* Wilkinson, "Ancient Egyptians," i. 138–142.

and welded Egypt into a compact kingdom (B.C. 671–617). He introduced several important reforms; had his son instructed in Greek letters; instituted a caste of interpreters, or dragomans, intermediatory between the natives and foreigners; and in the place of the militia established a regular army of Hellenic troops.

His successor, Nechao, Nekas, or Neco, the *Pharaoh Necho* of the Old Testament,* reigned sixteen years (B.C. 617–601). He carried on a great war against the Babylonian Empire, and defeated its ally, Josiah, king of Judah, at Megiddo; after which he entered Jerusalem in triumph, and set upon the throne Eliakim, the younger brother of Jehoahaz. He penetrated into Assyria, but after four years of victory, was defeated at Carchemish, or Circesium, on the Euphrates, by Nebuchadnezzar, and forced to flee into Egypt.

He was unquestionably a monarch of signal capacity and adventurous spirit. At his command a Phœnician fleet attempted the circumnavigation of Africa; and he constructed, or, at all events, commenced, a canal between the Red Sea and the Nile. It left the river near the modern town of Belbeis, and ran east and south to Suez.

Necho was succeeded by his son Psammis, or Psammetichus II. (B.C. 601–595), who restored the Egyptian supremacy over Ethiopia. Great calamities befell the empire in the reign of Apries, the "Uaphris" of the monuments, and the *Pharaoh Hophra* of the Scriptures. Lower Egypt was invaded by Nebuchadnezzar; and Western Egypt by the Greeks, who defeated him at

* 2 Kings xxiii. 29–34.

Irusa (*Ain Ersen*). Soon afterwards he was deposed and strangled by a successful soldier, Amasis, Amosis, or Aah-mes II., with whom we are familiarized by Greek history. He reigned forty-four years (B.C. 570–526); was in league with the Greeks; wedded a Greek beauty; was visited by Solon and Pythagoras; cultivated arts and letters; and promoted the well-being of his people.

Herodotus describes the close alliance that existed between him and Polycrates, the "king" or "tyrant" of Samos, until the Egyptian monarch grew alarmed at the latter's unchanging prosperity. He advised him, in order to avert the anger of the gods, to throw away some valuable possession; and Polycrates accordingly flung into the sea a costly signet-ring of curious workmanship. The day afterwards, however, a fisherman presented the king with a singularly large fish that he had caught, and in its belly was found a ring. Thereupon Amasis withdrew from all relations with a man whose ominously good fortune predestined him to some melancholy catastrophe.

The truth, however, would seem to be that the Greek *thalassocrat*, or "sea-king," broke the alliance and leagued himself with Persia, when the latter power bade more highly for his support.*

In the reign of Psammenitus, which only lasted six months (B.C. 525), the Persians invaded Egypt under their great king Cambyses, defeated the Egyptians at Pelusium, and reduced the country to the rank of a Persian province, or satrapy.

* Grote, "History of Greece." iv. 323.

β. THE PERSIAN ERA.

The 27th Egyptian dynasty, thus founded by the sword of Cambyses,* included eight Persian kings, and extended over a period of 124 years (B.C. 525-401), disturbed by constant revolts of the Egyptians against their foreign rulers.

During the reigns of Xerxes (B.C. 486-460), who crushed a dangerous revolt, and afterwards unsuccessfully attempted the invasion of Greece; and of Artaxerxes Longimanus (B.C. 460-413), the country was convulsed by the insults which the Persians offered to the ancient religion. An insurrection was quelled in B.C. 456 by the satrap Megabyzus.

It was during the rule of Artaxerxes that Herodotus visited Egypt, and at Heliopolis and Thebes collected those precious notes in reference to its history, religion, antiquities, and social life, which are of such value to the modern student. The Land of the Nile is photographed in his pages with a wonderful fidelity; and his graphic account of its refined civilization, and its miracles

HERODOTUS.

---

* Cambyses, pursuing his schemes of conquest, afterwards led his army into the deserts of Ethiopia, where it was destroyed. He then went mad with shame, and plunged into an excess of debauchery and cruelty.

of art and science, furnishes us with one of the most vivid and interesting pictures of the past preserved in ancient history. He describes the Egyptians as "extremely religious, and surpassing all men in the worship they rendered to the gods." They were so regardful of cleanliness that "they wore only linen, and that newly washed." Wheat and barley they considered to be food unworthy of men; beans they regarded as sacred. In health and constitution no people was to be compared with them. The women left to the men the management of the loom, while "they themselves were engaged abroad in the business of commerce." Their physicians were each confined to the study and treatment of one particular disease. There were no priestesses in Egypt, "in the service either of male or female deities." Their country, he adds, contained more wonders than any other, and there was no region in all the world where one could see so many works which were so truly admirable. He highly praises the sanitary arrangements of the people; their domestic morality, for each Egyptian was the "husband of one wife;" their industry, and inventive genius. In a word, it is evident, from the warmth and fulness of his elaborate descriptions, that he looked upon them as a superior race.*

The 28th dynasty contains only one name, that of Amyrtaeus of Sais (B.C. 413–407), who was overthrown in a successful rebellion of the Egyptians, slain, and interred in a superb sarcophagus of green breccia, now preserved in the British Museum. The revolt against the Persians was maintained by the kings of the 29th

---

* Herodotus, book ii., sections 35–96, *passim*.

and 30th dynasties, whose names are given by some authorities as follow :—

29th or Mendesian dynasty: Nepherches (B.C. 407-402); Achoris, or Acoreus (B.C. 402-387).

30th or Sebennytic dynasty: Nectanebus I. (B.C. 387-361); Tachos, or Teos, who employed Agesilaus of Sparta to fight against the Persians (B.C. 361-351); and Nectanebus II. (B.C. 351-350).

Nectanebus II.—the last of the Egyptian Pharaohs—was defeated by Bagoas and Mentor, the generals of Darius Ochus, and compelled to flee into Ethiopia. Thus terminated the succession of Egyptian kings, after enduring for a period of 3553 years.

γ. THE GREEK ERA.

The mission of Egypt in the great economy of the world's history may now be considered to have terminated. The spirit of the ancient race, long a flickering flame, died out completely after the conquest of Egypt by Alexander. The nation was well prepared for the change. A long commercial and military intercourse with Greece had saturated it with Greek ideas; though the Hellenes were not exempt from a reciprocal influence, and the literature, art, and religion of Greece had been coloured to no inconsiderable extent by the literature, art, and religion of the Land of the Pharaohs. Hellenic colonies had sprung up along the shore of the Red Sea. The Thebaid had been traversed by Greek historians and philosophers. Greek soldiers mustered in the Egyptian court. Greek settlements were planted about the fertile fields of the Delta. The condition of things obtaining in Egypt in the fifth and fourth centuries before Christ may, in truth, be compared to that which prevailed in England during the reign of Edward the Confessor; so that the people in each country underwent, as it were, a long preparation for the introduction of a new dynasty and an alien government. Just as England was Normanized before the Conquest, so, but to a far greater extent, Egypt was Hellenized before its subjugation to Alexander.

The Macedonian monarch invaded Egypt in B.C. 332. Pelusium received him willingly, and Memphis threw wide its gates. The politic respect he paid to the religion of the country secured him the hearts both of the priests and people; and his firm and equitable government was gladly welcomed after the vacillating despotism of Persian satraps. Nor could the Egyptians fail to be gratified by the evident interest he displayed in their manners, their customs, their history, and traditions. To Alexander himself Egypt was a land of no ordinary attraction, because it offered, as he believed, the solution of the question agitated from his very birth, whether he was not only the descendant of Hercules and Achilles, but the true and actual son of Jove? For this purpose he marched into the Libyan Desert, and consulted the famous oracle of the god, worshipped there under his most ancient name of Ammon (Amun). The response which he received entirely satisfied him. The god, it was said, saluted him as his son; and thenceforth his coins assumed the divine symbol of a ram's horn.

Alexander introduced no violent changes into the laws and local government of the Egyptians, while providing a firmer rule and a more even administration of justice. He restored the privileges of the priests, and repaired the temples of the deities. The defence of the country he intrusted to a Greek force: and he established two great military posts; one at Pelusium, as the key of the Nile Valley; and the other at Memphis, as the centre of Lower Egypt. Descending the river from the latter capital, he was struck by the capabilities of the little town of Rhacotis, situated on a narrow neck of land between Lake Mareotis and the Mediterranean, to become the site of a great commercial city; and connecting it with the isle of Pharos* by a causeway (called the *Heptastadium*, or three-quarters of a mile), he founded there *Alexandria* (B.C. 332). On each side of the causeway was a harbour, and the two ports were linked with each other by two channels through the Heptastadium, and by another with the Lake Mareotis, which, in its turn, communicated with the Nile by numerous canals. The city was laid out in two chief streets; one, running east and west, measured nearly four miles in length; the other, north and south, upwards of a mile. The ground-plan of the city was traced by Alexander himself, and carried out by his favourite architect Deinocrates.

ALEXANDER THE GREAT.
(Canini Iconografia.)

* From the lighthouse afterwards erected here by Ptolemy II., Philadelphus, every similar structure was afterwards called by Greek and Roman a *Pharos*.

On the death of the great conqueror in B.C. 323, the vast empire constructed by his genius fell to pieces, like a magnificent arch from which the keystone has been withdrawn; and in the division of spoil made by his chief captains, Egypt fell to Ptolemy Lagus, or Soter, the first of its Greek sovereigns. Under the sway of this able monarch the Land of the Nile was still further Hellenized. The old Egyptian names were replaced by Greek appellations: *On* became Heliopolis, the "city of the sun;" *This* was changed to Abydus; *Thebes* to Diospolis Magna; *Pilak* to Philae; *Petnieh* to Aphroditopolis; as *Chem* gave way to Ægyptus. In like manner, the abstract religion of the priests of Osirei and Ptah was dethroned; and a curious compound of the Old and the New, of ancient symbols to which novel meanings were attached, of a misty philosophical theurgy with a poetical mythology, of Egyptian gods with Greek attributes, reigned in its stead.

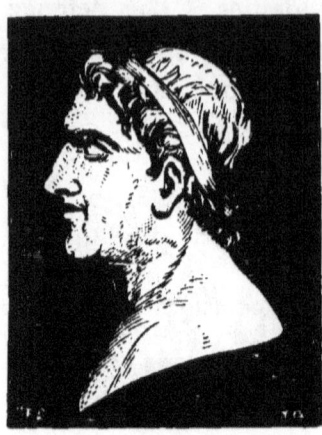

PTOLEMY SOTER.
(Visconti, Iconographie Grecque.)

That science and learning, however, which could no longer flourish under the sway of the rude soldier-kings of degenerate Greece, found a home in the refined court of the Ptolemys; and Alexandria gathered within its walls the erudition of the age. Ptolemy Philadelphus founded the celebrated Alexandrian Library; encouraged the Septuagint version of the Hebrew Bible; patronized the labours of the historian Manetho. The study of the arts and sciences was not less favoured by Philopater; while under the enlightened countenance of these cultivated princes commerce rapidly developed, and the Delta became a scene of prosperous and peaceful activity. Half Europe was supplied by its merchants with corn, and linen, and papyrus, with the products of Libya, and the rare treasures of the East. Philadelphus encouraged the river traffic by establishing a system of police from Cercasorum to Syene, and by completing the Pelusiac Canal which Necho had begun. He also rebuilt Aennum, or Cosseir.

PTOLEMY PHILOPATER.
(Visconti, Iconographie Grecque.)

Ptolemy III., surnamed Euergetes, or the "Benefactor," made war upon Syria, and extended his conquests as far as Babylon and Susa, while his fleets swept the Asiatic shores of the Mediterranean. But he did not neglect the "victories of peace." He largely increased the library of Alexandria; and among the worthies who adorned his court were Eratosthenes, Apollonius Rhodius, and the grammarian Aristophanes.

PTOLEMY EUERGETES.
(Visconti, Iconographie Grecque.)

In the reign of Ptolemy V., Epiphanes, the Romans began to interfere in Egyptian affairs. He proved a degenerate scion of a noble race; and his misgovernment dealt a death-blow at the prosperity of the kingdom. He was poisoned by some of his followers while preparing for an expedition into Syria.

The sixth of the race was Philometor, virtually a nominee of the Roman Senate, but a cultivated and generous sovereign. He was succeeded by the brutal Euergetes II., nicknamed Physcon, or the "Big Bellied," and Kakergetes, or the "Malefactor," whose reign was a prolonged Saturnalia of lust, greed, and cruelty. He married his sister Cleopatra, who was also his brother's widow; and on the bridal day murdered her infant son Eupator, who had been proclaimed king. He afterwards divorced Cleopatra, and married her daughter by her first husband, and consequently his niece. His subjects rebelled, and placed Cleopatra on the throne. He then murdered his and her son, and as a birth-day gift sent to her the poor lad's head and hands. Three years afterwards he recovered his crown. The equal of Nero and Tiberius in blood-thirstiness, he resembled them in his literary and artistic tastes, and wrote a work in twenty-four books, called *Hypomnémata* (Ὑπομνήματα), or "Memoirs."

Passing over some monarchs of less note, we arrive at the epoch of Ptolemy XII. The will of his father had placed the guardianship of the Egyptian kingdom in the Roman Senate, while it nominated him and his sister Cleopatra, both under age, as successors to the throne.* In accordance with the national custom, this

---

* Cæsar. "De Bello Civili," bk. iii., c. 108.

joint authority had been cemented by the marriage of the brother and the sister,—the former of whom was seventeen, the latter twelve years of age—a daring, ardent, able woman, and a dazzling beauty,—

"With swarthy cheeks and bold black eyes."

Having been driven from Alexandria by a popular insurrection, her brother's ministers took occasion to exclude her from her share in the sovereignty. But a new actor now appeared on the scene in the person of Julius Cæsar (B.C. 48). The dethroned queen obtained admission to his presence, and fascinated with her charms the conqueror of the world. He espoused her cause; reduced Pelusium, the key of Egypt; crossed the Nile at the head of the Delta; and totally defeated the army of Ptolemaeus, who, attempting to save himself by flight, was drowned in the river.* The Alexandrians then submitted to the victor, who placed a Roman garrison in the capital, and acknowledged Cleopatra as queen of Egypt.

JULIUS CAESAR.
(Visconti, Iconographie Romaine.)

It is not my intention here to trace the career of this extraordinary woman. It will suffice if I remind the

---

* Merivale, "History of the Romans under the Empire," ii. 322.

reader that after Caesar's death she threw the magic of her beauty and her address over Antonius, who loaded

MARCUS ANTONIUS.
(Visconti, Iconographie Romaine.)

her, and the children he had by her, with magnificent donations; that her fatal influence enticed him into the path of ruin and dishonour; that through her cowardice or treachery she lost him the battle of Actium and the dominion of the world; that she failed in her attempt to enthral his conqueror, the cold and wary Augustus; and finally, that to avoid figuring in a Roman triumph, she terminated her wild and passionate life by her own hand (B.C. 30).

The manner of her death, however, is not certainly known. It seems, says Canon Merivale,* that there were no marks of violence on her person, nor did any spots break out upon it, such as usually betray the action of poison. But the experiments she was reported to have made on the bite of venomous reptiles were remembered; these were coupled with the story of the basket of figs conveyed to her immediately before her death, in which such means of destruction might easily have been concealed. At last it came to be generally asserted and

CLEOPATRA.
(Visconti, Iconographie Grecque.)

* Merivale, "History of the Romans under the Empire," ii., 322.

believed that her arms were found slightly punctured as by the fangs of an asp. Such, too, was the account which Octavius himself circulated. And when the effigy of the Egyptian Beauty was carried in his triumph, she was represented recumbent on a couch, an asp clinging to either arm, and the sleep of death stealing slowly through every limb :—

> " Brachia spectavi sacris admorsa colubris,
> Et trahere occultum membra soporis iter." *

The chronology of the Ptolemys is as follows :—

B.C.
Ptolemy I., Lagus, or Soter.....................323
Ptolemy II., Philadelphus......................285
Ptolemy III., Euergetes........................267
Ptolemy IV., Eupator...........................222
Ptolemy V., Epiphanes..........................205
Ptolemy VI., Philometor........................181
Ptolemy VII., Physcon, or Euergetes II.........146
Ptolemy VIII., Lathyrus, or Soter II.......117-107
Ptolemy IX., or Alexander I.................107-90

Ptolemy VIII. restored, B.C. 90–81.

Ptolemy X., or Alexander II.....................81
Ptolemy XI., Dionysius, or Auletes..............80
Ptolemy XII., and Cleopatra.....................51

Defeat and death of Ptolemy XII., B.C. 46.

Ptolemy XIII., and Cleopatra....................46

Ptolemy is poisoned by his sister, Cleopatra, B.C. 43.

Cleopatra......................................43

Cleopatra commits suicide, B.C. 30.

* Propertius, lib. iii., xl., 53.

δ. THE ROMAN ERA.

After the battle of Actium and the death of Cleopatra, Egypt ceased to exist as an independent kingdom. It was incorporated into the Roman Empire, and governed by a prefect (*Praefectus Augustalis*), who held his appointment direct from the Caesar, and was only responsible to him. He was also selected from the equestrian order, the post being one of too great an importance to be bestowed upon a senator, whom it might have tempted to the assertion of independence. It was divided into three great districts, called *Epistrategiae*:— Upper Egypt (Thebais), capital, Ptolemais; Middle Egypt (Heptanomis); and Lower Egypt, capital, Alexandria. Each was subdivided into nomes, the nomes into toparchies, the toparchies into κῶμαι and τόποι (*kômai* and *topoi*). The military force consisted of two legions, who were principally stationed at Elephantine and Parembole in the south; at a strong fort on the frontiers of the Thebaid and Heptanomis; at Paretonium in Libya; and at Memphis and Alexandria in the Delta. With their usual energy the Romans largely developed the revenue and resources of the country, until it became the rich and abounding granary of the Empire. It was visited in the reign of Tiberius by his son-in-law Germanicus, who consulted the sacred bull Apis

GERMANICUS.
(From a medal in the Florentine Museum.)

and received an oracular response prophetic of his future misfortunes. At a later period the Emperor Hadrian ascended the Nile as far as Thebes, and in memory of his favourite, the beautiful Antinous, raised the city of Antinoöpolis on the east bank of the river (in lat. 26° 30' N.).

The first great revolt of Egypt against its foreign rulers occurred in the reign of Marcus Aurelius. It seems to have been promoted by, and, perhaps, was wholly confined to, the native soldiery. After lasting four years (A.D. 171–175), it was crushed by Avidius Cassius. The imperial authority was soon afterwards re-established.

In A.D. 193 Pescennius Niger proclaimed himself Emperor, but was defeated and slain at Cyzicus, A.D. 196. Egypt was then visited by Severus, who examined the memorials of antiquity at Thebes and Memphis. In the reign of Caracalla Egyptians were admitted to the Roman Senate; and the worship of Isis, which had long been established in the Roman cities, was publicly sanctioned.

In Egyptian history the next important event was the conquest of the land by Zenobia, the great queen of Palmyra, A.D. 269. She occupied it, however, for a few months only, and in A.D. 273 was herself conquered by the Roman Emperor, Aurelian. Immediately upon her downfall the standard of revolt was

ZENOBIA.
(From a medal in the Florentine Museum.)

raised on the banks of the Nile by her friend and ally, Firmus, a wealthy merchant of Egypt, and a native of Seleucia.* In the course of his trade to India he had formed very intimate relations with the Saracens and the Blemmyes, whose situation on either coast of the Red Sea gave them an easy introduction into Upper Egypt.† He excited the Egyptians with the hope of freedom, assumed the imperial purple at Alexandria, coined money, issued edicts, and raised an army, which speedily fled before the veteran troops of Aurelian. Firmus was captured, tortured, and put to death.

THE EMPEROR AURELIAN.
(From a medal in the Florentine Museum.)

A period of anarchy and confusion marked the reigns of Probus and Diocletian, who were frequently called upon to suppress the revolts of their Egyptian subjects. Afterwards, the country suffered severely from the rage of religious factions, who persecuted one another, as each alternately attained to power, with the unrelenting hate and cruel vengeance of fanaticism. A fierce warfare, moreover, was maintained between the rising power of Christianity and the decaying influences of Paganism. Christian monks dwelt in the Thebaid; Christian bishops ruled in Alexandria, which became the theatre of desperate and protracted hostilities between the respective

* Vopiscus, "Firmus," c. 5.
† Gibbon, "Decline and Fall of the Roman Empire," i. 379.

followers of Arius and Athanasius. In A.D. 379 the Emperor Theodosius I. published an edict prohibiting the worship of idols, and ordering the temples to be closed. Thenceforth the splendid edifices which crowded the banks of the Nile—or, at least, so many of them as had not been converted into Christian churches—were suffered to fall into decay, after being stripped of all their gorgeous decorations. So complete a revolution was not everywhere effected without opposition, and in Alexandria the votaries of Serapis, under the philosopher Olynthus, defended with arms the altar of their god. But the wrath of the Christians was stimulated by their archbishop, Theophilus, and the superb structure, raised by the first Ptolemy, which had so long been the pride and glory of the city, was levelled to the dust (A.D. 398).

The colossal statue of the god was involved in the fate of his shrine and religion. The story ran, that if any impious hand dared to profane its majesty, the heaven and the earth would straightway be reduced to their primeval chaos. An intrepid soldier, fired by religious zeal and wielding a heavy battle-axe, ascended a ladder; he dealt a vigorous stroke at the cheek of Serapis; it fell to the ground; yet the heavens did not fall, and the earth did not shake. He repeated his blows; the huge idol was shivered into fragments, and its limbs were ignominiously dragged through the streets of Alexandria amidst the shouts and derision of the populace. Even the Pagans acknowledged their contempt for a god who could not save his own image from destruction.*

* This incident is related by Gibbon, and by Milman in his "History of Christianity." The original authority is Sozomen, book vii.

It is to be regretted that on this occasion the valuable library of Alexandria was pitilessly ravaged.

ϵ. THE MODERN ERA.

Converted to Christianity, and permanently brought under the influences of Western civilization, the history of Egypt, as a peculiar and independent nation, with a distinct faith and an original literature, must be regarded as closed. Over its later annals the reader will be content to pass with rapidity. In A.D. 618 it was conquered by the Persians. In A.D. 640 it was subjugated by Amrou, the general of the Khalif Omar, and so completely, that Mohammedanism has thenceforth remained its established creed, and its entire polity has assumed a Mohammedan character. Previous to this great event the country had begun to decline in prosperity, and so much of wealth and commerce as it retained lingered only in Lower Egypt. Yet when Amrou described to the Khalif the condition of Alexandria, he could still report that the city contained 4000 palaces, 4000 public baths, 400 theatres, 40,000 Jews who paid tribute, and 12,000 persons who sold herbs.

Under the rule, first of the Arabs, and afterwards of the Turks, the decadence of Egypt was greatly accelerated; and the discovery, in 1497, of a passage to India round the Cape of Good Hope, by diverting the current of Indian commerce, dealt a fatal blow at its fortunes. For six centuries the virtual rulers of Egypt were those fierce and brutal soldiers of Tartar origin, the Mamelukes, who, from the epoch of their murder of the Sultan Selim in 1260, until they were finally crushed by Mehemet

MASSACRE OF THE MAMELUKES.

Ali in 1811, overawed and intimidated the Turkish lieutenants.*

Mehemet Ali was a man of extraordinary vigour and resolution, and after his confirmation to the pashalik of Egypt by the Sultan, he determined on ridding himself of those turbulent soldiery. For this purpose he devised a characteristic stratagem. He summoned the Mameluke Beys to Cairo, on the pretence that he wished to consult them with reference to a campaign against the Wahabees of Arabia. As his son Toussoun had just been invested by the Sublime Porte with the dignity of Pasha of the second order, the occasion was one of festivity as well as of policy. The Beys, therefore, mounted their finest horses and donned their richest apparel, forming the most splendid cavalry in the world (March 1, 1811).

After receiving a most flattering welcome from the Pasha, they were invited to parade in the court of the citadel. Without suspicion they defiled within its lofty walls; the portcullis fell behind the last of their glittering array; too late, they perceived, as Eliot Warburton remarks,† that their treacherous host had caught them in a trap, and they turned to effect their retreat.

In vain! Wherever they looked, their eyes rested only on barred windows and blank, pitiless walls. Nay; on something more, when incessant volleys poured from a thousand muskets upon their defenceless band. This sudden and terrible death they met with a courage

---

* They had previously suffered severely during Napoleon's invasion of Egypt in 1798, and were defeated in a great battle near the Pyramids. I may add that the French were finally expelled from Egypt by the British, under Abercromby, in 1801.

† Eliot Warburton, "The Crescent and the Cross," c. 5.

worthy of their past history; some with arms folded upon their mailed bosoms, and turbaned heads devoutly bent in prayer; others with angry brows, and flashing swords, and curses which were wasted on the desert air.

All that superb array of troopers sunk beneath the withering and deadly fire; all save one, named Emim Bey, who spurred his charger over a pile of his dead and dying comrades; sprang upon the battlements; the next moment he was in the air; another, and he released himself from his crushed and bleeding horse amid a shower of bullets. He fled; took refuge in the sanctuary of a mosque; and finally escaped into the deserts of the Thebaid.

Mehemet Ali, taking advantage of the growing weakness of Turkey, conceived the design of founding an independent dynasty in Egypt, and of annexing Syria to his dominions. He carried out his design with great energy, ably seconded by his son Ibrahim Pasha; but in 1840 England interfered. The English fleet, under Sir Robert Stopford and Charles Napier, captured the fortresses planted along the Syrian coast, and destroyed St. Jean d'Acre. A long negotiation ensued, with the result of securing the viceroyalty of Egypt in the family of Mehemet Ali, under the nominal suzerainty of the Porte.

Mental decay incapacitated this extraordinary man for the government of his country in June 1848, and his son Ibrahim Pasha was accordingly invested with the pashalik. On his unexpected decease in the following November, he was succeeded by his nephew Abbas, under whom the adoption of a more liberal and energetic administration promoted the development of the extraordinary resources of Egypt. The transit-trade between

ST JEAN D'ACRE.

England and her Indian possessions was also one great and foremost cause of its increasing prosperity in the last quarter of a century.

Abbas Pasha, in 1854, was succeeded by Said Pasha, under whose government the trade and commerce of Egypt developed considerably; but neither under him nor any other ruler was the deplorable condition of the fellaheen, or common people, ameliorated. They were loaded with a heavy taxation, which crippled all their efforts and reduced them to a miserable poverty. A host of Turkish officials lived upon their scanty earnings, and if there were any delay in responding to their exactions, the kourbash, or whip, and the prison were freely employed. A more corrupt, a more arbitrary, and a more despotic government than that which has oppressed Egypt for the last fifty years the world does not present. It did nothing for the education, or the material prosperity, or the moral well-being of its subjects.

On the death of Said Pasha, January 18th, 1863, the pashalik fell to his nephew, Ismail (born in 1816),—the eldest surviving son of Ibrahim Pasha, Mehemet Ali's distinguished son,—a man of much force of character and more than ordinary capacity, who visited France and England, and showed himself profoundly sensible of the resources and influence of Western civilization. He was also an ambitious man, and his reign was distinguished by events which have largely affected the history of Egypt and of Europe. The title borne by his predecessors was the Turkish one of "Vali," or Viceroy; but by a liberal expenditure of money at Constantinople, he obtained permission, in May 1866, to adopt the royal designation of "Khĭdĭv-el-Misr," or King of Egypt, or, as more generally received, the Khedive. And by the same firman, obtained on condition that he increased the annual tribute to the Sultan from £376,000 to £720,000, the succession to the throne of Egypt was made hereditary on the European principle—that is, from father to son, instead of descending, according to the Turkish custom, to the eldest heir. Another firman, dated June 8, 1873, virtually conceded to him independence, by granting the rights, hitherto refused, of concluding treaties with foreign powers, and of maintaining an army.

The luxurious ostentation of his court, the profligacy of his administration, the profuse hospitality which he exercised, the vast sums which he expended on his pleasures, prevented Ismail from lightening the intolerable burdens which pressed upon his subjects; yet was he not without some sentiment of public duty. And the successful construction and completion of the Suez Canal, the great water-way between the Mediterranean and the Indian Ocean, were in no small measure due to his liberal and enlightened encouragement. His ambition, however, in another direction, proved of evil import to his country and himself, and involved a series of remarkable and unexpected consequences to which history presents no parallel.

The southern boundary of Egypt proper is placed at Wady Halfa. Thence spreads to the southward a vast region of desert and wilderness, relieved here and there by tracts of fertility, known as the Soudan. It measures 1600 miles from north to south and 1200 miles from east to west. Owing to the want of

KHARTÛM.

water, it is almost inaccessible by the sea; and it has neither canals nor navigable rivers, except the Nile during a portion of the year, and its only roads are camel tracks. It is inhabited by Arab tribes, all holding the Mohammedan faith, and all brave and fond of war. Its eastern boundary is the Red Sea; its western, Darfur; its northern, Egypt; and its southern, the lakes of Central Africa. Almost in its centre, at the junction of the Blue and White Niles, is situated its capital, Khartûm, or Khartoum, which of late has acquired for all English-speaking peoples so romantic and pathetic an interest.* From this town to the ports of Suakim and Massowah on the Red Sea is about 400 miles. Descending the

---

* The following description of Khartûm is adapted from one written by Lieutenant-Colonel Stewart in 1883:—The capital of the Soudan, and the chief trade emporium for the whole country, it is built on a wide plain, barren and stoneless, on the western bank of the Blue Nile, and about a mile above its junction with the White Nile. At their lowest point both streams are from 600 to 800 yards wide, and are studded with cultivated islands. When in flood, the White Nile broadens to a very considerable extent; but not so the Blue Nile, as its banks are much steeper. Around Khartûm are several small villages. Both above and below the town flourish small plantations of date palms and plantains and a number of vegetable gardens. During the hot season, from the beginning of April till the middle of November, the heat is severe, averaging in the shade from 90° to 95° F. The rains generally begin about mid-July and last till mid-September, and at this time the barren ground between the two rivers is covered with grass, affording excellent pasture. The cold weather begins about the middle of December and lasts till the middle of February. The thermometer sinks sometimes as low as 46°. There is no rain except in the rainy season. The resident population is generally estimated at from 50,000 to 55,000 souls, of whom two-thirds are slaves. There is also (or was) a floating population, estimated at from 1500 to 2000, consisting of Europeans, Syrians, Copts, Turks, Albanians, and a few Jews. Both the free population (who are mostly Mukhars or aborigines, Dongolawees, and Shaghhiyés) and the slaves are all Mohammedans. They are very superstitious. In shape the town is very irregular, and in appearance very miserable. The houses are mostly built of sun-dried brick, and to prevent them from crumbling away, they are generally plastered over with dung every year before the rainy season begins.

Nile, in the direction of Egypt, we find two towns of importance—Berber, about 200 miles distant, and Dongola, about 350 miles. We may note, by the way, that the direct route from Khartûm to Egypt does not touch Dongola, but, leaving the Nile at Abu Hamed, 220 miles below Berber, where the river makes a great westward bend towards Dongola, strikes across the desert to Korosko, where it again takes to the Nile and follows it to Assouan, about 850 miles from Khartûm. Berber is a point of special importance, because it is there that the camel track across the desert from Suakim, the chief port of the Soudan, touches the Nile. The distance from Suakim to Berber is estimated at 280 miles, and this is the line proposed to be covered by a railway commenced by the British Government in 1885.

The principal product of the Soudan is—slaves. It had long been the chief hunting-ground of Zebehr and other great slave-dealers, and its possession was coveted by the Egyptian pashas because it would supply them with facilities for carrying on the inhuman traffic which filled their coffers. Its sovereignty was first seized by Egypt in 1819, when the internecine wars between its tribes furnished Mehemet Ali with an excuse for its invasion. Professing a disinterested desire to bestow on it the blessings of civilization, he despatched thither his son Ismail with a large force of regular and irregular troops. Ismail penetrated to Khartûm, and established there an orderly government; but he and all his followers were burned alive by a native chief, who first intoxicated them at his own table, and then set fire to his house over their heads. For this act of treachery a terrible vengeance was

KOROSKO.

taken by Mehemet Ali, and gradually the rule of Egypt was extended over Sennaar and Kordofan. In 1826, Kurschid Pasha was appointed Governor. During his vigorous administration, which lasted eleven years, peace and order prevailed in the Soudan. He established Egyptian sovereignty over Fushoda, and taught the inhabitants of Khartûm to substitute brick houses for their huts of skins and thatch. In 1841 a rebellion broke out at Kassala; it was suppressed, but broke out again in the following year, when it was put down with ruthless severity. At that time the Soudan consisted of seven provinces—namely, Fazaglow, Sennaar, Khartûm, Tokha, Berber, Dongola, and Kordofan. In 1856 Said Pasha visited the Soudan, and in his conviction that it was a burden upon the revenues of Egypt had almost decided upon its abandonment, but was overruled by the representations of the men whose fortunes depended upon the maintenance of the slave-trade. He directed that several reforms should be carried out, but on his return to Egypt his directions were systematically ignored.

In 1865 a formidable revolt broke out among the negro troops, some 8000 in number, stationed at Tokha. They had received no pay for eighteen months. A large military force was sent from Cairo by Korosko, and another body by Suakim, and the revolt was crushed in blood. The negro troops were sent to Egypt, and thenceforward the Soudan was held by Egyptian garrisons. In 1870 Ismail enlisted the services of the famous explorer Sir Samuel Baker and of the German traveller Munzinger, and by their efforts the rule of Egypt was extended over the Equatorial Provinces.

Sir Samuel Baker returned from the Equator in 1873, having honourably distinguished himself by his exertions to suppress or limit the trade in human lives; and in the following year, Colonel Charles Gordon, who had obtained great renown by his suppression of the Tai-ping rebellion in China, was appointed Governor-General of the Equatorial Provinces. Four years later he became absolute ruler of the Soudan; and in this capacity displayed those high moral and intellectual qualities which have invested his memory with enduring interest. He organized a system of just and equitable government, which provided for the welfare of all classes. Prior to his appointment he had warned the Khedive that he would render it for ever impossible for Turks and Circassians to misgovern the Soudan again. He kept his word. By dealing out even-handed justice to the people, by listening with sympathetic attention to all their grievances, by strongly repressing every violation of the law, he accustomed the Soudanese to a purer and loftier standard of administration than they had ever before known. During his sovereignty he effectually prevented the court at Cairo from intermeddling in the Soudan, whether that intermeddling took the form of native or European interference. He contrived to balance revenue and expenditure, so that the Soudan was no burden to the Egyptian exchequer, while at the same time a very light taxation was levied upon the native inhabitants. The suppression of the slave-trade was an object dear to his heart, and he laboured at it with all the resolution and courage and singleness of purpose that marked his character. The work was fraught with peculiar perils. As one of his biographers puts it :—" It demanded a tact, an energy, and a force of will almost superhuman. He had to deal not only with worthless and often mutinous governors of provinces, but with wild and desperate tribesmen as well; he had to disband 6000 Bashi-Bazouks, who were used as frontier-guards, but who winked at slave-hunting and robbed the tribes on their own account; he had to subdue and bring to order and rule the vast province of the Bahr Gazelle, then beneath the sway of the great slaver Zebehr.* It was a stupendous task: to give peace to a country quick with war; to suppress slavery among a people to whom the trade in human flesh was life and honour and fortune; to make an army out of perhaps the worst material ever seen; to grow a flourishing trade and a fair revenue in the wildest anarchy in the world. The immensity of the undertaking; the infinity of details involved in a single step towards the end; the countless odds to be faced; the many pests—the deadly climate, the horrible vermin, the ghastly itch, the nightly and daily alternation of overpowering heat and bitter cold—to be endured and overcome; the environment of bestial savagery and ruthless fanaticism,—all these combine to make the achievement unique in human history."

In the midst of his campaign against Zebehr and the other great slave-dealers, Gordon wrote :—" No man ever had a harder task than I, unaided, have before me; but it sits as a feather on me. As Solomon asked, I ask wisdom to govern this great people; and not only will

---

* This man, the so-called "king of the slave-dealers," was arrested in March 1885, by order of the British Government, on a charge of complicity with the Mahdi, and removed to Gibraltar.

He give me it, but all also besides. And why? Because I value not the 'all besides.' I am quite as averse to slavery, and even more so than most people. I show it by sacrificing myself in these lands, which are no paradise. I have nought to gain in name or riches. I do not care what man may say. I do what I think is pleasing to my God; and, as far as man goes, I need nothing from any one. The Khedive never had directly gained any revenue from slaves. I now hold his place here; and I, who am on the spot with unlimited power, am able to judge how impotent he, at Cairo, is to stop the slave-trade. I can do it with God's help, and I have the conviction he has destined me to do it; for it was much against my will I came here. What I have to do is so to settle matters that I do not cause a revolution or my own death. Not that I value life. I have done with its comforts in coming here. My work is great, but does not weigh me down. I go on as straight as I can. I feel my own weakness, and look to Him who is Almighty; and I leave the issue without inordinate care to him. I expect to ride 5000 miles this year if I am spared. I am quite alone, and like it. I have become what people call a great fatalist—namely, I trust God will pull me through. The solitary grandeur of the desert makes one feel how vain is the effort of man. This carries me through my troubles, and makes me to look on death as a coming relief, when it is his will......It is only my firm conviction that I am only an instrument put in use for a time that enables me to bear up; and in my present state, during my long, hot, weary rides, I think my thoughts better and clearer than I should with a companion."

Differences of opinion with the Egyptian Government led to Gordon's resignation of his post at the end of 1879. Meanwhile stirring events had taken place at Cairo, the issue of which we must rapidly trace before we return to the Soudan. Owing to a variety of circumstances, England and France conceived themselves to have just grounds of complaint against the Khedive Ismail, and in June 1879 they procured a firman from the Porte authorizing his deposition, and the appointment in his place of his son, Mohammed Tewfik (born November 19, 1852). The two great Western Powers pledged themselves to the support of Tewfik, so long as he maintained order and governed discreetly; and came to an agreement between themselves to supervise the financial system and domestic government of Egypt. This was known as the Dual Control, or Anglo-French condominium. Two Controllers-General were therefore appointed by England and France, and a decree of the new Khedive, dated November 10, invested them with considerable power in the direction of affairs. But the experiment did not work well. The objects of the two Governments were not in accord; for while England was simply desirous that the finances of Egypt should be honestly and prudently administered and the free navigation of the Suez Canal secured, France was solicitous that the interests of the bondholders should be protected, and aimed also, through her agents and officials, at obtaining an ascendency in Egyptian councils. An able journalist has briefly but clearly explained the situation:—"When, in 1879," he says, "the Governments of England and France deposed Ismail and set up Tewfik on the throne of Egypt, they committed themselves to a pseudo-protectorate of the Pashalik of the Nile. From the deposition of Ismail, England has been led on step by step to assume what now amounts to a virtual, although unacknowledged, sovereignty over Egypt. It is much easier even now to complain of this increase of our responsibilities than it is to indicate, with all the wisdom gained by experience, the precise point at which any English Government could have withdrawn from intervention in Egyptian affairs. Non-interference was possible, of course, but only on condition that English non-interventionists were willing to acquiesce in French intervention. English public opinion being unanimously hostile to the establishment of a French protectorate *à la* Tunis over the country commanding the Suez Canal non-intervention was impossible for any English Government. And if we were ready to go to war to keep the French out, it followed as a corollary that we must be equally ready to interfere to remove causes which would have justified and necessitated French intervention. Thus it came to pass that as we conquered India solely in order to forestall the French in the East, so we have occupied Egypt in order to render impossible the establishment of French ascendency on the highway to India...... The key of the situation lies in the necessity of preventing the Power that controls the canal becoming the mere creature of France."

The Dual Control could, under no circumstances, have existed long. It was dissolved, however, by a movement which belonged to the category of "the unexpected." To the Egyptian officials and the army it was necessarily unwelcome; and in the summer of 1882 a violent effort was made to get rid of it, and to expel foreigners from all positions of importance, by a colonel in the Egyptian service, named Arabi Pasha. He obtained a commanding influence in the Egyptian Ministry, occupied Alexandria with troops, placed the Khedive under close watch and ward, and proceeded to strengthen the fortifications of Alexandria with a view to resist foreign intervention. Alarmed for the safety of the Suez Canal, and pledged to uphold the authority of the Khedive, England prepared to interfere. She invited the co-operation of France. Fortunately this was refused, and she was free to do the work alone. The Mediterranean fleet, under Admiral Sir Beauchamp Seymour (now Lord Alcester), entered the harbour of Alexandria. An ultimatum was sent to Arabi Pasha demanding within forty-eight hours the surrender of the forts; and when this was ignored, the fleet, on Tuesday morning, July 3rd, opened fire and hurled a storm of shot and shell at the Egyptian batteries which speedily silenced the guns and reduced the fortifications to ruins.

The convicts, who had been purposely released from the prisons, profited by the disorder and terror that prevailed to gratify their lust of blood and greed of money. Hundreds of Europeans and wealthy Arabs were massacred, and the burning houses that flamed throughout the European quarter threatened a general conflagration. On Friday, the 7th, "two miles of fire" were visible. Admiral Seymour landed a body of marines and seamen, who patrolled the streets, and eventually succeeded in restoring order and arresting the ringleaders; but millions of property had been destroyed, and upwards of 2000 persons had lost their lives. Arabi retired upon Cairo; and in order to crush the rebellion, the British Government sent out a small but well-appointed army, under General Sir Garnet (now Lord) Wolseley, who, entering the Suez Canal, landed his troops at a point near Ismailia, struck into the interior, and by a bold and brilliant night march surprised the rebels at Tel-el-Kebir, and inflicted upon them a tremendous defeat. A few squadrons of horsemen, under Redvers Buller, then rode onward to Cairo, dashed into the alarmed city, and took possession. Arabi was made prisoner, and the rebellion suddenly collapsed. Arabi was afterwards tried before a Commission; and, on the 4th of December, having pleaded guilty of rebellion, was sentenced to death. Through the intervention of the British Government, the sentence was modified to one of perpetual exile from Egypt, and Arabi was sent to Ceylon.

While formally declaring its resolution neither to annex Egypt nor establish a protectorate over it, England felt compelled to undertake the responsibility of its administration, in conjunction with the Khedive and his advisers; and to maintain internal tranquillity, English garrisons were thrown into Cairo and Alexandria. On the 18th of January 1883, the Dual Control was abolished; and in its place the Khedive, on the recommendation of England, appointed a single European financial adviser, who should have a consultative voice in the Council of Ministers, but no direct power of interference in matters of internal administration. To this office Sir Evelyn Baring, K.C.S.I., was appointed in May; and circumstances having gradually extended the sphere of his influence, his present position may, perhaps, be fairly described as nearly analogous to that of a British Resident at the court of an Indian prince.

The Earl of Dufferin was sent to Egypt in the later months of 1883 to inquire into its domestic condition and investigate the administrative deficiencies and social evils under which it laboured. After several weeks of assiduous labour, he submitted to the English Ministry an exhaustive report, embodying a careful outline of the reforms needed in every department of the state, and suggesting numerous measures for the benefit of its inhabitants and the development of its resources. Already several of his recommendations have been acted upon, and have borne good fruit; but the reorganization of a state so supremely feeble as is Egypt must necessarily demand a considerable period.

Briefly speaking, the Egyptian constitution now stands as follows:—

The Khedive acts by the advice and through the agency of his Ministers, who are five in number: 1. The President, who superintends the departments of foreign affairs and justice; 2. The Finance Minister; 3. The Minister for War, Marine, and Interior; 4. The Minister for Public Works; and 5. The Minister for Education. Provincial Councils, created by an Organic Law, on May 1, 1883, are composed of members chosen on the principle of universal suffrage by indirect election. Their duties are to advise upon local questions, and to levy extraordinary supplies for local purposes. Then there is also the Legislative Council of 30 members, 16 of them chosen on the same principle as the

Provincial Councils, and 14 appointed by the Khedive. This Council takes cognizance of all petitions addressed to the Khedive, and advises him upon all important public questions; its advice being accepted or rejected by the Council of Members, who must give reasons for this acceptance or rejection. It is to be summoned on the first of each alternate month from February to December, and at such other times as the Khedive may direct. Its members are elected for six years. The Organic Law to which we have referred also creates a General Assembly, consisting of the 5 Ministers, the 30 members of the Legislative Council, and 46 delegate notables chosen by indirect election for certain towns and districts for a period of six years. This Assembly—the Egyptian Parliament, in fact—must be summoned at least every two years. It controls or introduces taxation; advises the Government on loans, public works, land-taxes, and other national questions; and offers its advice or opinion upon all matters of public importance, whether economic, administrative, or financial.

Egypt proper is divided, for administrative purposes, into eight governorships of principal towns and fourteen moudirehs or provinces. The *Governorats* are Cairo, Alexandria, Damietta, Rosetta, Port Said, Suez, El-Arish, and Kosseir; the *Moudirehs*—Behera, Charkieh, Dakahlieh, Gharbieh, Kalionbieh, Menoufieh, Assiout, Beni Souef, Fayoum, Guizeh, Minieh, Esneh, Guerga, and Kena.

The worthlessness and untrustworthiness of the Egyptian army having been abundantly proved, it was disbanded by a decree of the Khedive in September 1882. Three months later Major-General Sir Evelyn Wood, on whom was bestowed the title of Sirdar, was charged with the organization of a new army, in which he was assisted by twenty English officers supplied by the English War Office. The new army, the discipline and martial bearing of which are all that could be desired, but the military efficiency of which has not yet been tested, consists of eight battalions of infantry, four squadrons of cavalry, and four batteries of artillery,—in all, 5800 men.

Having thus briefly sketched the events which led to the occupation of Egypt by a British army, and the supervision of its administration by the British Government, we return to the Soudan. The position assumed by the British Government necessarily made England responsible for the defence of Egypt proper; but they declined to regard the Soudan as included within their sphere of operation, and advised the Egyptian Ministry to abandon a province which had always been a heavy burden on the resources of Egypt. The Khedive and his advisers, however, were reluctant to act upon this advice, and took such measures as were within their power to subdue the insurrection which had broken out there as early as 1881.

The original cause of this insurrection was undoubtedly the oppression exercised by the swarm of Turks and Circassians and Bashi-Bazouks which, on the departure of Gordon from the Soudan, was let loose upon its miserable inhabitants. But through the influence of an extraordinary man, it gradually assumed a religious character, extended over the whole of the Soudan, and developed into a great military movement for the extension of Mohammedanism. This man, now known throughout the world by his assumed title of the Mahdi, or Prophet, is named Mohammed Achmet, and is a native of the province of Dongola. In his boyhood he was apprenticed to his uncle, a boat-builder; but having one day received a beating from him, he ran away to Khartûm, and joined the free school, or "medressee," of a *faki*—that is, a learned man, head of a sect of dervishes—who resided at the neighbouring village of Hoghali. Here he for some time remained, immersed in religious studies, but making scant progress in the secular accomplishments of reading and writing. He completed his theological education at another free school, kept by a sheikh at a village opposite to Berber. In 1870 he became a disciple of another faki, Nur-el-Daim, who subsequently ordained him a sheikh, or faki; whereupon he withdrew to the island of Abba, near Kana, on the White Nile. Having made there a *khaliva*, or subterraneous retreat, he retired to it, several hours daily, to repeat one of the names of the Deity, accompanied by fasting, incense-burning, and prayer. His repute for sanctity soon spread far and wide; he became wealthy through the offerings of the faithful, married several wives, all of whom were influentially connected, and made a host of disciples. It seems to have been in the spring of 1881 that he began to write to his brother fakis, and to give out that he was the Mahdi whose appearance was foretold by Mohammed; that he had a divine mission to reform Islam, to establish a universal equality, a universal law, a universal religion, and a community of goods; and

A RELIGIOUS WAR. 99

that all who did not believe in him, whether Christian, Mohammedan, or pagan, should be destroyed. In an incredibly short period of time a large force was collected, pledged to obey his commands; a force, irregular indeed in discipline, and imperfectly equipped, but composed of the bravest warriors of the great Arab tribes—men whom fanaticism inspires with an absolute contempt for death.

His first military operations, however, were unsuccessful. In the winter of 1881 he was defeated in the south of Sennaar, but retreating up the Blue Nile he largely increased his army, whose faith in their leader had undergone no diminution. Having matured his plans, he made a fresh departure, and crossing the White Nile, invaded the country watered by the Gazelle river. In July 1882 his forces surrounded 6000 Egyptian soldiers under Yussuf Pasha, and massacred them to a man. In August he advanced upon the important town of Obeid, which was garrisoned by Egyptian troops. Three attempts to take it by storm were defeated with heavy loss; but he held his ground tenaciously, and cut off all its communications with the surrounding country, and on the 15th of January 1883 it surrendered unconditionally. The capture of Obeid invested the Mahdi with the prestige of success, while it convinced the Egyptian Government that if the insurrection were to be put down vigorous proceedings were indispensable. It collected all its disposable forces, and put them under the command of Colonel Hicks, a British officer who had seen much service in India. On the 1st of March 1883 he arrived at Berber. On the 29th of April he attacked a body of 5000 rebels near Duem, and defeated them with heavy loss. On the

5th of October he marched from Duem for the purpose of recapturing Obeid. A month later he encountered the hosts of the Mahdi at Kashgate, and after three days' fighting (November 2nd, 3rd, and 4th) his army was annihilated,—a disaster which compelled the Egyptian Ministry to act on the advice of the British Government and abandon its attempt to recover the Soudan. At the same time England pledged herself to undertake the defence of Egypt proper, and British military posts were thrown forward as far as Assouan and Wady Halfa.

In the Eastern Soudan, the insurrection was not less formidable than in the Western. Its leader, Osman Digna, a man of considerable military capacity, who had acknowledged the Mahdi and been appointed his lieutenant, raised the Arab tribes, with few exceptions, and in August they surrounded the Egyptian garrisons at Sinkat and Tokha, severing communications between Berber and Suakim, and threatening Suakim itself, where they were kept at bay only by the presence of British gunboats in the harbour. At the beginning of November a force of Egyptian soldiers was despatched for the relief of the garrison of Tokha; but on the 6th of November it was surrounded by the insurgents, and perished to a man. Valentine Baker, formerly a lieutenant-colonel in the British army, but holding the appointment of commander of a newly-formed force of Egyptian *gendarmerie*, was then sent to Suakim to relieve, if possible, the imperilled garrisons. But when about half-way between Suakim and Sinkat, in December 1883, his troops were met by Osman Digna's warriors, and with scarcely any attempt at resistance, threw down their arms. A terrible

SUAKIM.

massacre ensued; and it was with difficulty that Colonel Baker and a few of his officers effected their escape.

As it was impossible to permit the occupation of Suakim by the rebels, the British Government despatched a small army under General (now Sir Gerald) Graham, with orders to drive back Osman Digna. The result was the fierce battle of Tamai, in which a British infantry square was at one time actually broken into, but the steadiness of our troops retrieved the mishap, and after some hard fighting, the Arabs were totally defeated with great slaughter. It was supposed that the moral impression of this victory would prevent further aggression on the part of Osman Digna; but this sanguine anticipation was not fulfilled, and an expedition of 12,000 troops of all arms, including an Indian contingent of 3000,—the whole under Sir Gerald Graham,—was landed at Suakim in the early part of March 1885 for the purpose of crushing Osman Digna and advancing to Berber. Engagements with the enemy took place on the 20th, 21st, and 22nd, as Graham advanced along the hills towards Tamai, the scene of his former victory. In all these the British were successful; and the loss of the Arabs was so tremendous that Osman Digna was compelled to retreat to the hills. In the month of May, therefore, a great portion of the British army was withdrawn.

While recommending the abandonment of the Soudan, the British Government were desirous of doing all that could be done for the relief of the Egyptian garrisons scattered over that wide region. To Khartûm their attention was particularly directed; and they gladly accepted the offer of General Gordon to exert his immense personal influence to secure its peaceable evacuation. He left London on Friday, January 18, 1884. The instructions given to him by the Ministry are embodied in the following letter from Lord Granville :—

"SIR,—Her Majesty's Government are desirous that you should proceed at once to Egypt to report to them on the military situation in the Soudan, and on the measures which it may be advisable to take for the security of the Egyptian garrisons still holding positions in that country, and for the safety of the European population in Khartûm. You are also desired to consider and report upon the best mode of effecting the evacuation of the interior of the Soudan, and upon the manner in which the safety and the good administration by the Egyptian Government of the ports on the sea coast can best be secured. In connection with this subject, you should pay especial consideration to the question of the steps that may usefully be taken to counteract the stimulus which it is feared may possibly be given to the slave-trade by the present insurrectionary movement and by the withdrawal of the Egyptian authority from the interior. You will be accompanied by Colonel Stewart, who will assist you in the duties thus confided to you. On your arrival in Egypt you will at once communicate with Sir Evelyn Baring, who will arrange to meet you and will settle with you whether you should proceed direct to Suakim, or should go yourself or despatch Colonel Stewart to Khartûm *viâ* the Nile."

On General Gordon's arrival at Cairo, it was decided, after consultation with Sir Evelyn Baring and the Khedive, who conferred upon him the title of Governor-General of the Soudan, that he should immediately proceed to Khartûm *viâ* the Nile; and accordingly he set out, with no other companion than Colonel Stewart. At Khartûm he was warmly welcomed by the inhabitants, and with the energy and intelligence characteristic of the man, took immediate steps to establish order, administer justice, and prepare for a vigorous defence of the town against the Mahdi, for that a pacific settlement was impossible he soon convinced himself. He caused some surprise to his friends in England by a request that his old enemy Zebehr, the great slave-dealer, should be sent to Khartûm to assume the governorship. "I would take out the Cairo employés," he wrote, "and Zebehr Pasha would put his own men there. I would evacuate the equatorial Bahr Gazelle provinces, and hand over the troops to Zebehr Pasha, who would before the end of the year finish off the Mahdi." This startling request the British Government, however, did not feel able to grant.

Meanwhile the Mahdi's forces gradually closed around Khartûm, and that memorable siege began which for ten months excited so profound an interest, and in the military history of the world must always prove one of its most stirring and romantic chapters. The investment was complete on the 16th of April, so complete that messengers could neither enter nor leave the city, and it was not until the 29th of September that news of Gordon were again forthcoming. These were obtained through the diary of Mr. Power, the English consul at Khartûm, which began in March and continued its record of events to the 31st of July. Reaching England by way of Kassala and Massowah, it was published on the 29th of September. It bore testimony to the vigour with which Gordon had conducted the defence and to the plenitude of his intellectual resources. Despatches from Gordon were received in October. From these it appeared that he had sent, on the 17th of September, Colonel Stewart, Mr. Power, and the French consul, with a body of regular troops and Bashi-Bazouks, to recapture Berber, and he was daily expecting to hear of their success. It was afterwards ascertained that they *did* attack and capture Berber; that afterwards Colonel Stewart sent back the troops and steamers to Khartûm; and that he himself, with Mr. Power and M. Herbin, resolved to descend the river to Dongola in a small boat. Unfortunately it struck on a rock near Wady Gama, and the three Europeans were treacherously murdered by an Arab sheikh, in whose offers of hospitality they had confided. Thenceforward Gordon was alone in Khartûm, with a garrison whose fidelity might well be doubted, and surrounded by enemies whose attacks might at any moment prove successful.

That it would be needful to despatch an expedition to Khartûm for the rescue of Gordon was a conclusion at which the British Government reluctantly arrived in the course of the summer of 1884. Preparations were made accordingly throughout the months of August and September; and an army of 8000 men, under the command of General Lord Wolseley, began the ascent of the Nile in October. The difficulties of the route were enormous, but the skill of the commander and the resolution of his men triumphed over them, and the army arrived at Korti on the 16th of December. Here Wolseley received intelligence from

Gordon which showed that the defence could not be protracted beyond a few days; and he resolved therefore to throw forward a column across the desert to Metammeh, a point on the Nile about twenty miles below Khartûm, whence it would be easy to open up communications with its heroic defender. The hazard was great, for the country all around swarmed with rebels; but it was justified by the object in view. A strong position was secured at Gakdul Wells, and thence a body of about 1200 men, led by Sir Herbert Stewart, advanced upon Metammeh. On the 17th, this small force came into collision with 10,000 of the Mahdi's forces near the Abu Tlea Wells, and after a desperate hand-to-hand fight drove them back. It was on this occasion that Colonel Burnaby lost his life. After resting his men for a few hours, Stewart resumed his advance, and at Gubat, about five miles from the Nile, again encountered the enemy. He cut his way through them with splendid gallantry, killing and wounding some 2000 of the rebels, and at sunset reached the banks of the great river. Unfortunately he was severely wounded in the action, and the command of the little column temporarily devolved on Sir Charles Wilson, who, after a reconnaissance in force upon Metammeh, decided that with his handful of men an attack upon it would be dangerous, and therefore fortified his position at Gubat. On the 22nd five steamers arrived from Khartûm, sent by General Gordon; they had on board five hundred soldiers and five guns. After a most unfortunate waste of time in fruitlessly bombarding Shendy, Sir Charles Wilson, with a couple of steamers, ascended the river to Khartûm, experiencing a heavy fire at Halfiyeh and Omdurman, both which places were occupied by the Mahdi's soldiers. He succeeded in getting within a mile of the city, but only to find that, four days before, through the treachery of Faraz Pasha, one of Gordon's lieutenants, the rebels had poured into the city, and made themselves masters of it; that Khartûm had fallen, and that Gordon, the Christian hero, had been killed in the *mêlée* (January 27, 1885). Wilson then returned to Gubat, not without a narrow escape from falling into the enemy's hands. Lord Wolseley, on receiving this melancholy information, was compelled to change his plans. With the small force at his disposal, and the hot season rapidly approaching, when military operations are almost impossible for European troops, an attempt to recapture Khartûm he decided to be impracticable, and he hastened to recall Sir Herbert Stewart's column, and a detachment which, under General Earle, had been sent forward up the Nile to strike at Berber, to Korti, where his headquarters were stationed.* It should be added that General Earle won a brilliant victory over the enemy at Kerbekan, but was slain in the conflict.

The financial condition of Egypt has proved a serious obstacle to the British Government in the arduous task which it has undertaken of regenerating Egypt.

On the 5th of April, 1880, an International Commission was appointed to examine the financial condition of Egypt, and propose some satisfactory settlement of the relations between Egypt and her creditors. By that Commission, in concert with the Egyptian Government,

* The British forces have since been withdrawn from the Soudan, and concentrated at Wady Halfa.

BERBER, FROM THE DESERT.

the annual income of the country was estimated at £E8,411,622* for 1882 and after. Their estimate of the expenditure was :—

Government—		
Tribute	£E681,486	
Moukabalah annuity	150,000	
Interest to England on Suez Canal shares	193,858	
Daira Khassa	34,000	
Administrative expenses	3,641,544	
Unforeseen expenditure	197,000	
		4,897,888
Debt—		
Privileged Stock	1,157,718	
Unified	2,263,686	
		3,421,404
		£E8,319,292

The Commissioners assigned (1) to the payment of the interest on the Privileged Debt the railway and telegraph income and the port dues of Alexandria; and (2) to the service of the Unified Stock the customs revenues and the taxes of four provinces. But the financial results of the three years—1881, 1882, and 1883—showed a deficit of about two million on the budget assigned to the Government, which, in September 1884, was compelled to appropriate, for administrative purposes, a portion of the surplus of the revenues assigned to the debt. And it was calculated that on December 31st, 1884, the floating debt would amount to £E7,811,000. Thus :—

Ordinary deficit	£E2,238,000
Alexandria indemnities	4,130,000
Cost of evacuation of Soudan	1,000,000
Commutation of pensions	150,000
Cost of British army of occupation	293,000
	£E7,811,000

* £1 Egyptian equals £1, 0s 6d. sterling.

In order to pay off this floating debt and secure a balance in future budgets, the British Government proposed to a Conference of the Powers, held in London in June and July 1884, to guarantee a pre-preference loan of £8,000,000 to the Egyptian Government, with interest and sinking fund at the rate of $4\frac{1}{2}$ per cent. It also proposed the abolition of the existing Sinking Fund, and a reduction of one-half per cent. in the interest of the Preference and the Unified Stock, as well as on the interest paid to England on account of the Suez Canal shares. After a prolonged discussion, the Conference separated without coming to a decision, the other Great Powers looking unfavourably on the British propositions. In September 1884 the Earl of Northbrook was sent as High Commissioner to Egypt to inquire into and report upon the financial and general condition of the country; but his recommendations were not adopted by the Government. Early in 1885 France reopened the question, and another Conference was held, which, after protracted debates, formulated a convention and declaration accepted by all the Powers. Its main features may briefly be summarized:—The six Great Powers—England, France, Germany, Italy, Austria, and Russia—agree that the Khedive shall raise a loan of £9,000,000, at $3\frac{1}{2}$ per cent., to be guaranteed by them all, Russia only making the reservation that if a default should occur she will not pay more than her sixth. The Khedive is also authorized to place a tax of 5 per cent. upon the coupons of the Unified Debt and the Domains Debts for two years; to reduce the interest on the Suez Canal shares belonging to the British Government by a half per cent.; and to tax foreign residents like his own subjects. The international guarantee will not carry with it any right of international control; but at the end of the two years an international inquiry will determine whether the land tax of Egypt requires reduction, and whether the tax upon the coupons can be abolished. During the two years England will remain in occupation, and will receive £200,000 a year in part payment of her military expenses.

Briefly speaking, the arrangement may be described as a stop-gap which postpones for two years the final decision of Europe on the Egyptian question.

Egypt proper is divided into two great districts—"Musr-el-Bahri," or Lower Egypt, and "El Said," or Upper Egypt—which together comprise 394,240 English square miles. According to the census of May 3rd, 1882, the population amounted to 6,806,381 souls—3,965,664 in Lower Egypt and 2,840,717 in Upper Egypt. Of this total, 3,396,308 were males and 3,410,073 females. The number of foreign residents was :—Greeks, 37,301; Italians, 18,665; French, 15,716; Austrians, 8022; English, 6118; Germans, 948; other nationalities, 4116: total, 90,886.

The imports into Egypt in 1883 were valued at £E8,596,976; the exports, £E12,309,885. England imported Egyptian produce to the value of £E8,625,939, and exported British wares to the value of £E3,882,473.

The railway system of Egypt had a total length, in January 1884, of 1276 miles, and the telegraphs belonging to the Government of 2707 miles. The Eastern Telegraph Company have a line to Cairo 445 miles in length.

CHAPTER III.

THE RISE AND COURSE OF THE RIVER NILE.

> From thence, through deserts dry, thou journey'st on,
> Nor shrink'st, diminished by the Torrid Zone,
> Strong in thyself, collected, full, and one.
> Anon, thy streams are parcelled o'er the plain;
> Anon, the scattered currents meet again;
> Jointly they flow, where Philae's gates divide
> Our fertile Egypt from Arabia's side;
> Thence, with a peaceful soft descent they creep,
> And seek, insensibly, the distant deep;
> Till through seven mouths the famous flood is lost,
> On the last limits of our Pharian coast.
>   LUCAN, *Pharsalia*, book x., *Rowe's Translation*.

> Thus do they, sir: they take the flow o' the Nile
> By certain scales i' the Pyramid; they know
> By the height, the lowness, or the mean, if death
> Or prison follow.
>   SHAKSPEARE, *Antony and Cleopatra*.

> See where it flows, disgorging at seven mouths
> Into the sea.
>   MILTON, *Paradise Lost*.

AS the memorials of antiquity — the tombs, temples, and monuments of old Egypt—to whose description the following pages are dedicated, lie in the valley—that is, on the banks—of the Nile, it seems desirable we should briefly sketch the course of that remarkable river. Apart from

A LANDSCAPE ON THE NILE.

the physical phenomena attending its annual inundation, the mystery which so long hovered about its sources has always rendered it an object of wonder and curiosity, from the days of Herodotus and Diodorus, Heliodorus and Lucan, to those of Speke, Grant, and Sir Samuel Baker.

Everything in Egypt, as Miss Martineau remarks—life itself, and all that life includes—depends on the incessant struggle which the great river maintains against the forces of the Desert. The world has witnessed many conflicts; but no other so unresting, so protracted, and so sublime as the struggle of these two gigantic Powers. The Nile, ever young, because perpetually renewing its youth, seems to the inexperienced eye to have no chance with its stripling force—a David against a Goliath—against the Desert, whose might has never relaxed, from the earliest days till now; but the Goliath has not conquered it. Now and then he has prevailed for a season, and the tremblers whose destiny hung on the event have cried out that all was over; but he has once more been driven back, and Nilus has risen up again, to do what we see him doing in the sculptures—bind up his water-plants about the throne of Egypt.*

From the beginning, continues Miss Martineau, the people of Egypt have had everything to hope from the River, nothing from the Desert; much to fear from the Desert, and little from the River. What their *fear* may reasonably be, any one may conjecture who has looked upon a hillocky expanse of sand, where the little jerboa burrows, and the hyena prowls at night. Under these hil-

* Miss Martineau, "Eastern Life: Past and Present."

locks lie temples and palaces, and under the level sands a whole city! The enemy has come in from behind, and stifled and buried it. What is the *hope* of the people from the river, any one may witness who, at the regular season, sees the people grouped on the eminences, watching the advancing waters, and listening for the voice of the crier, or the boom of the cannon which is to tell the prospect or event of the inundation of the year. The Nile was naturally deified by the old inhabitants. It was a god to the mass; and at least one of the manifestations of Deity to the priestly order. As it was the immediate cause of all they had, and all they hoped for—the creative power regularly at work before their eyes, usually conquering, though occasionally checked—it was to them the Good Power; and the Desert became the Evil one. Hence originated a main part of their faith, embodied in the allegory of the burial of Osiris in the sacred stream, whence he rose, once a year, to scatter blessings over the earth.

The sources of this wonderful river—so intimately bound up with the fortunes and creed of a great people—were long involved in obscurity. Until partly solved by the labours of Speke, Grant, Baker, and Cameron, the problem was one which stimulated the curiosity and foiled the ingenuity of geographers. It would be interesting both for writer and readers to reproduce the story of the Nile from the days of Herodotus to those of Cameron, and to narrate the attempts of adventurous travellers to reach the mysterious source of its head-waters. But these pages must be devoted to other themes, and we must content ourselves with a statement of *results*.

The source of the *Blue* Nile was discovered by James

Bruce in 1770; but that of the more important *White Nile*, which is, indeed, the true Nile, remained enshrouded in obscurity. About 1840 three Egyptian expeditions were sent in search of it; but they devoted themselves to slave-hunting rather than to geographical research. In 1849 a Roman Catholic mission was established at Gondokoro, in lat. 4° 24′ 5″ N.; and thence as a starting-point several travellers, such as Brun-Rollet, Werne, and Malsay, endeavoured to penetrate farther southward. They were baffled by the nature of the country and by the animosity of the natives, who had suffered severely from the Egyptian slave-hunters; but they seem to have advanced as far as lat. 3° N., or within 220 miles of the Victoria, and about 90 from the Albert Nyanza.

In 1860, Captain Speke, accompanied by Lieutenant Grant, started on the same errand from Kazeh, on the east coast, and made his way to Lake Victoria, which he had discovered in 1858. There he learned of the existence of another lake, the Luta Nsige, now known as Lake Albert; and turning northward, he followed up the course of the Nile until he arrived at Gondokoro. All the information gained by later travellers has but confirmed the view propounded by Speke, that the great inland sea of the Victoria is the "reservoir, the headwater" of the Nile.

In 1863, Sir Samuel Baker, with his heroic wife, traced in a southerly direction that Upper Nile route which Speke had traced in a northerly. He came upon the Luta Nsige, which he re-named in honour of the late Prince Consort; and voyaging along its shores for sixty miles, he discovered that the Nile, after issuing from Lake Victoria, falls into it near its southern extremity, to flow out of it towards the north.

Colonel Chaillé Long, in 1874, advanced from Gondokoro to the Victoria, and examined a hitherto unexplored portion of the Nile's course, namely between Urondogani and Mrooli. He was followed in 1875 by M. Ernest Linant, who, however, added nothing to our knowledge of the Nile basin. Signor Gessi, in 1876, launched a couple of iron lifeboats on the Albert, and reached its northern extremity, determining it to be a lake 190 miles in length, with an average breadth of 50 miles. At the south end the water is exceedingly shallow, and the lake is skirted by dense forests. On the west great forests also occur, and the scenery is rendered grand by ranges of high mountains. On the east the lake receives a river which, on account of its rapid current, is described as unnavigable.

Mr. Stanley, who first acquired a reputation as the "discoverer of Livingstone," traversed, at the head of an expedition fitted out by the proprietary of the *Daily Telegraph* and the *New York Herald*, the equatorial regions of Africa in 1876 and 1877. He accomplished a complete survey of the Victoria, and discovered a stream which he called the Alexandra Nile, and a small lake, at a higher elevation than the Victoria, which, in honour of the Princess of Wales, he proposed to christen the Alexandra Lake. The river, however, is simply the comparatively unimportant stream called by Speke the Kitangulé, which flows into the Victoria.

MURCHISON FALLS.

We take, then, the Victoria as the head-waters of the Nile, which flows out of it on the north, just beyond the equator, in a channel (the Somerset of Speke) 150 yards wide, and pouring over a mass of igneous rocks, forms the Ripon Falls, 12 feet high, in lat. 0° 20' N. and long. 33° 30' E. Proceeding in a north-westerly direction, it forms the Karuma and the Murchison Falls, and joins the Albert N'yanza. Emerging from this second reservoir, the White Nile, or *Bahr el-Abiad* of the Arabs, still keeps to the north-west, and through a country recently opened up by Colonel Gordon and his lieutenants, goes onward to Gondokoro, the great depôt of the ivory dealers, 1900 feet above the sea. Over a gently undulating plain, with many windings, but no great descent, it strikes to the north-west, and afterwards to the north-east, for nearly 500 miles, receiving, in lat. 9° 15' N. and long. 30° E., its first great affluent, the Bahr el-Gazal, or Gazelle River, a slow and shallow stream from the west. Taking an easterly direction for 80 miles, and curving southward for 30 miles, it is augmented by the waters of the Giraffe and the Sobat; after which it takes a northerly course, with a full and tranquil current, and a breadth varying from 1700 to 3600 feet, for nearly 480 miles. Thus it arrives at Khartûm, the capital of Nubia, in lat. 15° 37' N. and long. 33° E.

Here it is that it receives the river which, for generations, was supposed to be *the* Nile; the river which the adventurous Bruce traced to its fountains; that is, the Blue Nile, or Bahr el-Azrek. It is formed by the junction of the Abai—which rises in Abyssinia, 50 miles from Lake Dembea, and 8700 feet above the sea—and the Blue River, which has its sources in the southern highlands, and is fed by the Dender and the Shimfa.

At Khartûm the Blue Nile is 708 yards broad, and the White Nile only 483 yards; but the latter is much deeper, and its flow of water more continuous. Flowing north for 60 miles, across wide pasture plains, and past Halfaia and ancient Meroë, the Nile arrives at its first "cataract," or rather rapid, the *seventh* counting from the river's mouth. Rolling onwards, it passes Shendy, and receives at El-Damer, in lat. 17° 45' N. and long. 34° E., the Atbara, or Tacazzé, or, as it is often called, in allusion to its muddy waters, the *Bahr el-Aswad*, or Black River.

From this point the great river traverses for 120 miles the rich, well-cultivated, and numerously inhabited country of the Berbers, to enter on a widely different region; a wilderness of sand, barren and desolate, where the ruins of antiquity lie overwhelmed by the sandstorms of centuries. Below the island of Mogreb (in lat. 18° N.) it bends sharply to the south-westward; three cataracts, or rapids, marking this part of its course. It then takes a north-westerly direction, crosses the desert of Bahiouda, forms another cataract, diverges to the north-east, and flows through the rapids of Wady Halfa; passes, in a much narrower valley, the ruins of Abou-Simbel, Derr, Ghirsché Housseyn, Dendour, and Kalabsché, and at Assouan (anciently Syene), in lat. 24° 5' 23" N., descends into Upper Egypt by its largest cataract, the seventh (or first). Note that these cataracts, as already hinted, are really *rapids*, which almost disappear when the Nile is at its height during the period of the annual inundation. They are caused by the encroachment of rocks upon the river-channel, which, dividing into several small streams, pours its waters through the craggy defiles with considerable fury.

The Nile in its later course passes successively the quarries of Silsileh on the east, Edfoo and Esneh on the west; the wonderful palace-temples and memorials of Thebes, with Luxor and Karnak, on the east, and Medinet-Aboo on the west; then Girgeh and Siout on the west, and the tombs of Beni-hassan on the east. In due time it reaches the ruins of Memphis and the Pyramids, all on the west bank, and leaving Cairo and the railroad on the east, spreads out into the numerous arms which form the celebrated region of the Delta. From Assouan to the sea its average fall is only two inches in 1800 yards, and its average velocity does not exceed three miles an hour. Its direction is almost due north, with occasional deviations to the east and northwest. The geological character of its valley undergoes many changes; beginning with limestone, passing into sandstone, thence again into limestone, and, below Gebel el-Mokattam, into the great alluvial deposits of the Delta. This triangular area, which derives its name from the Greek letter Δ, begins at a point about 120 miles from the two chief mouths of the river, the Rosetta and Damietta mouths, and stretches along the Mediterranean coast in a network of streams and islands for about 150 miles, between lat. 30° 10′ and 31° 30′ N.

The rise of the Nile is due to the periodical rains of eastern Abyssinia and the countries further south, and on their greater or less quantity depends the height of the inundation. This height is carefully noted, as the extent of land subjected to irrigation, and the length of time during which it will remain under water, are regulated by it; and hence the occurrence of a good or bad harvest may be predicted with certainty. The ordinary rise at Cairo is about 23 to 25 feet: less is insufficient, and more is dangerous, frequently overwhelming whole villages. A rise of only 18 or 20 feet means—famine; and a flood of the height of 30—ruin.

The land, thus strangely irrigated, will yield annually three crops; being first sown with wheat or barley; a second time, after the spring equinox, with cotton, millet, indigo, or some similar produce; and, thirdly, about the summer solstice, with millet or maize. The river begins to rise about the end of June, and attains its maximum between the 20th and 30th of September. At this time the country wears a very singular aspect. On the elevated bank you stand, as it were, between two seas; on one side rolls a swollen turbid flood of a blood-red hue; on the other lies an expanse of seemingly stagnant water, extending to the desert-boundary of the valley; the isolated villages, circled with groves of palm, being scattered over it like floating islands, and the *gise*, or dike, affording the sole circuitous intercommunication between them.* When the waters subside—a process which is very perceptible about the 10th of November—the valley is suddenly covered with a mantle of the richest green, and the face of the land smiles in the traveller's eyes with all the splendour of a new-created beauty.†

Bearing in his memory these few facts, the reader will

---

* Eliot Warburton, "The Crescent and the Cross," p. 21, *et passim*.
† The *minimum* depth of the river at Cairo does not exceed six feet.

come to understand the secret of the reverence with which the ancient Egyptian regarded the sacred river. The god Nilus, says Sir Gardner Wilkinson, is frequently represented with water-plants growing from his head, and binding up stalks or flowers, indicative of the inundation. In all the cities on the banks of the river certain priests were exclusively appointed to the service of this deity; and if a corpse were found upon the sacred shore, the nearest town was obliged to embalm and bury it with every mark of honour, though only a priest of the Nile could superintend the interment.

The Nile was a member of the first Ogdoad, or rank, of the Egyptian divinities, and placed in direct opposition to Phtah, or "Fire," while regarded as the companion and ally of Neith, or "Air,"—Zeus (or Amun), the principle of "Life,"—Demeter, the "Earth,"—Neph, the Spirit of the Deity—and Osiris and Isis, the "Sun" and "Moon." Thus it represented one of the most sacred essences, or primitive forces of Nature; had its own hieratic emblem on the monuments; and its special symbol, the tamed crocodile, typical of its power and yet beneficence. A festival, called Nilva, was celebrated at the summer solstice, when its rising waters gave the first promise of abundance to the thirsty land. Pictorially, it was imaged as a round plump figure, with female breasts and of a blue colour, in allusion to its fertilizing and productive powers.

A remarkable statue of the Nile was discovered among the ruins of Rome in the fifteenth century, and is now preserved in the Museum of the Vatican. It represents it surrounded by sixteen children, in allusion to the sixteen cubits at which the inundation of the river begins to irrigate the land; and its base is sculptured with carvings of the Nile boats, the ibis, the stork, the crocodile, the ichneumon, the hippopotamus, and the lotus in flower.

STATUE OF THE NILE.

The Nile boats, as pictured on the monuments, exhibit a great variety of size and form. There are the light

PAPYRUS SHALLOP.

papyrus shallop, rendered water-tight by bitumen; the canoe hollowed out of a single trunk; the square-rigged boat, with high bow and stern, a single mast, and shallow keel; and the large capacious *baris*, described by Herodotus, which was propelled by as many as forty rowers, and sometimes carried a burden of three, four, and even five hundred tons. It was built of the hard wood of the *sont* or acacia; its seams were caulked with oakum made of the fibres of that plant; and its sails were manufactured of papyrus.

The royal barges were of a far more splendid character, with rudder, cabin, and masts painted of a rich golden colour; the sails fringed and diapered, and glowing like the rainbow; reminding one of the gorgeous bark in which Cleopatra ascended the Cydnus:—

> " The barge she sat in, like a burnished throne,
> Burned on the water: the poop was beaten gold;
> Purple the sails, and so perfumèd that
> The winds were love-sick with them; th' oars were silver,
> Which to the tune of flutes kept stroke, and made
> The water which they beat to follow faster,
> As amorous of their strokes." *

Grand religious festivals and processions were celebrated on the Nile, reminding us, in some respects, of the water-pageants which the old Venetians celebrated on their "Grand Canal." A favourite pastime was to row rapidly in boats, and hurl at one another, as they swept by, blunt javelins or *jereeds*. At the great feast of Bubastis, or Pasht, it is said that as many as seven hundred thousand persons would assemble upon the river, delighting themselves with the music of pipe and cymbal, and joining in loud hymns of gladness and triumph.

The fauna and flora of the Nile are necessarily identical with those of the Egyptian Valley, to which we have already alluded; except that to its animal life we must add the crocodile and hippopotamus. The former is now very seldom met with below 27°, or the latter further south than the second cataract. Fifty-two species of fish

* Shakspeare, " Antony and Cleopatra," a. ii., s. 2.

are described as belonging to the river; of these the genus *Silurus* is most abundant.

The water of the Nile is exceedingly wholesome, and in its most turbid condition always capable of filtration. Between the highest and the lowest periods of the yearly flood it is not less remarkable for its purity than for its transparency.

The word *Nilus* is probably of Semitic origin, and, like the Hebrew *Sihhor*, the Egyptian *Chemi*, and the Greek epithet μέλας (*mĕlas*), may have referred to the dark hue of its waves. The natives called it *p-iero*, or "the river of rivers," as if no other could claim comparison with it in grandeur, beauty, or fertility.

Lastly, we may point out the powerful influence exercised by the Nile on the character and genius of Egyptian art. As its waters might not be polluted with dead bodies, the rocks of the Desert were converted into tombs; and this circumstance suggested those *angular forms* peculiar, in the first place, to Egyptian architecture, but which have been adopted in every succeeding style. The ornaments of shaft and capital were borrowed from the river-plants; everywhere, in tomb and temple, the traveller sees the graceful outline of the rose-coloured lotus. How important a place the great river occupied in the Egyptian Olympus we have already hinted at. Its annual overflow suggested the allegory of the burial of Osiris in the hallowed stream, and his resurrection, once a year, to scatter blessings over the earth. Moreover, it typified to the Egyptians the "river of death," across whose silent wave the dead were ferried, attended by the conductor of souls, the god Anubis.

CROCODILES OF THE NILE.

The Greeks afterwards availed themselves of this imagery, —which, appropriate enough in Egypt, became singularly inappropriate in Hellas—and converted Anubis into Charon, and the Nile into the gloomy Styx. How many of our own ideas of the other world may have been borrowed from the Nilotic worship of the Egyptians!

THE MYSTIC FERRY-BOAT.

When we speak of the darkling stream which separates Time from Eternity we are employing an Egyptian image, and, unknown to ourselves, perhaps, referring to the mysterious river of a mysterious land — the great and glorious Nile!

Book Second.

CHAPTER I.

ALEXANDRIA—POMPEY'S PILLAR—CLEOPATRA'S NEEDLES.

> Obelisks graven with emblems of the time.
> TENNYSON.

THE traveller's exploration of the Land of the Nile begins at Alexandria, the celebrated city and port which was founded by the genius of the Macedonian hero (B.C. 332), and which for so many centuries became the treasury of Oriental commerce. Its ancient opulence and prosperity may be inferred from the fact that its port-dues alone amounted in B.C. 63 to the vast sum of 6250 talents, or a million sterling. Its population about the same time was estimated at 300,000 free citizens, and at least an equal number of slaves and casual residents. To its singular beauty willing evidence is borne by the writers of antiquity. Much was due to its happy position and genial character; but much to the skill of man, which embellished it with buildings of marble,—with palaces and temples and public baths,—with museums, libraries, and obelisks,—with long colonnades of the costliest marble yielded by the Egyptian quarries, with leafy groves and blooming gardens. Among the more celebrated of these architectural achievements I find enumerated: the Palace of the Ptolemys; the Library, containing 700,000 vol-

ANCIENT PHAROS AT ALEXANDRIA.

umes of inestimable value; the Museum, which numbered among its professors Euclid, Callimachus, Aratus, Aristophanes, Aristarchus, Clemens and Origen, Theon and his famous daughter Hypatia, whose sad story has been so graphically told by Canon Kingsley; the Caesareion, or Temple of the Caesars, where divine honours were paid to the emperors, dead and living; the Mausoleum of the Ptolemys, where were interred the body of Alexander the Great, in a coffin of gold, afterwards replaced by one of glass, and the remains of Marcus Antonius; the Arsinoeum, raised by Ptolemy Philadelphus to the memory of his beloved sister Arsinoë; the Serapeion, dedicated to the great god Serapis, or Osirei-Apis; and the Pharos, or Lighthouse, which consisted of several stories, and is said to have been four hundred feet in height.

Very different is the aspect of the modern Alexandria from that of the capital of the Ptolemys—from that of the city which afterwards had Cyril for its bishop, and witnessed the feuds of Arians and Athanasians. It is now a very lively, dirty, bustling, semi-European town, with an extensive commerce, a flourishing trade, a curious Babel of languages, and a motley population of some 70,000 souls. Copts, Arabs, English, Scotch, Armenians, Greeks, Turks, French, Indians; almost every nation under the sun, and every creed of every nation, have here their representatives. In truth, it is best defined as the meeting-point of East and West, of the old and the new civilizations; but the Western element predominates, and the customs of the Frank are rapidly encroaching on those of the Oriental. There are camels and mules,—palms, orange-trees, and bananas,—turbaned Moslems, eunuchs, and the veiled inmates of the Harem; but there are also dockyards and arsenals, steam-engines, steam-cranes, steam-boats on the river, mills, factories, a railway, and a score of other tangible indications that the "Old

ALEXANDRIA, BEFORE THE BOMBARDMENT.

order" has changed, and is yielding to the New. It has lost all its ancient beauty, except its transparent atmosphere and sunny sky; and the principal object of the traveller who visits it is to get out of it again with all possible celerity. Of its magnificent edifices few memorials, as we shall see, are extant; and after cursorily examining these, the European invariably hastens to commit himself and his fortunes to the charge of the river Nile. The most that can be said for Alexandria, remarks Mr. Kennard, is, that it is an inferior continental town; its streets peopled with Englishmen, Greeks, French, Italians, whose wives dress in bonnets and Paris mantles, and go out shopping in the afternoon in one-horse clarences and pony-phaetons.

This, perhaps, is too depreciatory an estimate. Some of the "sights" in Alexandria are such as no European city can boast of, and recall to the traveller the legends he has read of "the days of Haroun-al-Raschid." A recent writer speaks of them as utterly strange and unwonted, fairy-like, and Arabian-Night-like.* Here came a file, he says, of tall camels laden with merchandise, stalking with deliberate, solemn step, through the bazaars; there rode a grand-looking native gentleman, in all the pride of capacious turban and flowing robes; yonder passed a lady on her donkey, enveloped in black silk *habura*, and the more remarkable white muslin veil,—which universal out-of-door costume of Egyptian ladies only suffered two dark eyes to gleam from behind the hideous shroud. And if the carriages we saw, continues our authority, had a smack of Europe, they were driven and

* Rev. A. C. Smith, "The Nile and its Banks," i. 20, 21.

ARAB WOMEN IN THE STREETS OF ALEXANDRIA.

attended by men in Oriental dress, and—even stranger still—were preceded, even at their best pace, by a barelegged running Arab, who shouted to the passengers to get out of the way—the shrill cries of this active *avant-coureur* resounding on every side; and fortunate is the stranger who escapes being run over in the narrow streets by some cantering donkey, or knocked down by some tall camel laden with heavy boxes, as he stands staring at the unwonted scene—his whole attention rivetted on the everyday life of an Oriental city.

We may borrow another picture from a different source, to find in it the same general characteristics.* Take, for instance, the platform of the Alexandria railway-station. Here you find the same mixture of East and West, of old and new: a motley crowd of wily Greeks, dusky Arabs, and soft-featured Syrians ferments before you; men, women, and children in every variety of costume, and no costume; water-sellers, sweetmeat-sellers, bread-sellers persistently pestering everybody; ghostly women in white, visible as human by their flashing dark eyes and naked feet, flitting hither and thither in frantic search for a lost husband or friend. You will see solemn Turks and crafty-looking Jews, and, perhaps, a batch of recruits for the Khedive's army,—Abyssinians, fine brawny powerful fellows in white tunics, with bare black legs, chubby faces, and dark lustrous eyes.

Yet the associations of Alexandria are well calculated to impress the mind of the thoughtful stranger. Its very name carries the imagination back over the dim gulf of centuries to the days when all the known world trembled at the nod of the Macedonian hero. It was founded by him, as we have said, on the site of a little town called Rhacotis, though not completed until the reign of the

---

* Howard Hopley, "Under Egyptian Palms," pp. 3, 4.

second monarch of the Lagid line, Ptolemy Philadelphus.* By each succeeding sovereign of that dynasty it was enlarged and embellished, until it assumed the general outline of the cloak, or chlamys, common to the Macedonian cavalry. That is, its ground-plan was an oblong, rounded at the south-east and south-west extremities. From east to west it measured about four miles; from south to north, nearly a mile; its circuit completed fifteen miles. The interior was laid out in parallelograms, the streets crossing one another at right angles, and two great thoroughfares, each 200 feet in breadth, striking across them to connect the four main gates— namely, the Canobic, east; that of the Necropolis, west; that of the Sun, south; and that of the Moon, north.

A volume would barely suffice for an outline of the history of this once-famous city. It prospered under the wisdom of Ptolemy Soter and the genius of Philadelphus, but declined under the corrupt government of Philopater, who was the slave of his eunuchs, his favourite courtiers, and his mistresses. Enervated by vice and luxury, it was unable to preserve its independence; was involved in the disasters and convulsions of the great struggle between Julius Caesar and Pompey, Mark Antony and Augustus; and finally surrendered its last vestige of freedom at the bidding of the victor at Actium.

Under the Emperors it became one of the principal granaries of Rome. At an early period after the death of Christ, many of its inhabitants embraced the new religion, which flourished to such an extent that the bishopric

* The plan, designed by the architect Deinocrates, was completed by Cleomenes of Naucratis.

of Alexandria became one of the most important, probably, in the whole Christian Church. It gained a melancholy celebrity as the scene of the sanguinary conflict between Arians and Athanasians. It suffered severely in the still more desperate struggle between Paganism and Christianity, which was nowhere fought out with greater intellectual activity or more heroic resolution. The persecution ordered by the Emperor Severus claimed its hundreds of martyrs. Alexandria, at that time, was the ripe and pregnant soil of religious feud and deadly hatred. It was divided into three hostile factions: Jews, Pagans, Christians. These were continually blending and modifying each other's doctrines, and forming schools in which Judaism was transmuted into Platonism, and Platonism into Christianity, while Christianity at various points acknowledged the Platonic influence. Nevertheless, all three awaited the signal for persecution, and for license to draw off in sanguinary legions, who might settle their controversies by the sword, the rope, and the stake.* Under Severus came the triumph of Paganism. Priests were burned and virgins tortured. For a while the professors of the new creed were compelled to bow their heads, and take refuge in the sandy wildernesses of the great deserts.

But the Pagan world was tottering to its fall, and after the death of Severus, Christianity rose again from the dust, more vigorous than ever, and began its final wrestling with the powers of darkness. The battle was virtually decided before Constantine the Great announced himself a Christian; and after that memorable event,

* Dean Milman, "History of Christianity," ii., 157, 158.

Paganism covered its head, and, amid dust and ashes, yielded up the ghost.

This grand conflict between the Roman Empire and the Christian Church lasted for upwards of four centuries; yet at the outset the combatants were so unequally matched that one might have supposed the issue could not be long delayed. The weapons of the Empire, as Mr. Kingsley observes,* were not merely an overwhelming physical force, and a ruthless lust of aggressive conquest, but, even more powerful still, an unequalled genius for organization, and an uniform system of external law and order. But against its preponderant forces the Church, armed only with its own mighty and all-embracing message, and with a holy spirit of purity and virtue, love and self-sacrifice, fought the good fight, and conquered. The weak things of this world confounded the strong. In spite of relentless persecution; in spite of the contaminating atmosphere of vice which surrounded her; in spite of the seeming feebleness of the recruits whom she gathered from the dregs of society; in spite of internal dissensions on points of doctrine and ceremony; in spite of a thousand counterfeits which sprang up around her and within her, claiming to be parts of her, and alluring men to themselves by that very exclusiveness and party arrogance which disproved their claim;—in spite of all, she conquered. At last, the very Emperors espoused her cause. Julian's final attempt to restore the fallen creed of ancient Rome only sufficed to prove that it had lost its hold on the hearts of the masses. At his death the great tide-wave of new opinion rolled on un-

* Kingsley, Preface to "Hypatia," p. viii.

checked, and bore onwards with its current the rulers of the earth; who, in words at least, accepted as their own the laws of the Church; acknowledged the supreme power of the King of kings; and even trembled before the priests who declared themselves His representatives and ministers.

As the seat of the intellectual and moral activity which accomplished this grand result; as the residence and episcopal city of Clemens, Athanasius, Origen, and Cyril; as the scene of the apostolic labours of the Evangelist Mark; and as the place where toiled the learned Seventy, to whose devotion and genius the world is indebted for the Septuagint version of the Old Testament—no less than by its past imperial power, its antiquity, its monuments, its rising fortunes— Alexandria ought to command the earnest attention of the thinker.

Towards the close of the fifth century, however, Alexandria shared the common doom of the great Roman Empire. The shadow of decay fell upon it; its Jewish and Greek merchants and money-dealers abandoned it; its harbour was no longer thronged with masts; its streets no longer echoed with the sounds of all languages, from Cadiz to the Crimea. Yet when, in 640, it was conquered by Amrou and his Arabs, it still contained its palaces, and public baths, and theatres, and Jews who paid tribute, and venders of herbs.* Under the blighting influence of Arab rule, its decline was greatly accelerated; it shrank yearly within narrower and yet narrower limits; its quays and its warehouses were deserted; the glorious relics spared by its conquerors fell into irretrievable

---

* Eutychius, "Annales," vol. ii., p. 316, cited by Gibbon.

desolation. The final death-blow to its fortunes was the discovery, in 1497, of the passage round the Cape of Good Hope, which changed the direction of the commerce of the East; and it is only within recent years that it has again lifted up its head, owing to a second change in the current of Oriental traffic produced by the establishment of the Overland Route. It is now a busy and a prosperous city; one of the great connecting links between the East and the West; one of the principal posts or landmarks on the grand highway from England to Calcutta. And with the Suez Canal practicable for large vessels, it must become of further importance, notwithstanding the rivalry of Port Said. Nay, it is even possible that the splendour of its future may outshine the glory of its past.

Its ruins are, unfortunately, to a great extent mere shapeless masses of masonry, of shattered columns and capitals, to which the most vivid fancy, informed by the most profound erudition, cannot give "a local habitation and a name." Vestiges of baths and buildings, and portions of ancient cisterns, and fragments of pottery and glass, may indeed be traced; but the only remains which can be said to possess a real interest are Pompey's Pillar and the Obelisks.

POMPEY'S PILLAR, as it is absurdly misnamed,—the *Amood è sowari* of the Arabs,—is a monolithic column of red granite, situated on a solitary mound which overlooks the Lake Mareotis and the modern city. Its fluted Corinthian shaft measures 73 feet in height; the total height, including the capital and base, is 98 feet 9 inches; the circumference, 29 feet 8 inches. It should properly be designated Diocletian's Pillar, having been erected, as the inscription on its base records, by Publius [*quaere*, Pompeius?], the Eparch of Egypt, to commemorate the siege and capture of Alexandria in A.D. 297, when it had declared in favour of the usurper Achilleus, by the Em-

POMPEY'S PILLAR.

peror Diocletian. The shaft, capital, and pedestal are apparently of different ages, the capital and pedestal being of later and inferior workmanship than the shaft.

According to the Arab historian, Abdallatif, cited by Mr. Lane, it is the sole existing relic of the famous

Serapeion—the gorgeous temple destroyed through the bigot zeal and iconoclastic enthusiasm of the Archbishop Theophilus. The four hundred columns which had embellished and enclosed the magnificent structure were ruthlessly overthrown, and piled up as a break-water on the sea-shore; all save the one stately pillar, the loftiest of the four hundred—the "pillar of the colonnades," as the Arabs emphatically term it—which is now the cynosure of European pilgrims.

Its present site is a scene of desolation, far different from the glowing picture which surrounded it of old, when the Nile was thronged with gilded barges, and the waters of the Mediterranean were gay with Phœnician argosies, and the light of the Pharos was the guiding star of the world's commerce. To reach it you must pass, as Miss Martineau reminds us,* through the dreariest of cemeteries, where all is of one dust-colour, even to the aloe fixed upon every grave. And the view from the base is very curious. Groups of Arabs labour in the hot, white, crumbling soil, with soldiers watching over them. To the south-east spreads Lake Mareotis, whose slender line of shore seems liable to be broken through by the first ripple of its waves. A strip of vegetation—marsh, field, and grove—somewhat relieves the dreary landscape; and the eye rests with pleasure on a lateen sail occasionally gliding among the trees.

At the eastern extremity of Alexandria—that is, in a directly opposite direction to Diocletian's Pillar, and formerly in the vicinity of the Palace, the Museum, the Library, the Market, and the Docks, all of which have

* Miss Martineau, "Eastern Life," i. 13, 14.

perished—stood the Sebaste Caesareum, or Temple of Caesar, whose site was long marked by two obelisks of red granite, one erect, the other prostrate on the sand.* These were the so-called Cleopatra's Needles,† though in no wise connected with that "serpent of old Nile," whose fatal beauty enchanted the Roman triumvir, and cost him the sovereignty of the world. Long before the dynasty of which she was the last representative reigned over Egypt, they were raised at Heliopolis—the centre of Egyptian art and science—by Thothmes III. They date, therefore, fully twelve centuries before the Christian era. Their removal to Alexandria was effected by Julius Caesar, to adorn his temple.

One of them—that which had fallen—was presented to the British Government in 1820, by the then ruler of Egypt, Mehemet Ali, with the view of its being transported to England and placed on some conspicuous site in London. But constant delays and difficulties, on the score of expense, &c., arose on our part, till in 1867 the land on which the Needle lay was disposed of by the Khedive to a Greek merchant, who insisted upon the monument being removed. At last, chiefly by the noble exertions and liberality of Professor Erasmus Wilson, an eminent English physician, the enormous mechanical difficulties of the enterprise were overcome, and the obelisk placed on board the *Cleopatra*, a vessel constructed specially for the purpose. This vessel, taken in tow by

---

* Madox, " Excursions in Egypt, the Holy Land," &c., i. 99.
† *Meselleh*, " a needle," is the Arabic word usually applied to an obelisk. Many of the great works of Alexandria are ascribed by the Arabs to Cleopatra, who holds in their memory much the same place as Cromwell in that of the English peasants, or Wallace among the Scotch.

the steamer *Olga*, left Alexandria on September 21st, 1877. A terrible hurricane was encountered in the Bay of Biscay on October 14th; and after the lives of some brave men had been vainly sacrificed, the *Olga* was compelled to cast off and abandon the *Cleopatra* and her precious freight. But the strange craft did not sink, though sorely buffeted by wind and waves, and was, after the storm, rescued by another ship and towed into the harbour of Ferrol. On January 16th, 1878, the *Cleopatra* was again taken in tow by a steamer sent from London, and in a few days safely reached the English shores. The Needle, placed on the great Thames Embankment, now tells its old tale of wonder and mystery to countless multitudes of visitors and passers-by. Gazing upon its tapering spire, one cannot but have one's mind filled with thoughts of her whose name is associated with it—her strange, wild history; the subtle spell of her loveliness; the "chance and change" of her romantic, semi-barbaric career; the pride of her luxurious splendour, when she charmed "great Caesar's soul;" and the deep shadow that gathered about her tragical end.

The other obelisk has been made over to America, and arrived not long since without accident at New York. It is the larger of the two—seventy-three feet high.

The other memorials of ancient Alexandria are of comparatively little interest, consisting of numerous tanks for supplying the city with Nile water; vestiges of baths and mansions; fragments of pottery and glass; and shattered capitals and columns. The Catacombs, or remains of the old Necropolis, which lie beyond the western gate, are remarkable for their extent.

It only remains to add that the Modern Alexandria* does not exactly occupy the site of the ancient city, but stands on the mole called the Heptastadium, formerly connecting the island of Pharos with the mainland. Successive alluvial deposits have widened and enlarged this mole into a broad neck of land between the two harbours, of which the eastern is called the New, and the western the Old Port.

* Population, in 1882, 208,755.

CHAPTER II.

CAIRO: ITS MOSQUES—THE CITADEL—THE PYRAMIDS—
THE SPHINX—HELIOPOLIS, AND ITS OBELISKS.

> The sphinx,
> Staring right on with calm eternal eyes.
> ALEXANDER SMITH.

ACROSS the broad expanse of the Delta the traveller is now borne by the "iron horse" towards the Egyptian capital. At first he skirts the shores of Lake Mareotis, stretching away to westward, like a Venetian lagoon; yet *unlike* a Venetian lagoon, in its flocks of pelicans, which ever and anon rise in the air like dense clouds of dazzling snow.

The landscape, as we speed along, is somewhat monotonous, or would be, if not occasionally relieved by strange glimpses of Oriental life: of boys selling sugarcanes; of women pacing slowly along, with water-vessels gracefully poised upon the shoulder; of mud-villages, the homes of wretched *fellahs;* and long strings of loaded camels, carrying cotton or corn to Alexandria. Long before we reach Cairo, however, we become sensible, so to speak, of the Desert,—the wild, dreamy, mysterious Desert,—with its intense tranquillity, its awful silence, its

CAIRO.

gorgeous atmospheric effects, and wonderful flushes of colour.

Soon after crossing the Nile at Old Cairo, or Boulak, we come in sight of the Pyramids, rearing their triangular heads above the flat alluvial plain in the distance, clear and vivid, with "sharp blue shadows," standing out in majestic outline against the soft and glowing sky. Seen thus, they apparently belong to the mysterious days of Anakim and giants; to the age of fable, and legend, and strange romance, when—

> "All the powers of nameless worlds,
> Vast sceptred phantoms, heroes, men, and beasts,"

inspired the imagination of the seer and the poet. One may well be forgiven for associating with them the most fantastic dreams!

Cairo itself, backed by its white citadel and the yellow range of the Mokuttam hills; the "great Al Cairo," as Milton calls it; the city of Saladin and the Arabian Nights—is an ever-changing panorama of life and interest. It preserves a true Oriental air, and, as you examine its bazaars and ramble through its streets, you seem carried back, in body and spirit, to the days of Haroun Al-Raschid. Its streets are so narrow as scarcely to admit of two camels passing abreast; its bazaars glow with the richest productions of the looms of the East; its mosques and minarets are apparently innumerable; and its fountains fill the air with an enduring freshness. The richly-carpeted shops are enclosed in front by a divan, and in the midst sits a venerable Turk or a wealthy Arab, smoking a splendid narghileh of gold and silver, and surveying with complacent gaze his costly wares: jewellery from Paris, chibouques from Constantinople, tobacco from Latakia, dainty muslins from India, keen bright swords of "Damascene steel," and rustling silks from the land of the Celestials. Meanwhile, the ways are thronged in every part, and it is with difficulty the pedestrian escapes a rude jostle from the donkeys, which pass him every moment, laden with sand, and flour, and water; or with a happier burden, in the person of some beauty of the harem, closely veiled, and attended by watchful guards. Then comes the water-carrier, calling shrilly, "Moira, moira!" or a stately Turk making his way to his favourite baths; or some tawny East Indian hero, returning to England, stalks imperturbably through the excited crowd; or one of the Pasha's guards dashes by, mounted on a richly caparisoned steed.

The visitor to Cairo is at first bewildered by the novel scenes which crowd upon him, and some time elapses before he is able to disentangle his confused impressions, and realize each feature of the marvellous picture. After awhile he begins to understand that he is, at length, in a purely Oriental city—the *Musr el Kaherah*, or the "victorious capital" of the Arabs—and to combine, in an orderly manner, his recollections of its past history with his knowledge of its present condition. Then he comes to the conclusion that its peculiarities, whether architectural or social, must be examined *seriatim*, and he leisurely examines its buildings, and curiously investigates its customs. Afterwards he puts together his notes in some such fashion, perhaps, as the following:—

Cairo (p. 368, 108) lies in lat. 30° 2′ N., and long. 31° 16′ E., on a sandy level between the right bank of the Nile and the range of the Mokuttam Hills. It was founded, eastward of Old Cairo, by Touloun, a Moslem governor of Egypt, in A.D. 868; but removed still further eastward—that is, to its present site—by the Fatimite khalif, El Moez, in A.D. 923. It remained the capital of the Fatimite rulers until 1171, when the famous Saladin—the "Bayard" of the East—usurped the throne. In 1220 it was unsuccessfully besieged by the Crusaders. In 1250, Moosa-el-Ashref was deposed by the Mamelukes, who retained possession of the city until 1517, when it was stormed and captured by Sultan Selim. Though it has lost much of its original importance, it is still a thriving and prosperous city, with a population (mostly Mohammedan) of 250,000; and may be considered as the great centre of the learning of the Eastern world, its celebrated university being presided over by men of acknowledged erudition, and annually attended by some two thousand students.

Its remarkable edifices are its citadel, its minarets, and its mosques. The citadel, as already stated, dominates over the whole town from its elevated position on a bold ridge of sandstone. Its walls—within which the massacre of the Mamelukes took place, and whose battlements were crowned by Napoleon's victorious standards—are of great solidity, and, in some places, one hundred feet in height. The works were enlarged and strengthened by Mehemet Ali, who resided here during the greater part of his reign. The prospect it commands is of a very extensive and impressive character; including not only the carved domes and fantastic minarets of Cairo,

TOMBS OF THE KHALIFS, AND CITADEL OF CAIRO.

but the sequestered valley with its tombs of the Mameluke sultans; the rich deep verdure of the distant Delta; the sharp clear outlines of the mysterious Pyramids; the yellow frontier-belt of the Desert; the sweet meanders of the tranquil Nile; and everywhere a soil that has been swept by successive waves of revolution, from the days

MOSQUE OF THE SULTAN HASSAN AT CAIRO

MUEZZIN ANNOUNCING THE HOUR OF PRAYER.

of Menes and Rameses to those of Napoleon, Sir Sidney Smith, Abercromby, and Nelson; a soil that it is no exaggeration to say seems haunted by

"The shape and shadow of mystic things."

The Cairene minarets are justly eulogized by travellers as the most beautiful of any in the East; exquisite creations of the strange dreamy Arabian genius; towering to an extraordinary height, built of courses of red and white stone, and ornamented with balconies, from which the muezzins announce the hour of prayer. Of these, the most ancient adjoins the great mosque of the Sultan Touloun, or Tuyloun, built in A.D. 879, soon after the foundation of the city. Two others belong to the magnificent mosque of the Sultan Hassan, which is situated in the palace of the Roumayli, near the citadel, and was completed about A.D. 1362.

The general character of the mosques is admirably sketched by Lady Duff Gordon.* She describes that of the Sultan Touloun as exquisite, noble, and simple; what ornament there is, the most delicate lacework and embossing in stone and wood. This Arab architecture, as she observes, is even more lovely than our Gothic. The mosque of the citadel is like a fine modern Italian church; but Abbas Pasha stole the alabaster columns, and replaced them by painted wood. The mosque of Sultan Hassan is a singularly majestic building, and the beauty of the details quite beyond belief to European eyes; the huge gates to his tomb are one mass of the finest enamel ornaments.

It is to be regretted, however, that these "fairy edifices" are so shamefully and grievously neglected.

Let us now venture into the streets of Cairo; if we keep our eyes open, we shall be amused by the various scenes they present. One of them is the "zikr," or performance—if we may use the expression—of the dancing or whirling Dervishes. It takes place within a railed

* Lady Duff Gordon, "Letters from Egypt" (1863–65), pp. 17–21.

A STREET IN CAIRO.

enclosure, like the arena of an equestrian display; the space around, and the galleries above, being open to spectators, Europeans as well as Orientals. At the further end of the arena is seated the sheikh of the Dervishes, dressed in dark green robes, edged with fur, and with a tall, brimless, conical hat upon his head. Then enter some score or so of men and lads, of various ages, from gray-bearded manhood to smooth-chinned childhood, all dressed in flowing garments of lively colours, and in quaint brown felt caps, which resemble nothing in the world so much as our English flower-pots. A chapter of the Koran having been read, they circle round the enclosure in dignified order, making low obeisances to the sheikh. The whirling then begins, to the accompaniment of a drum and two fifes. One by one, and with astonishing gravity, each individual rotates—his arms held out horizontally, with the palm of one hand and the back of another uppermost—his eyes bent down, and nearly closed—his heels kept close together—and the whirling motion performed not on the toes, but on the soles of the feet. By degrees the rotation grows more rapid, until the whole company are spinning round and round, like so many animated balloons, with their arms extended, and their sweeping garments raising quite a current of air; no individual, however, touching or in any way incommoding his neighbours. Those in the

DANCING DERVISH.

THE ASS-DRIVERS OF CAIRO.

centre keep nearly the same spot—at least, to the careless eye they appear not to move; but if closely watched it may be seen that they too, though with great dexterity, and with a subtle gliding movement, accomplish the circuit of the ring.

With two brief intervals of three to five minutes each this extraordinary performance, which makes the spectator dizzy to look upon it, lasts for a full half hour—the drum and fifes, meanwhile, maintaining their harsh, discordant, ear-splitting sound. At the conclusion, another Dervish repeats a chapter from the Koran, and the sheikh goes through some ceremony apparently analogous to a benediction; after which the whirling wonders retire, and the spectator, with a giddy brain and aching eyes, gladly seeks the open air.*

Quite an institution in Cairo are the donkeys and their drivers. But you must not suppose that the Cairene ass is as patient, depressed, and dismal-looking a quadruped as his European congener. He has a smattering of pride about him, pricks up his ears with an air of intelligence, indulges in impetuous fits, but is also given to prolonged "pauses of meditation." In mere personal appearance, as Mr. Hopley remarks,† he is more of "a swell" than his northern brother. His owner shaves him upon the back like a poodle dog. He carries a high and humpy saddle, covered with scarlet leather and tinsel trappings; so that, on the whole, he can sniff up the wind proudly beside the statelier camel, or run unabashed in presence of his high-born kinsman, the horse. But even a Cairene

---

* Rev. A. C. Smith, "The Nile and its Banks," i. 65, 66.
† Howard Hopley, "Under Egyptian Palms," p. 41.

donkey is not without his failing; he is not "the perfect monster which the world ne'er saw." He will lie down at inconvenient times, kick up his heels, and grovel in the dust. And this is the more strange, since he appears thoroughly aware of the folly of such an escapade. He invariably rises with a guilty look, perfectly conscious that he is about to receive a beating; and yet the temptation to do evil is always irresistible.

Not less original than the animal is the animal's owner. Now in Cairo every little proprietor keeps a donkey, which is as much a sign of respectability in the East as "payment of rates and taxes" in the West. The proprietor is not always the driver; but whether he owns the beast or not, the driver is as fond of him as the Bedouin of his camel; runs beside him, stimulates him with kind words, and takes care he is comfortably fed and housed. His own dress is light and airy; a scarlet tarboosh or white turban of few folds for the head, a blue cotton tunic reaching barely to the knees, and a long scarf for the waist. He is as eager for a customer as any London cabman; and your appearance on the steps of your hotel is the signal for a general rush towards you of donkey-drivers and donkeys.

Of course, for the European visitor, one of the "lions" of Cairo is a real Oriental harem; but it is not every stranger who can obtain admission to one, and when that admission *is* obtained, the impression produced is generally painful. These luxurious dark-skinned beauties, gorgeously apparelled, reclining on their soft, billowy divan, like so many dusky Venuses, and laboriously whiling away the hours with the scented *narghilehs*—with occasional songs and dances—with a daily promenade through the streets and bazaars;—what thoughts can they suggest to the thoughtful spectator, except that so lethargic a life must stimulate the passions at the expense of the intellect, and that until the relations of the two sexes are wholly altered, the civilization of the East can never attain its due development?

As soon as the European has become familiar with the "thousand and one" curiosities of Cairo, he determines on an expedition to the Pyramids, which lie about twelve miles distant from the city, and six or seven miles from the bank of the Nile.

These "memorials of the world's youth" are the principal objects in a singular landscape, which, checkered by such features as the great winding river; the purple city, with its forts, domes, and spires; the green fields, and palm groves, and speckled villages; the plains either covered with verdure, or glistening with shining inundations,—stretches far, far away, until it is lost and mingled in the golden horizon.*

Despite of all that has been written about them, despite of the innumerable sketches which crowd our albums, the Pyramids are ever attractive, ever fresh, and ever new. From our very boyhood they work upon our imagination with a subtle charm. I know that for my own part they have often haunted my dreams, and that in silent moments their image frequently rises upon the brain unbidden. Like the spells of the old necromancers, they invoke a host of spectres from the shadowy graves of the Past. They are probably more familiar to us, by book and

* Thackeray, "From Cornhill to Cairo" (edit. 1869), p. 510.

picture, than half the architectural monuments of our own land. Their mighty masses seem to convey to us from afar a singular impression of awe, majesty, and strength ; and with them we insensibly associate I know not what ideas of august mystery and wonder. They belong to the earliest ages of the human race—to days before History began—when the "world's gray forefathers"

THE PYRAMIDS.

—to use Vaughan's fine expression—roamed at will over the boundless pastures, and the angels had hardly ceased to visit the "daughters of men." Abraham may have gazed upon their giant forms, Joseph have reposed in their shadow. Generations have come and gone; dynasties have risen like stars, and, like stars, have sunk below the horizon ; the arts and sciences of Egypt have transferred their glories to Western empires; but still, on the edge of the broad and dreary Desert, and still, looking out upon the "blown valley" of the Nile, are securely seated these giants of the Unknown Time, as if to mock the men, and things, and littlenesses of To-day!

Who built them? What purpose were they intended to serve? The first question, through the researches of Champollion, Vyse, and Lepsius, we can answer with tolerable accuracy; to the second, no fully satisfactory reply has yet been given. We are told they were the granaries erected by Joseph; temples of Venus; ancient observatories; reservoirs for purifying the Nile waters; mausolea of the Egyptian kings; while Professor Piazzi Smyth has recently attempted to prove that the Great Pyramid was erected to preserve certain standard measures of capacity and dimension.* After reading all the ingenious arguments the Scotch astronomer puts forward in support of his hypothesis, I still believe the more reasonable conclusion is that which General Howard Vyse arrived at;—that they are the tombs of Egyptian monarchs who flourished from the 4th to the 12th dynasty;† solid mounds raised over sepulchral chambers, like the cromlechs of the Celtic tribes. Now, Death-in-Life was the great principle of the religion of the Egyptians. All life was spent in a steadfast and methodical preparation for death. The unseen world was their daily thought; the visible world of no regard, except as the porch or vestibule of the Temple of Eternity. Every man, if his

---

* Prof. Piazzi Smyth, "Our Inheritance in the Great Pyramid," *passim*.
† The etymology of the word "Pyramid" is uncertain, but there can be little doubt it means a tomb or sepulchre.

need was not too great, began the preparation of his tomb even in his early youth. He looked forward eagerly to joining the " great congregation " of those who had gone before. And this was especially the case with the Egyptian kings. Each one of them lived solitary; and it was only when he died that he would enter among his peers. He went from the solitude of the busy, peopled Egypt, to the sanctified society of the Valley of Death. To him, as Miss Martineau remarks, this was the great event, to which he was looking forward during the best years of his life ; and he devoted his wealth, his thoughts, and the most sacred desires of his heart, to preparation for his promotion to the society of kings, and the presence of the gods. There, an abode would be prepared for him. On the walls of his tomb he attempted to paint the succession of mansions in the great heavenly house which he was to inhabit at last: but, meanwhile, he was to dwell, for a vast length of time, in the long home in the valley, with his peers (whether asleep or vigilant) all round about him.*

Thus, then, as soon as a king began to reign, he began the erection of his mausoleum. Gangs of labourers were brought together from all parts of the empire : in those days labour was cheap, and a royal command irresistible. A shaft of the size of the intended sarcophagus having been first excavated in the rock, at such an incline as permitted the sarcophagus to be readily lowered, then, at a suitable depth, a cell or chamber was hollowed out for its reception. Over this chamber was built up the pyramidal mass of masonry, of square blocks,—the mouth

* Harriet Martineau, " Eastern Life," i. 325-327.

of the shaft being left open. As long as the sovereign lived, this pyramid was increased in height and breadth, and, at his death, completed by facing or smoothing its exterior. The latter operation was performed in a very simple manner: courses of long blocks were

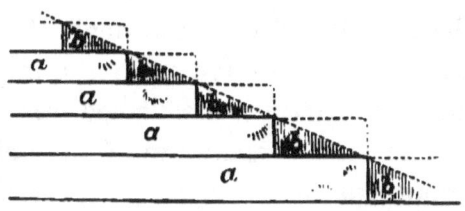

a, Original masonry. *b*, Additional work of exterior.

added to each step or gradation of the mass, and the whole cut down to an uniform surface, beginning from the apex.*

It was long a matter of wonder how such immense masses of masonry had been elevated to their respective places, but the discovery of large circular apertures in many of the stones, seems to show that the Egyptians were assisted by some kind of machinery. Not the less must our admiration be freely given to the artisans who

ANCIENT EGYPTIAN MODE OF CONVEYING STONES.

accomplished so much with means and appliances apparently of the simplest order. How great must have been the ingenuity—how supreme the perseverance—how vast

* Sir Gardner Wilkinson, "Modern Egypt and Thebes," *passim*

the toil! Alas, for the hewers of wood and drawers of water, who were dragged from their far-off homes to perish, perhaps, under the incessant labour! Where did *they* sleep the last sleep, I wonder? What sepulchre enshrined *their* dust? Not for them the mighty pyramid and the historic memory: their meed was forgetfulness.

The stones made use of were either brought from the granite quarries of Syene, or, more frequently, quarried on the spot. The entrances were filled up with anxious care, and ingress to the last resting-place of the king prevented by barriers of solid stone.

Egypt contains seventy Pyramids, all between 29° and 30° north latitude, the most remarkable being situated either at Memphis or in the neighbourhood of Cairo, and all on the west bank of the Nile. Their sides face the cardinal points, and their entrances are on the north. The three largest, or those of Ghizeh, are the best known and most celebrated.

The first, or *Great Pyramid,* was mainly erected by "Cheops," who flourished, according to different chronologists, about 3229, 3095, or 2123 B.C., and was the Chenebes or Chemmis of Diodorus, and the Shufu of Manetho. Its height was 480 feet 9 inches, and its base 764 feet square; that is, it occupied an area equal in extent to Lincoln's Inn Fields, or about 543,696 square feet, with a mass of building higher than St. Paul's Cathedral. Its slope or angle was 51° 50', but its external effect has been much injured by the spoliation of the exterior blocks for the erection of Cairo. The entrance is about 40 feet from the ground, and 4 feet high. The passage is on a considerable incline, 320 feet in length, and conducts to the mortuary chamber, excavated out of the solid rock, and measuring 46 feet by 27 feet, and 14 feet 6 inches in height. At the distance of 106 feet from the entrance it is closed by a block of granite, and an upper passage proceeds from this point at an angle of 27°.* Climbing by a few steps into the second passage, you ascend to the entrance of the Great Gallery, from whence a

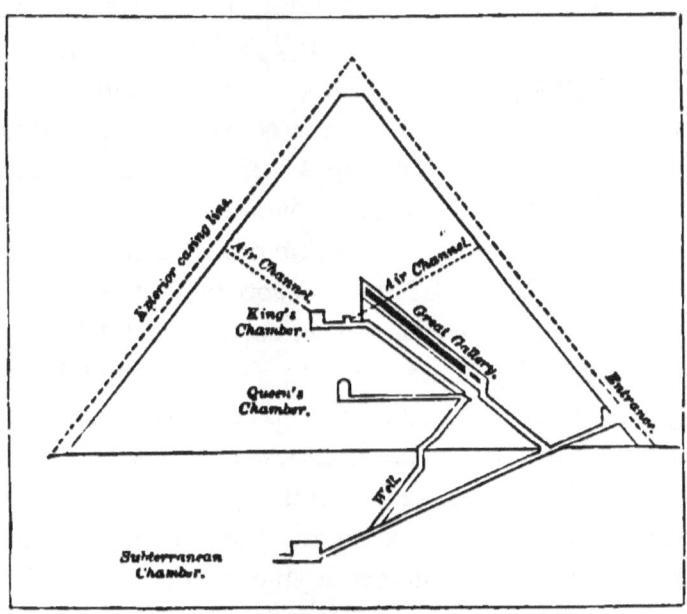

SECTION OF GREAT PYRAMID OF GHIZEH.

horizontal passage leads into what is called the Queen's Chamber, which has a triangular roof, 20 feet 3 inches high, and is 17 feet in length by 18 feet 9 inches in breadth. There is a niche in the east end, where the Arabs have broken the masonry in search of treasure;

* General Howard Vyse, "Observations on the Pyramids of Ghizeh" (London, 1840–43).

and Sir Gardner Wilkinson is of opinion that if the pit where the king's body was deposited exists in any of these rooms, it should be looked for beneath this niche, which is nearly in the centre of the Pyramid.

Returning to the Great Gallery, we come, at its base, to the mouth of what is called the Well—a narrow funnel-shaped shaft leading down to the subterranean chamber. As it is useless to descend thither, we continue our course along the gallery for 158 feet, arriving at a horizontal passage where four granite portcullises, descending through grooves, once arrested the steps of the intruder and guarded the repose of the dead. These obstacles, however, have been overcome, and you are now enabled to enter the principal chamber in the Pyramid—the King's Chamber—constructed entirely of red granite, and containing a sarcophagus of the same material, 7 feet 6½ inches long, 3 feet 3 inches broad, and 3 feet 5 inches high. We have called it a "sarcophagus," but later authorities are not in accord as to its uses, and Prof. Piazzi Smyth asserts that it was jealously preserved as a standard measure of capacity, of which the British quarter is the fourth part. The reasons, however, which the Scotch astronomer advances in support of his opinion can hardly be described as more than *plausible*.

The King's Chamber measures 17 feet 1 inch by 34 feet 3 inches, and 19 feet 1 inch in height.* It is ventilated by two small air-channels, or flues, about 9 inches square, which ascend to the north and south sides of the Pyramid; and its walls and roof are lined with superb

---

* J. Fergusson, "History of Architecture" i. 88.

slabs of syenite. Above it, and accessible only by a narrow passage, is a small chamber, discovered by Mr Davidson, 3 feet 6 inches high; and above *this*, four other similar niches or chambers were explored by General Vyse. In one of these he found the cartouche containing the name of the founder Shufu, or Cheops, worked in red paint.

Shufu, and his brother Num-Shufu (or Sensuphis) reigned for some years conjointly, and conjointly erected the Great Pyramid. Their reigns extended over sixty-six years. During this long period, upwards of 100,000 men, relieved every three months, were employed upon the mighty work.*

The second Pyramid, generally attributed, though on no hieroglyphical authority, to Chephren (perhaps Sha-fre, or Sephres, of the 5th dynasty), is of later date, and of ruder construction than that of Cheops. It stands on higher ground, and consequently has an appearance of greater height. Its actual elevation, however, is only 454 feet; the square of its base 707 feet. It is distinguished by retaining a portion of that outer and smoother casing which all the pyramids once possessed. In its interior arrangements it differs from the Great Pyramid, the sarcophagus of the founder being sunk in the floor. It appears to have been broken into by the Khalif Alaziz Othman Ben-Yousouf, 1196 A.D., but the honour of throwing it open to modern exploration is due to the enterprise of Belzoni.

The account which that intrepid and sagacious tra-

---

* Herodotus, bk. ii. 123, 124.

veller furnishes of his explorations, may even now be perused with interest by the reader. Having discovered an entrance, he caused his hired troop of Arabs to clear away the rubbish about it, and cut through the massive stones of the Pyramid, until admission was obtained into the shaft or passage already described. Further labour conducted him to a portcullis, a fixed block of granite, which seemed to render impossible his progress into the interior. It stared him in the face as a *ne plus ultra*, putting an end to all his projects. But enthusiasm never believes in the impracticable. A closer inspection of the stone revealed that at the bottom it was raised about eight inches from the ground, while at the top a groove had been opened in the wall to admit of its elevation when required. With great toil it was lifted up into this recess, and a tunnel excavated high enough for a man to pass underneath. Belzoni, with a thrill of triumph, pressed forward, and, after thirty days of wonderful perseverance, was rewarded by finding himself in the road to the central chamber of the second Pyramid.

As it was his desire to reach the centre, he continued his advance along a corridor excavated in the solid rock, 6 feet in height, and 6 feet 6 inches broad. He then arrived at a large chamber, and paused to collect his scattered thoughts. Where was he? What was the object of the cell or apartment in which he found himself? "Whatever it might be," he says, "I certainly considered myself in the centre of that Pyramid which, from time immemorial, had been the subject of the obscure conjectures of many hundred travellers, both ancient and modern. My torch, formed of a few wax candles, gave

THE PYRAMID OF CHEPHREN, AND THE SPHINX.

but a faint light; I could, however, clearly distinguish the principal objects. I naturally turned my eyes to the west end of the chamber, looking for the sarcophagus, which I strongly expected to see in the same situation as that in the first Pyramid; but I was disappointed when I saw nothing there. The chamber, he continues, has a pointed or sloping ceiling, and many of the stones had been removed from their places, evidently by some one in search of treasure. On my advancing towards the west end, I was agreeably surprised to find that there was a sarcophagus buried on a level with the floor."

This sarcophagus is 8 feet long, 3 feet 6 inches wide, and 3 feet 2 inches deep in the inside. It is manufactured of the finest granite, but does not exhibit a single hieroglyph. The fragments of bone found in the interior belonged to an animal of the bovine species, and have been generally supposed to be the remains of the sacred bull—the type of the god Apis—so highly venerated by the Egyptians. The chamber is 46 feet in length, 16 feet 3 inches in width, and 23 feet 6 inches in height.

Such were the most important discoveries which rewarded Belzoni's energy. He also found a well or shaft, as in the Pyramid of Cheops, and from thence a passage running towards the north at an angle of 26°. It continued in this direction for $48\frac{1}{2}$ feet, and then opened upon a horizontal passage 35 feet long. Off this gallery turns an avenue or corridor 22 feet long, with a descent of 26° towards the west, which leads into a chamber with a pointed roof, 32 feet long, 9 feet 9 inches wide, and 8 feet 6 inches high.* Chephren, according to Manetho, reigned sixty-six years.

The third Pyramid, smaller than the others, but admirably constructed, was built by Men-ka-ré or Mycerinus, who reigned sixty-three years. It is only 218 feet high, by 354 feet 6 inches square. It has two sepulchral chambers, excavated out of the solid rock. The lower, modelled after a palace, has a pointed roof, cut like an arch inside. It contained the sarcophagus of Mycerinus, —a curious work of art, also modelled in imitation of a palace; but its cedar coffin, and the mummy belonging to it, had been removed to the upper apartment by some unknown spoliator. The débris of the coffin, and the remains of the mummy, were afterwards conveyed to England, where, in the British Museum, they now attract the attention of thousands. The stone sarcophagus was unfortunately lost off Carthagena, in the wreck of the vessel on board of which it had been embarked.

It seems desirable to add that six other pyramids of inferior dimensions are situated at Ghizeh; one at Abou-Ruweysh, five miles north-west, in a ruined condition, built by Venephes, of the first dynasty; another decayed memorial, built of limestone, stands at Zowyet-el-Arrian; and another, supposed to have been built by King User-en-Ra, or Busiris, at Rugar. There are three pyramids at Abou-Seir, one connected with King Shura, and another with a monarch of the third dynasty. Eleven are extant at Sakkara; five at Dashour—the northernmost of which is believed to have been erected by the King Asychis of

* Belzoni, *" Researches and Operations in Egypt and Nubia,"* i. 410, *et seq.*

Herodotus.* Others are at Biahmo, at Meydoon, and at Illahoon, and some small ones of brick, belonging to kings of the eleventh dynasty, at the Drah Aboo Negger, near Thebes. Wherever found, it has been ascertained that none were erected later than the era of the twelfth dynasty, and almost all of them may be described as forming a part of the great Royal Necropolis of Memphis.

All things dread Time, says the proverb, but Time dreads the Pyramids.†

---

* This king boasted greatly of his erection, perhaps because it was of brick "Wishing," says Herodotus, "to surpass all the kings who had reigned in Egypt before him, he left for a monument a pyramid of brick, with this inscription cut upon a stone: 'Degrade me not by comparing me with the pyramids of stone. I am as much above them as is Amun above all other gods: for I have been built of bricks made with the mud brought up from the bottom of the lake. This is the most notable thing that Asychis did."—*Herodotus*, bk. ii. § 136.

† The youthful student may be referred, for fuller information, to General Howard Vyse's "Observations on the Pyramids of Ghizeh;" Gliddon's "Egyptian Archæology;" and Bunsen's "Egypt's Place in Universal History." We may add that Sir G. Cornewall Lewis seems to intimate that none of the pyramids were anterior to the building of Solomon's Temple (1012 B.C.); while astronomical dates would certainly place the erection of the Great Pyramid eleven centuries earlier, or in 2123 B.C. At that time the star γ Draconis was the pole star, and passed the lower meridian at Ghizeh at an altitude of 26 or 27 degrees— the inclination at which the straight passages on the north side of the Great Pyramid descend.

The Pyramids have their legends: of a lighter character, in truth, than would seem to become such grave and hoary piles. Of one, the erection is ascribed to a princess of the Pharaonic race. Her father taunted her one day with the uselessness of the personal charms she possessed in no ordinary measure, and was not unnaturally vain of. She vowed, in her anger, that she would raise, by the power of her beauty, a monument as lasting and as grand as any that her ancestors had erected by the power of their armies. The number of her lovers, says Warburton, was thereupon increased by all who were content to sacrifice their fortune for her smiles. Her memorial, a massive pyramid, rose rapidly: to prove their devotion, her lovers ruined themselves; but the fair architect secured the renown she desired, and was afterwards enshrined in Sappho's tender song. Another legend relates that a fair Greek girl, named Rhodope, was once bathing in the Nile, while the very birds of the air hovered round her, entranced in ad-

An examination of these marvellous structures involves us in a labyrinth of thought. No one, for instance, can possibly penetrate into the interior of the Great Pyramid, as Mr. Fergusson remarks,* without being struck with astonishment at the wonderful mechanical skill displayed in its construction. The immense blocks of granite brought from Syene—a distance of five hundred miles—polished like glass, are so fitted that the joints can hardly be detected. Nothing can be more wonderful than the extraordinary amount of knowledge displayed in the construction of the discharging chambers over the roof of the principal apartment, in the alignment of the sloping galleries, in the provision of ventilating shafts, and in all the wonderful contrivances of the structure. All these, too, are carried out with such precision, that, notwithstanding the immense superincumbent weight, no settlement on any part can be detected to the extent of an appreciable fraction of an inch. Nothing more perfect, mechanically, has ever been erected since that time; and we ask ourselves in vain, how long it must have taken before men acquired such experience and such skill, or were so perfectly organized, as to contemplate and complete such undertakings.

Wonderful, continues Mr. Fergusson, as all this matu-

---

miration of her loveliness. An eagle, more rapturous than the rest, as might be expected of the bird of Jove, flew away with one of her dainty pantoufles in its talons; but, startled by a sudden outburst of Egyptian loyalty, let fall the precious souvenir at the feet of Pharaoh, who was holding his court in the open air. Our reader's imagination will supply the remainder of the story. Pharaoh commanded an instant search for the owner of so small a slipper. She was found; she was wooed; she was won; and within a pyramid erected to her glory now lies her dust.—*Eliot Warburton*, " *The Crescent and the Cross*," chap. xvi

* Fergusson, " History of Architecture," i. 81-83.

rity of art may be when found at so early a period, the problem becomes still more perplexing when we again ask ourselves how long a people must have lived and recorded their experience before they came to realize and aspire to an eternity such as the building of these pyramids shows that they sacrificed everything to attain. One of their great aims was to preserve the body intact for three thousand years, in order that the soul might be again united with it when the day of judgment arrived. But what taught them to contemplate such periods of time with confidence? and, stranger still, how did they learn to realize so daring an aspiration?

Such are some of the questions which a study of Egyptian monuments naturally suggests, but which, in our present state of knowledge, we are unable to answer satisfactorily.

In front of the Pyramids—a solemn and majestic apparition, rising, Pharos-like, above the surging sands which gather round it,—the billows of a petrified sea,—the traveller beholds the SPHINX, mutely tranquil and immovably serene, as in the days when religious processions marched up between its colossal paws to the temple which it sheltered in its all-embracing bosom. It is, perhaps, the most impressive of the Egyptian monuments; and the traveller never wearies of gazing upon the " stony calm of its attitude," the weird beauty of its repose, the unutterable meaning of its eloquent countenance. The Arabs expressively name it Aboolhol, " the father of terror," or " immensity." Bartlett compares it to " some mysterious pre-Adamite monarch," or " to one of those gigantic genii of Arabian fiction which make their abode in the desolate places of the earth." Miss Martineau speaks of its "long, well-opened eyes—eyes which have gazed unwinking into vacancy, while mighty Pharaohs, and Hebrew lawgivers, and Persian princes, and Greek philosophers, and Antony with Cleopatra by his side, and Christian anchorites, and Arab warriors, and European men of science, have been brought hither in succession by the unpausing ages to look up into those eyes—so full of meaning, though so fixed."

"There was something," says Dean Stanley, "stupendous in the sight of that enormous head—its vast projecting wig, its great ears, its open eyes, the red colour still visible on its cheeks, the immense projection of the lower part of its face. Yet what must it have been when on its head there was the royal helmet of Egypt, on its chin the royal beard; when the stone pavement by which man approached the Pyramids ran up between its paws; when immediately under its breast an altar stood, from which the smoke went up into the gigantic nostrils of that nose, now vanished from the face, never to be conceived again! All this is known with certainty from the remains which actually exist deep under the sand on which you stand, as you look up from a distance into the broken but still expressive features."

The eloquent author of "Eōthen" has expressed the admiration which it awakens in every thoughtful observer with yet greater faithfulness, and in language of singular force.

Comely the creature is, he says,* but the comeliness

* A. W. Kinglake, "Eōthen; or, Traces of Eastern Travel."

is not of this world; the once-worshipped beast is a deformity and a monster to this generation: and yet you can see that those lips, so thick and heavy, were fashioned according to some ancient mould of beauty—some mould of beauty now forgotten—forgotten because that Greece drew forth Cytherea from the flashing foam of the Ægean, and in her image created new forms of beauty, and made it a law among men, that the short and proudly-wreathed lip should stand for the sign and main condition of loveliness through all generations to come. Yet still there lives on the race of those who were beautiful in the fashion of the elder world; and Christian girls of Coptic blood will look on you with the sad, serious gaze, and kiss your charitable hand with the big pouting lips, of the very Sphinx.

"Laugh and mock, if you will," continues our authority, "at the worship of stone idols; but mark ye this, ye breakers of images, that in one regard the stone idol bears awful semblance of Deity — unchangefulness in the midst of change—the same seeming will and intent, for ever and ever inexorable! Upon ancient dynasties of Ethiopian and Egyptian kings; upon Greek and Roman, upon Arab and Ottoman, conquerors; upon Napoleon dreaming of an Eastern Empire; upon battle and pestilence; upon the ceaseless misery of the Egyptian race; upon keen-eyed travellers, Herodotus yesterday, and Warburton to-day;—upon all and more this unworldly Sphinx has watched, and watched like a Providence, with the same earnest eyes, and the same sad, tranquil mien. And we, we shall die, and Islam wither away; and the Englishman, straining far over to hold his loved India, will plant a firm foot on the banks of the Nile, and sit in the seats of the Faithful; and still that sleepless rock will lie watching and watching the works of the new busy race, with those same sad, earnest eyes, and the same tranquil mien everlasting. You dare not," says Eōthen, "you dare not mock at the Sphinx."

The colossal figure is hewn out of the rock, excepting the fore-paws, which are built of squared stone: an enormous couchant monster, with gigantic arms, between which formerly nestled a miniature temple with a platform, and flights of steps for approaching it. In the old time, its head bore either the royal helmet or the ram's horns. It measures, from the belly to the highest part of the head, 56 feet; its length is 172 feet 6 inches; and the circumference round the colossal brows, 102 feet. Over the temple and altar of sacrifice the grand head of this tutelary deity towered from an altitude of 60 feet. The granite tablet above the altar is still visible, but the temple itself lies buried beneath the drifted sand.

From a tablet which M. Mariette has discovered, it would appear that some repairs were effected on this extraordinary monument by Suphis, or Shufu, the chief founder of the Great Pyramid.* In that case, the Sphinx must have existed before the Pyramids; and, in truth, if it then required renovation, must have existed long prior to those venerable piles. And, therefore, it is not only the most colossal, but the most ancient idol of which we have any knowledge. In the Egyptian hieroglyphs it is always referred to under the name of *Neb*, or "Lord," and *Akar*, or "Intelligence;" so that when we consider its

* Renan, "Revue des Deux Mondes," 1865, pp. 675, *et sqq*

curious combination of the lion's body with the human head, we may, perhaps, be allowed to suppose that it symbolized Intellect and Strength.

The Sphinx* of Ghizeh is the largest in Egypt. Caviglia, who carefully explored it in 1816, ascertained from three hieroglyphical tablets in its temple, that the said temple was dedicated to it, under the name of Haremakhu, or "Sun on the Horizon," by Thothmes III. and Rameses II. Before the altar, apparently a Roman addition, extended a *dromos*, or paved esplanade, repaired in the reigns of Marcus Aurelius and Lucius Verus, May the 10th, A.D. 160. Various votive inscriptions were discovered; and, especially, on the second digit of the left paw, the following, in Greek pentameters, by Arrian :—

> "Thy form stupendous here the gods have placed,
> Sparing each spot of harvest-bearing land;
> And with this mighty work of art have graced
> A rocky isle, encumbered once with sand,
> And near the Pyramids have bid thee stand."

Some further particulars were obtained by M. Mariette in 1852, who caused the vicinity to be carefully excavated. He laid open a peripolos, or outer wall, designed to protect it from the ever-shifting sands; and ascertained that only the head of the Sphinx was sculptured. To the south he found a dromos leading to a temple, built, in the era of the fourth dynasty, of huge blocks of red granite and alabaster. Here, in the midst of the great chamber, were discovered seven statues—five mutilated, and two entire—of the monarch Chephren, or Sha-fre, which were very finely executed.

* The word is from the Greek, and signifies "the Strangler."

A short distance to the south-east of the Pyramids, and on the bank of the river, a few mounds—a few shapeless ruins and mummy pits—indicate the site of the old capital of the Memphite kings, MEMPHIS.

It was known to the Egyptians as *Men-nefer*, or the "Good Station;" the Hebrews named it *Noph;* and by the modern Arabs it is called *Memf.* If Herodotus may be credited,* it was founded by the first monarch of the first dynasty, Men or Menes, who diverted the course of the Nile, and raised an embankment of one hundred stadia in length, to protect his new city from inundations. The remains of this work, by whomsoever constructed, are still visible at Kafr-el-Tyat, which represents the centre of ancient Memphis, and the site of its most famous temple. A palace built by Menes, was enlarged by his son Athothis, and, when the seat of empire was removed to Thebes, became the residence of the viceroy.

Long before Athens or Rome existed, Memphis was celebrated for its wealth, its population, its influence, and its commercial greatness. It was here the Persian conqueror Cambyses received the splendid embassies that came from all quarters of the known world,—

> "From India and the golden Chersonese,
> And utmost Indian isle Taprobane,
> Dusk faces with white silken turbans wreathed."†

In those its palmy days, its circumference was computed at sixteen miles.‡ Owing to its important position, it was frequently exposed to the storms of war during the

---

* Herodotus, book ii. § 99.   See also Diodorus, book i. c. 4.
† Milton, "Paradise Lost."
‡ Sir G. Wilkinson, "Topography of Thebes," p. 340.

repeated revolts of the Egyptians against their foreign rulers. It was plundered and devastated by Ochus after his defeat of Nectanebus. Something of its former prosperity had returned when it was visited by Alexander, who, after worshipping the Apis in its sacred temple, descended the Nile in a gilded galley to its Canobic mouth. The Greek conqueror's body was brought hither by Ptolemy, before its final removal to Alexandria. The early monarchs of the Lagid dynasty were crowned in the Serapéion; but the city was destroyed by Ptolemy VIII. With that extraordinary vitality which sometimes distinguishes great cities, it revived under the Roman rule; but after the conquest of Egypt by Amrou the Arab, finally sunk into decay, and contributed by its enormous ruins to the foundation of Cairo and Fostat. They were still of considerable importance and extent when visited by the Arab historian Abdalatif, in the thirteenth century. The scanty remains are now to be found at Koum-el-Uzyzeh on the north, and Metrahenny on the west.

It was a curious feature of the ancient Egyptian worship, that each large city or nome had its own Triad, or assemblage of three gods, whom it more particularly adored. The Triad of Memphis consisted of *Ptah*, or "Fire"—identical with the Greek *Hephaestos; Pasht*, or Bubastis, who may be identified with the *Artemis* of the Greeks; and the ox-god *Apis*. There would consequently be temples erected to these divinities; but owing to the ruined condition of the city their sites cannot now be discovered, with the exception of that of Apis.

The foundations of the last-named were discovered by M. Mariette in 1850–51. This was the magnificent Serapéion, built by the Greeks on the site of that ancient "abode of Osor-hapi," or the "Osiris-Apis;"* which the Egyptians had for ages regarded with peculiar reverence. It was approached from the city by an avenue of sphinxes —which, even in the time of Strabo, was partially buried in the sands—and consisted of four temples, respectively dedicated to Serapis, Astarte, Anubis, and Imouthos (or Aesculapius). Close at hand stood the *Apeum*, or sanctuary of the sacred bull, where he was carefully tended, as well as the cow from which he had sprung. As each bull died, his mummy was stored away in one of the corridors extending underground for a considerable distance, and known as the "Mummy-pits of Apis;" and in which were preserved the remains of all the bulls from the reign of Amunophis III. (about B.C. 1400). The year in which he was born, when he was set up in the place of honour in the Apeum, and when interred in his subterranean sepulchre, were recorded on a tombstone or monumental tablet; and as these tablets range from the 19th dynasty to the epoch of Ptolemy III., Euergetes, in 247 B.C., their chronological value is very great. They number about twelve hundred, but the most important have been removed to the Louvre at Paris.† The priesthood of the Serapéion formed a peculiar order, living wholly within the confines of the temple, and supported by the oblations of the devout.

The mummies are arranged in two principal galleries, of which the more ancient is also the smaller; the second,

---

* This, however, is doubted by some authorities, who think that the Apeum stood south of the gateway of the Temple of Pthah.
† Mariette, "Serapéum de Memphis (4to, Paris, 1856).

THE SERAPEION, MEMPHIS.

in point of time, was begun in the fifty-third year of Psammetichus I., and contains about twenty-four magnificent granite sarcophagi. Its walls are covered with vivid decorations of the usual character. The other corridors are of inferior character, and their monuments and decorations display no artistic merit.

The Temple of Osiris-Apis, or Osor-hapi—that is, the

BRONZES OF THE EGYPTIAN GOD APIS.

"Osirified" or "dead Apis"—was called by the Greeks the Serapéion, simply because they identified the Egyptian god with the deity Serapis, whose image and worship they translated from Sinope in Pontus to Alexandria, in consequence of a vision of Ptolemy I. (Soter). This new deity found great favour in the Greek cities founded in Egypt, and forty-two temples were raised to his honour.

The three most famous were those of Alexandria, Canobus, and Memphis. The Egyptian Apis, or divine bull, was worshipped as a symbol of Osiris. He was attended by a retinue of priests, and sacrifices of red oxen were offered to him. All his changes of appetite, his movements, and choice of places were watched as oracular. He was not allowed to live longer than twenty-five years. If he died a natural death before that age, his body was embalmed as a mummy, and interred in the subterranean tombs. Otherwise, he was secretly put to death, and buried by the priests in a sacred well. A new animal was then sought for. It was necessary he should be marked with a white square on his forehead, an eagle on his back, and a knot like a cantharus under his tongue. When found, he was conveyed with great pomp to Nilopolis, where he remained for forty days, attended by naked women, and was then removed to Memphis.*

The ancient city also boasted of the *Iseion*, a magnificent temple completed by Amasis II., about 526 B.C; of a temple to Ra, Re, or the Sun—throughout Egypt an object of peculiar reverence; of the *Nilometer*, or standard which gauged the flood and ebb of the Nile, removed by

---

* After the defeat of the Persian army in the Libyan Desert, Cambyses returned to this city (B.C. 524), to find its inhabitants rejoicing at the discovery of a calf marked with the mystic characters which declared it to be the divine bull. Supposing the public joy to be over his own defeat, Cambyses summoned the magistrates before him. They endeavoured to pacify him by relating the discovery of Apis, but were immediately condemned to death as liars. He then ordered Apis and his priests to be brought into his presence; "he would soon know," he said, "whether a tame god had really come to dwell in Egypt." Drawing his dagger, he stabbed the calf in the thigh, and sentenced the priests to be scourged. All his subsequent excesses and disasters were supposed by the Egyptians to be the penalty which the gods inflicted for this sacrilegious act.

Constantine to Byzantium, but restored to Memphis by Julian the Apostate; of a temple to Ptah, which was probably one of surpassing magnificence; the mysterious shrine of the Cabiri; and the huge colossal statues of Rameses II. The most signal evidence of its past grandeur is afforded, however, by the remains of its superb Necropolis, which, extending for miles along the frontier of the Desert, includes seven-and-sixty pyramids, and among these the three great marvels of Ghizeh.*

There is one other memorial of ancient Memphis to which the traveller's attention should be directed. Herodotus tells us how Sesostris—that is, Rameses III.—erected in front of the great gateway a colossal statue of his royal self. And deep in a thick wide grove of palms, in a little pool of water left by the inundation which annually covers the spot, lies a gigantic effigy, its back upwards. The name of Rameses is carved upon its belt. The face lies downwards, but is visible in profile, and quite perfect, with a wonderful expression of repose and tranquillity.

The reader should also be reminded, as we take leave of the capital of Menes, that it was once visited by the patriarch Abraham, was afterwards the residence of Joseph, and perhaps the birth-place of the Hebrew lawgiver, Moses.†

Another excursion from Cairo, not to be neglected by

---

* Lepsius, "Reise Egypten," pp. 51–63. The pyramids form four principal groups: those of Ghizeh, the oldest and largest, Abou-Seir, Dashour, and Sakkara.

† According to Manetho, Moses was born at Heliopolis; yet the princess who rescued him from the Nile is said to have been the wife of "Chenephres," king of Memphis.

the traveller, is to HELIOPOLIS, where, in a remote antiquity,—

"An imperial city stood,
With towers and temples proudly elevate;"

but whose site is now only marked by a circuit of mounds, and by an obelisk, supposed to be the oldest in Egypt.

The road leads through fertile gardens, and irrigated fields of corn and rice, and, for the most part, under "the shade of melancholy boughs." As the tourist follows it, he pauses to examine the celebrated sycamore, under whose venerable branches tradition declares the Holy Family rested on their journey towards the south.

Little now remains of Heliopolis, says a recent writer,* but a vast accumulation of débris and piles of refuse. It is strange, he adds, to trace the sites of the most ancient Egyptian cities by these immense heaps of crumbled and broken bricks, which alone, in many instances, indicate where they once flourished. These bricks, though still hard and sometimes angular, are invariably of unburned earth, for there was no burned brick in Egypt before the time of the Roman dominion; yet so tenacious is the mud and slime of the Nile of which they are composed, and so baking are the powerful rays of the sun in those latitudes, that the ancient bricks are almost as hard as stone.

Heliopolis, as the oldest capital in Egypt, is rich in historical associations. Its Egyptian name was *Ei-n-Re*, "the Abode of the Sun;" from which came the Hebrew *Aôn* or *On*. Its chief temple was dedicated to the sun-god. It was, in truth, the sanctuary of the learning and

* Rev. A. C. Smith, "The Nile and its Banks," i. 100, 101.

wisdom of the Egyptians—the Egyptian Oxford—a cluster of temples and colleges, where the priests taught the mysteries of their faith. Here Joseph took to wife Asenath, the daughter of Poti-pherah, priest of the Sun. Here Moses was taught, by command of Pharaoh's daughter—the Pharaoh being Apophis, one of the Shepherd Kings—the doctrines of the Egyptian religion. Here, in a day of darkness and woe, Jeremiah wrote his Lamentations over the decline of Judah. And here Eudoxus and Plato resided for thirteen years; the latter imbibing that sublime belief in the immortality of the soul which he afterwards expounded in the glorious eloquence of the *Phaedo*. And here grew the famous *Amryllis Gileadensis*, yielding the fragrant balsamic resin of the " balm of Gilead" which the Queen of Sheba presented to Solomon.*

BALM OF GILEAD.

Of old-world Egypt, Heliopolis was the sacredest city, the very focus and centre of its active religious life, the source whence flowed, as it were, the higher impulses of its civilization. And now a solitary obelisk and " a circuit of mounds" are all that exist to remind us of its " local habitation." It is this that renders Egyptian tra-

* Josephus, "Antiquities," book viii. 6. 6; Eliot Warburton, "The Crescent and the Cross," c. v.

vel so mournfully impressive; everywhere the eye rests on the most striking testimony of the mutability of human things, and the most eloquent proofs of the vanity of human ambition.

The "solitary obelisk" to which I have referred is of

THE OBELISK.

red granite, and therefore must have come from the quarries of Syene, distant five hundred miles; but who excavated it, who sculptured it, or how it was transported to its present site, and erected, are questions not to be answered by the most learned Egyptologist. Exclusive of the top, it measures 67 feet in height, and it bears the name of Osirtesen I., the most illustrious member of the twelfth dynasty, who reigned over both Upper and Lower Egypt. Its base is buried several feet in earth, gradually deposited by successive overflows of the river, which now pours into the area of the city, though in ancient times considerably below its level.

It should be noted, as a rule with scarcely any excep-

CARTOUCHE OF THOTHMES III.

tion, that while all the pyramids stand on the west bank of the Nile, which was considered preferable for purposes of sepulture, the obelisks were raised on the east. As these monoliths seem to have been principally dedicated to the sun-god, their position may have had some emblematic reference to the quarter in which he first appeared.

Several of the obelisks which anciently adorned Heliopolis were removed by the Romans: one now rises before the church of St. John Lateran; another in the Atmeedan or Hippodrome of Constantinople. Both of these bear the well-known cartouche of Thothmes III. A third, in the Piazza del Popolo at Rome, originally erected by Menephthah, was transported to Rome by order of the Emperor Augustus. That of the Monte Cavallo was brought from Egypt by Claudius, A.D. 57.

Heliopolis, I may add, is situated on the east side of the Pelusiac branch of the Nile, about twenty miles northeast of Memphis.

DAHABEEYAH, OR NILE-BOAT

CHAPTER III.

BENI-HASSAN, AND THE TOMBS—ANTINOOPOLIS—SIOUT—GIRGEH—DENDERA, AND ITS TEMPLE.

> Monarchs—the powerful and the strong—
> Famous in history and in song
> Of olden time.   LONGFELLOW.
>
> A reverend pile,
> With bold projections and recesses deep.
>   WORDSWORTH.

AFTER our excursions to the Pyramids and Heliopolis, let us return to Cairo. Here we engage a *dahabeeyah*, or Nile-boat, and prepare for our voyage up the "sacred river." And a more delightful excursion it is difficult to imagine! There is a splendour in the sky, an elasticity in the air, to which the pilgrim from the cloudy West is wholly unaccustomed. The scenery through which he is carried easily and not too rapidly is of a striking and varied character. Villages of mud huts, embowered in groves of palm; sandy shoals, alive with wings, and gay with the plumage of the flamingo and the ibis; quaint native barges, of all sizes and types, carrying dusky passengers in brightly-coloured attire; a yacht or two, belonging to some adventurous European or wealthy Moslem; men paddling along on rafts of pottery or water-melons; little busy cafés, nestling in the shade of far-spread sycamores; creaking *sakias*, or water-wheels, used for the purpose of irrigation; and beyond the emerald strip of fertile valley the yellow boundary of the Desert;—all these combine to form a picture as splendid as it is rare.

Nor will the animal life which swarms upon the riverbanks fail to attract the traveller's gaze, from its abundance, its variety, and its newness. Water-fowl of several species; *grallatores* and *natatores*, waited on by *raptores*, for death always attends life very closely, in the East as in the West: vultures and kites, hawks, kestrels, buzzards, and harriers, sweep by in swift succession. Here may be seen the carcass of a dead camel, with dogs rending it on one side, and vultures on the other, and hooded crows at hand to claim their portion of the booty. There the ploughman plods on his way, driving a team of camels, or a pair of cows, or a camel yoked with a cow, or even a tall gaunt camel mated with a diminutive donkey, while herons and spoonbills follow in a lively but grotesque procession. Sand-pipers and little ringed plovers are running on the shallows, and flocks of geese and ducks quacking among the reedy marshes; while, until we get too far inland, the occasional shadow of a gull or a tern flits like a cloud above our heads.*

Passing through the narrow channel which separates the island of Rhoda † from Boulak (where, let me ob-

---

* Rev. A. C. Smith, "The Nile and its Banks," i. 41, 42.

† At Rhoda stands the famous Nilometer, which, for centuries, has marked the rise of the inundation. It is also said to be the spot where the infant Moses was rescued by Pharaoh's daughter.

THE SAKIA, OR EGYPTIAN WATER-WHEEL.

serve parenthetically, there is an admirable museum of Egyptian antiquities), we emerge upon the full broad river, rolling its waters between thick-clustering groves of palm. Yonder, across the level valley, loom the blue masses of the Pyramids, stretching far along the horizon from Ghizeh to Memphis; and in the distance a warm rosy haze floats over the sands of the Libyan Desert. We pass, first, the Pyramids of Sakkara (two in number); and next, those of Dashour (also two); and in due time heave in sight of the plantations and minarets of *Benisouef*. Here the traveller may land for the purpose of visiting Lake Moeris and the fertile district of the Faioum. Leaving behind us its palms, with their rich burden of golden dates, and its fluttering bowers of acacia, we sail onward, through ranges of barren cliffs, the offshoots of the Arabian and Libyan chains of mountains, to the cliff called *Gebel e Tayr*, or the "Mountain of the Birds." Here, according to an Arab legend, all the birds of Egypt congregate annually on a certain day; and after a lively debate, all set out in a body, with the exception of a solitary sentinel left in charge of the spot until the return of his congeners in the following year.

Yonder gleaming little town, encircled in date-groves, is called *Minyeh:* the river-channel at this point is considerably obstructed by dangerous sand-banks. Next we arrive at *Beni-hassan*—the "Speos Artemidos" of the Greeks—where everybody lands to explore the celebrated TOMBS, situated high up among the gloomy rocks, which have been laboriously excavated to furnish the dead with resting-places. They seem to have served as the necropolis, or public cemetery of the Hermopolite *nome*.

These tombs, thirty in number, are unique; unique on account of their antiquity, their architecture, and their representations of Egyptian manners and customs; and unique, because, unlike all other Egyptian sepulchres, they are situated on the *east* bank of the river.

They are among the oldest known monuments in Egypt, and many of them must have received their tenants before Joseph rose into Pharaoh's favour—a thousand years, perhaps, before Joseph was born. It is not improbable that in the first place they were employed as the residences of the living.* At all events, one of them is of peculiar interest. It bears date from the early time of Sesortesen I., and consists of an arched cavern, whose walls are everywhere covered with pictorial language.† It has a vaulted portico, with two shapely pillars of the kind which the Greeks afterwards called Doric, each 23 feet high. Throughout its chambers the basement is painted a deep red; and on this basement, as well as on the architraves, the hieroglyphics are green; the general effect commending itself to the spectator's eye. The central avenue has a low coved ceiling, and at its extremity a large niche or recess. It is divided from the aisle on either hand by a row of columns, resembling those of the portico.

In this painted chamber, or crypt, which is 30 feet square, occurs a remarkable procession, erroneously supposed, by some authorities, to represent the arrival of Joseph's brethren in Egypt. But, apart from other

---

* Fergusson, "History of Architecture."

† The walls are covered with a thick coat of some kind of cement, and on the smooth surface thus presented, the paintings have been executed.

MINEH.

evidence which tends to show that the tomb was closed ten centuries before that event, there is enough in the procession itself to prove that it has no connection with Hebrew history.*

At each end of the row stands a great man. The principal figure is named Neoothph, who was governor of this district, on the east side of the Nile, and, no doubt, the owner of the tomb. To him, as the old play-

BENI-HASSAN :—NEOOTHPH'S TOMB (EXTERIOR).

book says, comes a dreary train of seven-and-thirty captives; captives with white complexions, tunics, sandals, and long beards; the women with dishevelled hair, and shod in ankle-boots. They bring with them offerings to appease the great man's wrath—a wild goat, a gazelle, a flock of ostriches, and one ibis.

* Kenrick, "Ancient Egypt," i. 47, *et sqq.*

Others of the tombs are sculptured with the old Egyptian symbols, the lotus and the papyrus; some have slightly-vaulted roofs, some smaller inner chambers; all are alive, as it were, with the ancient life, with the manners and customs, the occupations and the pastimes of a nation which flourished four or five thousand years ago. There is nowhere else in the world so curious a history of a people, written or painted by themselves.

BENI-HASSAN:—NEOOTHPH'S TOMB (INTERIOR).

We have here, says Miss Martineau,—and we shall freely avail ourselves of her animated description,*—the art of writing as a familiar practice, in the scribes who are numbering the stores on every hand. There are ships [including the *bari*, or high-prowed barge] which would look handsome in Southampton Water, any sunny

* Miss Harriet Martineau, "Eastern Life," ii. 35-41.

day. There are glass-blowers who might be from Newcastle, but for their dress and complexion. There are

EGYPTIANS SPINNING. EGYPTIAN WEAVING.
(From the Monuments.)

flax-dressers, spinners, weavers, and a production of cloth which an English manufacturer would study with

EGYPTIAN POTTER.

interest. There are potters, painters, carpenters, and statuaries. Here a doctor attends a patient; there a herdsman physics cattle. The hunters employ arrows, spears, and the lasso. The lasso is as evident as on the pampas at this day. You may see the Nile full of fish, and a hippopotamus among the ooze. Yonder is the bastinado for the men; and the flogging of a seated woman. Nothing is more extraordinary than the gymnastics and other pastimes of the females. Their various games of ball are excellent. The great men are attended by dwarfs and buffoons, as in a much later age; and it is clear that bodily infirmity was treated with contempt—deformed and decrepit personages appearing in the discharge of the meanest offices. It was an age when this might be looked for; when war would be the most prominent occupation, and wrestling the prevailing sport, and probably also the discipline of the soldiery; when hunting, fishing, and fowling would be very important pursuits. But then, what a power of representation of these things is here! and what luxury co-existing with those early pursuits! Harpers may be seen with their harps of seven strings; and garments and boat-sails with elegant patterns and borders—where, by the way, angular and regular figures are pointedly preferred; and the ladies' hair, disordered and flying about in their sports, has tails and tassels, very like what may have been seen in London drawing-rooms in no very remote times. The circumstance which most reminds one of the antiquity of these paintings is, that the name of bird, beast, fish, or artificer is written above the object delineated. It is the resource—not needed here, however—of the artist who wrote on his picture, "This is a man," "This is a monkey." Another barbarism is, that the great man, the occupant of the tomb, has his greatness signified by bigness, being a giant among middle-sized people. There are brick-makers also, who are shown going through the different processes of their craft; and other trades and occupations receive the fullest and most vivid illustration.

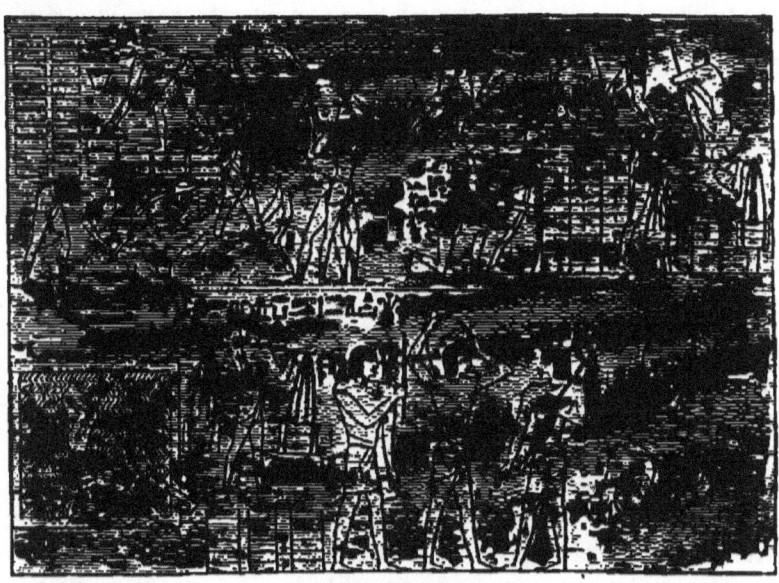

BRICK-MAKERS.
(From a Tomb at Beni-hassan.)

Such are the glimpses of Egyptian life which the traveller obtains in the tombs at Beni-hassan.

We resume our voyage; sailing up the stream to the loud and discordant choral music of the Reis and his boatmen, and enjoying the magic changes of the landscape at sunrise and sunset—the bright light which, at dawn, kindles up the palm groves and the distant hills— the after-glow, which, when the orb of day has paled its fires, illuminates minaret, and grove, and garden, and rippling waves with an indescribable glory. Yonder lies the village of *Sheikh-Abadeh*, near the site of that *Antinoöpolis* which the Emperor Hadrian founded in honour of his handsome favourite Antinous;* there rise, in awful grandeur, the dark abrupt precipices of Djebel Aboufodde, pierced with innumerable caverns, the asylum, in old times, of Christian anchorites, and, on one occasion, the refuge of the great Athanasius. On a high bank of earth above the river stands *Manfalut*. Next we come in sight of *Siout*, the capital of Upper Egypt, and the depôt of the slave-caravans from Darfur. It is a considerable town, with handsome mosques, respectable bazaars, and a fertile country around it.

About twenty-four miles from Girgeh lie the ruins of *Abydus*, or *This*, including the hoary remains of two temples, founded by Osirei and his son Rameses the Great. Very pleasant is the scenery between Girgeh and *Keneh*, the Neapolis of Herodotus; a fertile plain, covered with luxuriant crops of sugar-cane and Indian corn, and brightened with rich clusters of the fan-leaved doum or Theban palm. A crocodile or two are now occasionally seen among the dark herbage that fringes the sand-banks. This is the nearest point which the Nile attains to the Red Sea. It is only one hundred and twenty miles from Kosseir, and consequently a principal rendezvous with the Mecca pilgrims.

We next arrive at DENDERA—the "Tentyra" of the Greeks—whose temple is considered by many travellers

---

* The direction of its principal streets may still be traced. The town seems to have measured about a mile and a half in length, and half a mile in breadth.

SCENE AT SIOUT.

the noblest in Egypt.* It is thrown into fine relief by the dark woods of palms which gather in its rear. The façade is vast and sombre, with four rows each of six massive columns, the capital of each consisting of the head of the goddess Athor, the Venus of the Egyptians;—different, indeed, from the loose-zoned, laughing goddess

PROPYLON OF THE TEMPLE OF DENDERA.

of the Greeks, and wearing an expression of "bewitching half modesty," which might well impress the worshipper with admiration. The temple is in excellent preservation—as if, says Mr. St. John,† the Power in whose

* Hamilton, "Aegyptiaca," pp. 196-204.
† J. A. St. John, "There and Back Again in Search of Beauty."

honour it was built still sheltered its shrine from utter destruction.*

The great portico is a specimen of the later Egyptian art, having been erected as late as the reign of Tiberius. Its ceiling exhibits a representation of the zodiac, which our antiquaries, says Mr. Sharpe, once thought of great antiquity, though the sign of the Scales should have taught them that it could not date further back than the reign of Augustus, who gave that name to the group of stars formerly included in the Scorpion's spreading claws.†

It is impossible not to admire the zeal of the Egyptians by whom this work was finished. They were treated as slaves by their Greek fellow-countrymen; they, the fallen descendants of the conquering kings of Thebes, had every third year their houses ransacked in search of arms: the Romans only ruled to drain the province of its wealth, and the temple was perhaps never heard of by their Emperor, who cannot have been aware that the most lasting monument of his reign was being raised in the distant province of Egypt. Who will refuse his tribute of respect to a people who, denying themselves all beyond the coarsest food and clothing as luxuries, thought a noble temple for the worship of the gods the supreme necessity of their lives?

To the great portico succeeds a hall of six columns,

---

* Important excavations, however, are taking place here under the superintendence of M. Mariette.

† It is exceedingly doubtful whether this so-called Zodiac has any real astronomical signification. There seems reason to believe that it rather represents a procession of the Tentyrite Triad (Isis, Athor, and her son Horus or Ehôou) and their cognate deities.

TEMPLE OF DENDERA

with three rooms on either side. Then comes a central chamber, communicating on one side with two small rooms, and on the other with a staircase. Passing through another similar chamber, with two rooms on the west and one on the east side, we enter the "holy of holies"—the *naos*, or sanctuary—which has a corridor around it, and communicating with three rooms on either hand.

The total length of the temple is about 220 feet; its width, 41 feet; or, across the portico, 50 feet. The walls are everywhere covered with a profusion of elaborate hieroglyphics,* mostly relating to the worship of the Egyptian goddess, who had here her most sacred abode (Dendera = Thy-n-Athor, the abode of Athor). She ranked in the second class of deities, as the daughter of Ra, the Sun, and was identified by the Greeks with their Aphrodite. Her symbol was the cow, and in hieroglyphics she generally appears with the head of that animal, bearing between her horns the figure of the solar disc. In the earlier Egyptian mythology she seems to have symbolized the creative principle of the world; at a later period she became simply the goddess of "the laugh, the jest, and the song."

ISIS OR ATHOR, WITH THE INFANT HORUS.

The other buildings at Dendera are of inferior importance, though not unworthy of examination. Behind

* Among them are a few historical portraits, as those of Cleopatra and her son Cæsarion.

the south-west angle of the great temple stands the *Iseion*, or Temple of Isis, erected in the reign of Augustus, and consisting of one central and two lateral chambers, with a corridor in front. The names of Augustus, Claudius, and Nero are found among its hieroglyphics.

About three hundred feet to the north is situated the *Typhoneion* so named from the figures and emblems of Typhon upon its walls. Champollion observes, however, that every other design has some reference to the birth of Ehôou, the son of Athor; and suggests that this was one of the sacred places called "Mammeisi," or "lying-in-chambers," in commemoration of Athor's delivery. If this suggestion be correct, Typhon is simply introduced in the sculptures as symbolizing that chaos or primeval darkness which precedes creation or birth.*

The building contains two outer chambers, and a central and lateral adytum. A range of twenty-two columns embellishes it on the sides and rear.

* Champollion, "Lettres sur l'Egypte," ii. 67

CHAPTER IV.

THEBES: ITS HISTORY—THE RAMESEION—THE AMUNO-PHEION—THE COLOSSI—THE THOTHMESEION—THE PALACE OF RAMESES—THE TOMBS OF THE KINGS—MEDINET-ABOO—LUXOR—KARNAK—THE THEBAID.

> High towers, faire temples, goodly theaters,
> Strong walls, rich porches, princelie pallaces,
> Large streetes, brave houses, sacred sepulchers,
> Sure gates, sweete gardens, stately galleries,
> Wrought with faire pillours and fine imageries;
> All these (O pitie!) now are turned to dust,
> And overgrown with black oblivion's rust.
>
> SPENSER.

 A RECENT traveller has described the feeling which creeps upon the Nile voyager when, after a sail of about five-and-twenty miles from Dendera, he turns a certain angle of the river, and sees before him the plain of ancient Thebes—Thebes the magnificent—the "populous No" of the prophet Nahum—the great city of which Homer wrote as

> "Royal Thebes,
> Egyptian treasure-house of countless wealth,
> Who boasts her hundred gates, through each of which,
> With horse and car, two hundred warriors march."*

All that is left of her lies here, here on the wreck·

---

* Homer's "Iliad." book ix., Lord Derby's translation, i., 206.

strewn plain. Yes, the multitudes are gone, and the city lies desolate; but the forms of the landscape are fixed as the everlasting hills. The multitudes are gone, says Mr. Hopley,* but that circling barrier of rock-mountain which rises in the west is their prison-house—Thebes is still peopled with the dead. Yonder, for the ancient Theban, lay the region of the sunset—Amenti, the world beyond the grave. And between rolled the River of Death, the Funereal Lake. See it now in the distance, gleaming in the soft glow of twilight! There, beyond it, on the mountain, hundreds of tombs gape open, planted thickly in sheltering niches, under towering crags, and upon inaccessible heights. Wherever the eye wanders it rests on the city of the dead. And in that mountain's shadow, age after age, sits Memnon on his throne of rock—type of steadfast Faith—patiently awaiting the coming of the Day. Is it a dream of the brain, that silent, shining river flowing through the crimson evening,—that pillared and many-templed shore? Nay; it is, in truth, the Nile that you gaze upon, and the ruins of that mighty Thebes, into which, as Dean Stanley says,† for two thousand years—from the time of Joseph down to the Christian era—the splendour of the Earth was poured. As one thinks of all this vanished glory, the burden of the past becomes almost too heavy to endure.

The name of THEBES is formed from the Tape, or T-ape —that is," the head"—of the old Egyptian language. It was also called *Amunei*, or the "abode of Amun" (Ammon, or Zeus, the ram-headed god); whence the Greeks

---

* Hopley, "Under Egyptian Palms," p. 127.
† Dean Stanley, "Sinai and Palestine," Introd., p. xlii.

designated it Διοσπολις ἡ μεγάλη, or Diospolis Magna—
the great city of Zeus. It is the *No* and *No-Ammon* of the
Hebrew Scriptures.* The
name "Thebes" applied
to the whole city on both
banks of the Nile, but the
western quarter bears the
distinctive appellation of
Pathyris, or Tathyris, from
its being under the special favour of Athor.

Its situation was admirably adapted to favour
the development of a great
city. Planted on the
banks of a navigable river,
near the main routes that
led through the littoral
hills to the Red Sea, on
the one hand; and, on the
other, across the Libyan
wilderness to the Great
Desert; it became the entrepôt, until Alexandria rose into existence, of the commerce of Eastern Africa. It was also celebrated for the
industrial capacities of its inhabitants; for its manufactures of linen, pottery, and glass; and its wealth was
further increased by the resort to its temples of all who
worshipped the sun-god, Amun-Ra.

Alone of the Egyptian cities, as Dean Stanley observes,

AMUN-RA, THE SUN-GOD.

---

* Ezekiel xxx. 14; Nahum iii. 8.

was Thebes beautiful by nature as by art. For the first time the monotony of the two mountain-ranges—Libyan and Arabian—assumes a new and varied character. They each withdraw from the river so as to encircle a wide green plain; the western rising into a bolder and more massive barrier, and shutting in the plain at its northern extremity as by a natural bulwark; the eastern, further retired, is a loftier and more varied chain, rising and falling in almost Grecian outline, though cast in the conical form which marks the hills of Nubia in the south, and which perhaps suggested the Pyramids. Within the circle of these two ranges, thus peculiarly its own, the green plain stretches on either side the river to an unusual extent; and on either side of the river—in this respect unlike Memphis, but like the great city of the further East on the Euphrates,—like the cities of northern Europe on their lesser streams—spread the city of Thebes, with the Nile for its mighty thoroughfare. "Art thou better than No 'Amon,' that was situated by the 'rivers of the Nile,' that had the waters round about, whose rampart was 'the sea-like stream,' and whose wall was 'the sea-like stream?'" *

The hundred-gated Thebes was a mighty city even in so remote an antiquity as the days when Abraham led his flocks to drink of the Nile's sweet waters. A thousand years had rolled over its monuments and palaces when the Greek warriors encamped before the walls of Troy. Its era of magnificence, however, really commenced with the eighteenth dynasty of the Pharaohs, when its sovereign, Aah-mes I., expelled the last of the

---

* Dean Stanley, "Sinai and Palestine," Introd., pp. xl., xli.

Shepherd kings from Lower Egypt, and brought Memphis and the Delta under his dominion. Each successive monarch afterwards contributed to the embellishment of the ancient capital, until both banks of the river glittered with palaces and temples whose like the world has never since beheld. The second founder of the kingdom was Amunophis I., who seems to have been apotheosized, and who carried his victorious arms both into Syria and Ethiopia. Then came the illustrious Thothmes II., who began the series of splendid edifices to which we have referred, and founded the immense pile of the Royal Palace. Thothmes II. is supposed to have converted Ethiopia into a principality of the empire, which was governed by a member of the royal family. To his sister, and, perhaps, colleague in the monarchy, Nemt-Amen, are ascribed the great obelisks of Karnak. Next came Thothmes III., who ruled from Mount Sinai on the east, to the Second Cataract on the south; who completed the Palace of the Kings, covered Thebes with obelisks and sphinxes, and enriched all the towns of the Thebaid with splendid buildings. As we have stated in our historical introduction, he won a great victory at Megiddo, subjugated Syria and Mesopotamia, and exacted tribute from Phœnicia, Babylon, Assyria, and the fair islands of the Archipelago. From an extant astronomical record it is believed that the year B.C. 1444 fell in the reign of this able and successful monarch,—the "Edward the First" of Egypt,—a great administrator, and a famous warrior.

His successor and son, Amunophis II., like all of his race, was a great builder. Amunophis III., whose name is found at Toumbos, near the Third Cataract, enlarged the frontiers of his kingdom to Soleb, and increased its resources. He embellished Thebes with two magnificent palaces—one on either bank of the Nile; and founded the splendid structures whose ruins encumber the plain at Luxor. He is designated in the sculptures "the Conqueror of the Mennahoun," and the "Pacificator of Egypt." So world-wide was his fame that the Greeks celebrated him as Memnon, son of Amun-Ra, and in his honour were erected the Memnonian colossi. After his death divine rites were paid to this extraordinary man.

Passing over Rameses I., the founder of a great dynasty, we come to Sethi or Seethee I. (Setei Menephthah), who built temples at Amada and Silsilis, and conquered five Asiatic nations. His tomb was discovered by Belzoni in the Bab-el-Melook. Under Rameses II. the empire continued to flourish, and its boundaries were maintained, if not enlarged. Rameses III. is the Sesostris of Herodotus: he raised Thebes to the climax of its prosperity and power, and by his genius, his successes, and his fame so impressed the imagination of the Egyptians that, in later times, they ascribed to him the great achievements of many other monarchs, and involved his genuine history in a cloud of legend and fable. Diodorus was informed that he could lead into the field 600,000 infantry, 27,000 chariots, and 24,000 cavalry. All that can be safely asserted is, that he carried his victorious arms further than any of his predecessors; that he was remarkable for his valour, ability, and majestic person; that he built the Rameseion, or "monument of Osymandyas," on the west bank of the Nile; that he ascended the throne when a minor, and reigned upwards of sixty years. In the annals of Egypt no hero fills a more conspicuous place.

And yet with this great conqueror terminated the glorious days of Thebes. That fate which, or soon or late, overtakes every empire, fell upon the Egyptian kingdom, and the Tanite and Bubastite sovereigns of Lower Egypt rose into power. Of these, one of the most eminent was *Sheshonk*, the *Shishak* of the Bible, who defeated Rehoboam, and plundered Jerusalem, bringing back to Thebes the golden shields that had shone upon the walls of Solomon's Temple (B.C. 972). Then came an Ethiopian dynasty, marking a period of foreign conquest, and the seat of government was transferred to Sais in the Delta.

The invasion of Cambyses was the first great calamity which Thebes experienced. He rifled its tombs, overthrew its temples, and destroyed the statues of its early rulers. Yet, as in all imperial cities there is a surprising vitality, we need not be surprised that Thebes once more regained, if not its political importance, at all events its wealth and splendour. It was at this time visited by Hecataeus of Abdera, who had served in the army of Alexander. He explored its antiquities, and wondered at its opulence. The Rameseion was still erect in all its stateliness, and the temples were computed to hold the immense sum of three hundred talents of gold, and two thousand three hundred talents of silver. He saw also the other three palace-temples of Thebes, now called by the names of the villages in which they stand—Luxor (Luqsor, or El-Uksor), Karnak, and Medinet-Aboo.

The Theban priests showed Hecataeus the large

wooden mummy cases of their predecessors, ranged in order round the walls of the temple, to the number of three hundred and forty-five; and when the Greek boasted that he was the sixteenth in descent from Jupiter, they silenced him with the remark, that those three hundred and forty-five priests had governed Thebes in succession from father to son, each a mortal and the son of a mortal, and that so many generations had passed since the gods Osiris and Horus had ruled over Egypt. We cannot now determine the amount of exaggeration in this statement; but it is certain that the antiquity of Greece, as compared with that of Egypt, was as the antiquity of Britain compared with that of Greece.

The Ptolemys scarcely contributed to the architectural grandeur of the hundred-gated city by introducing many of the modifications suggested by the Greek taste, for they did not harmonize with the severe magnificence of the Egyptian monuments. In the reign of Ptolemy Lathyrus, Thebes rebelled. Intrenched within their temples, its inhabitants defied for three years the armies of their sovereign. Famine, and overwhelming numbers, and superior military weapons, eventually compelled them to yield; and a terrible revenge descended upon their heads. Numbers were sold into slavery; and the glorious memorials of their glorious history—the stately monuments which so eloquently bore witness to the genius, industry, and opulence of their ancestors—were broken down by hammer and pickaxe, and shattered into piles of débris.*

---

* Sir Gardner Wilkinson, "Modern Egypt and Thebes," ii. p. 225, *et sqq.*; Kenrick, "Ancient Egypt," i. pp. 150, 151, *et sqq.*

Thebes, however, remained for some centuries the headquarters of the Egyptian priesthood, until the ancient worship disappeared before the progress of Christianity, and the proselytes displayed the ardour of their faith by destroying the idols and shrines spared by previous depredators. Then came the Saracenic invasion, and the heavy hand of the Arab consummated its ruin.

The site of ancient Thebes is now marked by four small villages—*Luxor* and *Karnak* on the eastern, and *Gurneh* and *Medinet-Aboo* on the western bank of the Nile. The latter is chiefly occupied by the remains of the great necropolis, "the tombs of the kings," the palaces, temples, and sphinx-avenues of the Egyptian capital; on the eastern bank seem to have been situated its edifices of a secular character, and here, too, the mass of the inhabitants appear to have dwelt. Our survey will begin with the western quarter, and at its northern angle.

About three-quarters of a mile from the river moulder the remains of a building which Champollion calls the *Menephtheion*, from the occurrence of the name of Setei-Menephthah among the inscriptions on its walls. It formed a palace-temple, to which access was gained by a *dromos* (or avenue) of 128 feet in length.

Next we arrive at the RAMESEION—the *Memnonium* of Strabo, and the "tomb of Osymandyas" of Diodorus.

If it were possible for the spirits of the dead to revisit the "glimpses of the moon," and haunt the scenes most dear to them during their earthly existence, surely the old Egyptian kings would nightly roam among those hoary ruins, and lament the vanished splendours of their creed and dynasty!

The Rameseion was both a palace and a temple—the residence of the sovereign and his gods. It was unworthy of neither, for never did even Egyptian architecture create a more splendid pile. What art "inconceivable to us" erected, violence inconceivable to us has overthrown; and the huge heaped-up blocks are a more powerful commentary on the nothingness of human ambition than the homilies of a thousand moralists.

It is finely situated on the lowest grade of the hills as they begin to ascend from the plain, and its various parts occupy a series of terraces, one rising above the other in a singularly impressive and majestic fashion. Its propylon, or outer gateway, is grandly massive. Sculptures embellish it, very quaint and vivid. It formed the entrance to the first court, whose walls are destroyed. Some picturesque Ramessid columns remain, however; and at their foot lie the fragments of the hugest statue that was ever fashioned by Egyptian sculptor! It was a fitting ornament for a city of giants; such an effigy as might have embellished a palace built and inhabited by Titans! Unhappily, it is broken from the middle; but when entire it must have weighed—what think you, reader?—about 887 tons, $5\frac{1}{2}$ cwts.; and have measured 22 feet 4 inches across the shoulders, and 14 feet 4 inches from the neck to the elbow. The toes are from 2 to 3 feet long. The whole mass is composed of Syene granite; and I offer it as a problem to engineers and contractors

THE RAMESEION OF THEBES, AND COLOSSAL STATUE OF RAMESES.

of the present day,—How were nearly 900 tons of granite conveyed some hundreds of miles from Syene to Thebes? It is equally difficult to imagine how, in a country not afflicted by earthquakes, so colossal a monument was overthrown.

The second court was divided into aisles or avenues, by rows of huge Ramessid and circular columns, covered with emblematical and historical carving. Three flights of steps led up from its sun-lit area into the northern corridor of Ramessid pillars. On each side of the central one stood a black granite statue of Rameses. The head of one of them, called "the young Memnon," is now preserved in the British Museum. This was a fit introduction to the splendours of the Grand Hall, which seemed like some stately forest petrified into stone, with the lotus, the papyrus, and other river-plants all suddenly frozen in the midst of their budding life. The lighting of this hall, which, according to Champollion, was used for public assemblies, is beautiful. The roof in the centre, says Miss Martineau,[*] was raised some feet above the lateral roofing, so that large oblong spaces were left for a sight of the blue sky; and when they admitted the slanting rays of the rising and setting sun upon this grove of pillars, and, through them, kindled up the pictured walls, the glory must have been great. This roofing rested upon forty-eight pillars; a roofing painted blue, and studded with golden stars, like the sky of night. Twelve central pillars were larger than the others. All the capitals were sculptured in imitation of the graceful bell-shaped flower of the papyrus; and the decorations, de

---

[*] Harriet Martineau, "Eastern Life," i. 294.

signed from the stalks and flowers of different plants, painted in blue and green, and often exquisitely beautiful.

The sculptures which cover the walls are all devoted to the glorification of Rameses. He is represented as paying his homage to the gods, and receiving from them various privileges. Amun the Supreme is here, with the other two who complete the highest triad; and the god of letters, Thoth, notes the dates of the royal victories on his palm-branch. Elsewhere we see him honoured with the priceless gifts of life and power; or he is intrusted with the sword and the sceptre, to smite his foes with the one and to rule his subjects with the other. The use he made of his gifts is also illustrated. We are shown his battles, his sieges, his triumphs, his numerous captives: nor are his twenty-three sons or his three daughters forgotten. An inscription on one of the architraves of the Great Hall describes the splendour and beauty of the edifice, and dedicates it to the king's father, the Supreme, who says, "It is my will that your structure shall be as stable as the sky." Alas! Time has painfully falsified the boast. And Isis adds, "I grant you long life to govern Egypt." *

The next chamber is supposed to have been the Library, or "Dispensary of the Mind," described by Strabo. An astronomical subject was blazoned on the ceiling; and an inscription, alluding to the value of the apartment, still speaks of the "books of Thoth." The Egyptian Mercury is here attended, as Champollion records, by a figure with one eye in his face labelled "Source of light;" and the goddess Saf, the "lady of letters," is in

---

* Champollion, " Lettres sur l'Egypte."

like manner attended by a figure with an ear labelled "Source of hearing;"—signifying, perhaps, that man arrives at knowledge through the ear and the eye.

Of nine chambers which lay in the rear of the Hall, only two remain—the Library, and another in which Rameses is sacrificing to various Theban divinities.

OPERATIONS OF A SIEGE.
(From the Monuments.)

The sculptures on the exterior walls breathe only of battle and strife—the pride, pomp, and circumstance of victorious war. Rameses is represented as standing aloft in his war-chariot, and drawing his huge bow. In the battle a lion rages hither and thither. The conqueror drives headlong over bound and prostrate captives, while his enemies fall around him in all the attitudes of despair and degradation. A phalanx of gallant spearmen bear down the hostile forces with irresistible vigour.

A curious scene describes an attack upon a rock-built fortress named "the strong town of Watsch." Under cover of the *testudo* or shield—a frame-work large enough to shelter several men—the Egyptian warriors, led by the king's sons, are engaged in mining, and planting scaling-ladders against the wall. The defenders, meanwhile, are hurling down darts, and stones, and spears; and yet, as if conscious of the fruitlessness of further resistance, are waving signals of surrender, and despatching their heralds to implore the conqueror's clemency.

Such was the Rameseion. It looked towards the east, facing the magnificent temple at Karnak. Its propylon, in the days of its glory, was in itself a structure of the highest architectural grandeur, and the portion still extant measures 234 feet in length. The principal edifice was about 600 feet in length and 200 feet in breadth, with upwards of 160 columns, each 30 feet in height. A wall of brick enclosed it; and a dromos, fully 1600 feet long, and composed of two hundred sphinxes, led in a north-westerly direction to a temple or fortress, sheltered among the Libyan hills.

Our attention will now be directed to the *Koum-el-Hattam* ("sandstone mountain") of the Arabs—the ruins of the AMUNOPHEION, or palace-temple of Amunophis III., the "Memnon" of the Greeks. About five hundred yards nearer the river are situated the two Colossi, or gigantic statues of the king—called *Tama* and *Chama* by the natives—which, sitting alone amidst the wide sea of verdure, keep vigilant though silent watch over the mysteries of the Past.* There they sit, says Miss Martineau, hands on knees, gazing straight forward, seeming, though so much of the faces is gone, to be looking over to the monumental piles on the other side of the river, which became gorgeous temples after these throne-seats were placed here—the most immovable thrones that have

THE COLOSSI, OR RAMESSIDS.

ever been established on this Earth. He who is popularly called "the Memnon," and is the more northerly of the two, has been greatly dilapidated; either by Cambyses, or, as Strabo reports and the prophet Ezekiel foretold,† by an earthquake. One would like to think, with

---

* English travellers have jocosely christened them, says Mr. A. C. Smith, "Lord Dundreary and his Cousin Sam."
† Ezek. xxx. 16—" No shall be rent asunder."

Miss Martineau,* that Nature, rather than Man, had done it: but how came the earthquake to leave the mass of the throne and body unhurt, while shattering the head and shoulders? It is improbable that the whole was overthrown and then re-erected, the twin-giant remaining uninjured.

These statues are composed of a coarse, hard breccia, mixed with pebbles of an agate character. The pedestals are sculptured with numerous figures and hieroglyphs.

The old tradition ran that from the northern Memnon, when the sun rose over the purple Arabian mountains, a strain of music issued:

> "Morn from Memnon drew
> Rivers of melody" (*Tennyson*)—

a sweet, melancholy cadence, like that of the Æolian wires—

> "Soft as Memnon's harp at morning,
> Touched with light by heavenly warning"—(*Keble*).

The Greeks fabled that this morning music was Memnon's welcome to his mother Aurora. How the sounds were produced has long been a matter of controversy: perhaps by the artifices of the priests, who in some hidden niche may have smitten the sounding stone with a rod of iron; or by the passage through its chinks and crannies of light gusts and breaths of air; or, not improbably, by the sudden expansion of aqueous particles, enclosed within the solid mass, under the influence of the sun's rays.†

* Miss Martineau, "Eastern Life," i. 305.
† Dr. Richardson, "Travels along the Mediterranean and Parts Adjacent," ii. 41.

During the annual inundation of the Nile these statues tower above the watery expanse like carved islands of stone. Anciently a *dromos* of eighteen similar statues extended to the Amunopheion; and the river waters not overflowing so high as they do now, the entire avenue, with its solemn giants, must have stood upon elevated ground conspicuous from afar. The present height of

THE COLOSSI DURING AN INUNDATION.

the Pair is 53 feet above the soil, and the pedestals are sunk about 7 feet deep in the sand. From the elbow to the fingers' ends each colossal arm measures 17 feet 9 inches; and from the knee to the plant of the foot each leg measures 19 feet 8 inches. The foot was 9 feet 10 inches long. The pedestal of Tama is 33 feet long by 18 feet broad; the throne, nearly 15 feet in height and breadth.

Continuing in a south-westerly direction, we reach the village of *Medinet-Aboo*, situated on a lofty mound composed of the ruins of the THOTHMESEION—now choked with weeds, and frequented by the loathsome scorpion. And here we ought to remind our readers that, as every Christian church must have its chancel, so every Egyptian temple had its gateway—a pylon, or propylon—formed of two sloping, pyramidical towers, with a high perpendicular façade between. In this manner the temple and palace of Medinet-Aboo were each approached by a pylon: they were also connected by a dromos of statues. The temple was built by successive monarchs of the name of Thothmes; but among the ruins are found inscriptions relating to Tirhakah, Nectanebus, Ptolemy Soter, and Antoninus Pius—each of whom, probably, did something for the decoration of this locality.

Connected with the Thothmeseion by a dromos 265 feet in length, stands the PALACE-TEMPLE OF RAMESES—the Southern Rameseion of Champollion—a structure of vast dimensions and surpassing splendour. It is upwards of 500 feet in length; while the cella (or nave) measures nearly 150 feet broad without the walls, which are literally crowded with designs. In one place you see the coronation of the Pharaoh—the "visible God upon earth" of old Egypt. He sits on a canopied throne, borne along by his twelve sons. A grand procession follows of princes, priests, official personages, and soldiers. A scribe is reading from a scroll; the high-priest perfumes the air with incense; a band of musicians performs triumphal music. The accompanying hieroglyphs explain that the king has assumed the crown of the Upper and Lower Kingdoms ; and carrier-pigeons fly to convey the news to the north, south, east, and west.

Some vigorous battle-pictures illustrate the power of the great monarch. His scribes count out before him

THE THOTHMESEION AT MEDINET-ABOO, THEBES.

numerous heaps of human heads, each heap containing three thousand. There are also piles of human tongues. In other places a naval engagement is represented between the Egyptians—whose galleys bear a lion's head at the prow—and some Asiatic people ; in others, towns are beleaguered by masses of struggling warriors ; in others, gorgeous processions celebrate some day of peculiar festivity; and in all, the deities are introduced, approving and befriending the favoured race.*

The Temple of Medinet-Aboo may be described as facing that of Luxor, on the opposite bank of the river; while that of the Rameseion confronted the superb pile of Karnak. Hence all these magnificent structures formed so many stages or halting-places in the religious processions of the priests. Though the tabernacle of Amun was generally enshrined at Karnak,† yet every year it was carried across the river to remain for a few days in Libya; and we can fancy what pomp and splendour of ceremonial accompanied this solemn translation—how the hills and the plains resounded with harp and cymbal and song—and how the interminable train of priests and worshippers moved through the vast avenues of crio-sphinxes and colossal statues in a passion of enthusiasm! ‡

In the rear of the undulating area occupied by these various monuments of a vanished creed and empire—that is, from Gurneh to Medinet-Aboo—the Libyan hills for nearly five miles have been converted into a labyrinth of sepulchres,—into one immense and thickly-populated Necropolis. Here, in the lower ground, are interred the humble dead, along with the animals which they accounted sacred; the papyrus-roll, containing ritualistic

---

* Heeren, "Historical Researches," ii. 247, *et sqq.*

† The triad, or three supreme gods, of Thebes were—Amun-Ra, or the Sun god; Mant, the mother of all things—the Latona of the Greeks; and Khonso.

‡ Dr. Richardson, "Travels along the Mediterranean," ii. 94, 96.

BAB-EL-MELOOK, OR VALLEY OF THE TOMBS OF THE KINGS, THEBES.

directions for the soul's guidance; and corn, bread, fruit, bows and arrows, personal ornaments, boots, and the like;—so that the dead, when they awoke from their long sleep at the bidding of Osiris, might gaze upon familiar and favourite objects. Higher up, in the sacred solitude of the mountains, lay the noble and the wealthy, in richly-decorated tombs; their mummies carefully

"Packed to humanity's significance"—

their surroundings of the most gorgeous description. And still higher up, in two deep narrow gorges which strike into the very heart of the hills—one entirely shut in among them, the other opening up from the lower plain—are respectively situated the Tombs of the Kings and the Tombs of the Priests.

Ascending the first of these two gorges, we find it to be the very ideal of desolation—bare rocks, before and behind and on either side, overhanging and enclosing you; rocks utterly bare, and without a strip of vegetation to relieve their dreariness. Such is the last resting-place of the Theban kings, and it is impossible to imagine a scene of more extraordinary wildness.

Entering the sculptured portal in the face of the wild dark precipice, you find yourself in a long lofty corridor, which opens or narrows, as the case may be, into successive halls and chambers, all covered with a hard white stucco, and this stucco with colours as vivid now as they were thousands of years ago. Forty-seven were known to the ancients in the time of Diodorus; twenty-one of these have been discovered by modern explorers, but only three are complete and perfect as when they received their royal occupants—namely, those of Amunophis III., Rameses Meiamun and Rameses III. Some are much more magnificent than others; seven being, in truth, most gorgeous palaces, hewn out of the solid rock, and embellished with the richest decorations. Here "all the kings lie in glory, every one in his own house," the Pharaohs of Thebes, from the eighteenth to the twenty-first dynasty.

It is needful the reader should bear in mind the peculiar tenets of the Egyptians, to understand the motive which induced the construction of these remarkable sepulchres. Death, to the Egyptian, was the portal of life; of the Future in which he would receive such recompense or punishment as the divinities saw fit to award. To the Egyptian king, who was regarded as of a semi-divine nature, it was a long, long sleep; and when Osiris awakened him from it, his soul regained its body—its original tabernacle—and entered upon a career of unclouded happiness in the companionship of his immortal ancestors. Hence it was requisite that the body should be preserved uncorrupted, and the tomb wherein it was enshrined carefully concealed from profane eyes or disturbing touch.

Every Egyptian king began his reign by making ready his sepulchre, which was more or less magnificent according to the length of his reign, and which was immediately closed up at his death. Closed up, as the Egyptians fondly supposed, until the end of the world. Not only was the entrance sealed, but, in several cases, the approaches were cut in the most devious direction, and so walled up as to give the appearance of a termination long before you arrived at the actual burial-chamber.

In the sculptures and decorative designs of the tombs we seem to recognize, as Dean Stanley points out,* two leading ideas: First, the attempt to reproduce, as far as possible, all the details of human life, so that the dead monarch, whether in his prolonged sleep or on his awakening, might see around him the old familiar objects. Second, to conduct the king to the world of Death. And the further you advance into the great tomb, the deeper you become involved in continuous processions of jackal-headed gods and monstrous forms of good and evil genii; and the goddess of Justice, with her single ostrich feather; and barges carrying mummies across the sacred lake; and, more than all, incessant convolutions of serpents in every possible form and attitude—human-legged, human-headed, crowned—entwining mummies—enwreathing or embraced by processions—extending down whole galleries, so that meeting the head of a serpent at the top of a staircase, you must descend to its very end to reach his tail. And at length you reach the close of all, the *ne plus ultra*, the vaulted chamber in whose centre lies the immense granite sarcophagus which once contained the body of the king. Here the processions—above, below, and around—attain their climax, their culminating point; meandering on every side and in all directions—in white and black, and red and blue—legs and arms and wings spreading over roof and walls in enormous and fantastic forms.

All these tombs, then, are interesting, all afford matter

---

* Dean Stanley, "Sinai and Palestine," xliii., xliv.

for meditation; but our limits compel us to restrict most of our observations to one of them; and we shall select that which Belzoni explored with so much tact and energy, and whose occupant is supposed to have been Osirei, Seethee, or Sethos I., the father of Rameses the Great.

The explorer, after descending a flight of ruined steps to a perpendicular depth of 25 feet, finds himself in a passage whose walls are covered with inscriptions relative to Osirei. Next comes another staircase, decorated with grotesque figures of genii, and leading into a second passage or chamber, of large dimensions, very beautifully painted. Here we observe the emblems—a boat and a serpent—of Kneph, "the Spirit of the Supreme, which moves upon the face of the waters;" and of Ptah, the patron or tutelary deity of the occupant of the tomb. Ten steps conduct us into another superb chamber, from whence you pass into the so-called "Hall of Beauty," a cell or apartment 24 feet by 13, richly embellished with sculptures and paintings—a species of Egyptian Pantheon, where all the gods and goddesses are met in solemn conclave. The roof, which four square columns support, blazes with golden stars, and the walls are covered with processions of a curious character;—an immeasurable serpent being carried on the shoulders of a train of personages in one place; and in another, four different groups appearing, each consisting of four persons of different complexions: four red, namely, Egyptians; four primrose-coloured, Asiatics; four black, Nabasi or Africans; and four pale-yellow, with long flowing robes, and feathers in their hair, Europeans or Northmen.

Proceeding further, the traveller enters Belzoni's "Hall of Pillars," 28 feet long by 27 feet broad, containing six huge pillars in two rows. On either side opens out a small chamber; one on the right, having the figure of a cow painted on the wall, is known as the "Hall of Isis" (10 feet by 9); that on the left, from its allegorical drawings, is named the "Hall of Mysteries" (10 feet 5 inches by 8 feet 9 inches). At the end of the hall we pass into a large saloon with an arched roof or ceiling, and measuring 32 feet long by 27 feet broad. Various passages and chambers lead out of it, which it is unnecessary to describe; but we may add, that the entire extent of this subterranean labyrinth penetrates the solid rock to a length of 320 feet.*

Returning to the saloon, we may remember that it was here Belzoni discovered the sarcophagus of Osirei,† now one of the curiosities of Sir John Soane's museum. He describes it as made of the finest Oriental alabaster, 9 feet 5 inches long, and 3 feet 7 inches wide. Its thickness is only 2 inches, and a light placed in the interior lights it up like a transparency. Within and without, it is sculptured over with hundreds of figures, from one to two inches in height, representing the funeral procession, and religious ceremonies in honour of the deceased.

Such are the places, says Miss Martineau, where, in the words of Isaiah, "the kings of the nations, even all of them, lie in glory, every one in his own house;" and such are the regions supposed by him to be moved at the

---

* Belzoni, "Narrative of Operations," &c., i. 360-366.

† The mummy, however, had been already stolen; that is, if ever deposited in the sarcophagus.

approach of the tyrant, and to stir up their dead to meet him who has become as weak as they, and must now be brother of the worm, and be brought down to Hades, to the sides of the pit. From Egypt this mode of burial spread far over the East, and the caverns of the hills contained the successive generations of many peoples besides the Hebrews, who had, in their civilization, followed the ideas and methods of Egypt. In God's mysterious providence, not only the *forms* spread, but the *ideas* which had suggested them. After the example of Egypt, men preserved, amidst more or less corruption, a belief in the Supreme God; in a divine moral government; in a future life; in compensation and retribution; and in that highest of all truths, that moral good is the greatest good, and moral evil the deepest evil. So from the Valley of the Nile this mysterious faith spread into many lands, disguised, but never wholly concealed; working good in its generation—assuredly more good than evil—until, becoming incrusted with later superstitions, and its true meaning passing out of the memories of men, it was time that a purer and fuller revelation should be made, and the Star of Love appeared to the watchers in the East!

Before we quit this solemn spot, we must glance at the *Harpers' Tomb*, first mentioned by Bruce, and therefore often called by his name. It penetrates about 400 feet into the rock, and its small lateral chambers are decorated with glowing pictures of life in Ancient Egypt. Here, cooks knead bread or slaughter cattle; there, gardeners toil in blooming parterres: here, walls are gay with arms and standards; there, clothed in rich tapestry, and illuminated with graceful lamps. The tomb obtains its dis-

ILLUSTRATIONS OF EGYPTIAN LIFE. 257

tinctive appellation from the figures of ten harpers, playing before the god Ao, or Hercules. They are attired in white garments striped with red, and each carries a harp of ten strings.*

· The tombs of the Theban Pharaoh who reigned, it is supposed, in right of his wife Taosiri, and of the Pharaoh who pursued the migrating Hebrews to the Red Sea, have their peculiar features of interest. In the former, the king appears both as man and spirit, in his past and present conditions of being; the scarabaeus, or sacred beetle, with head downwards, representing the resurrection by which the two are linked together. In the latter, the wide extent of the monarch's dominions is indicated by five lines of tribute-bearers—black, red, light and red, brown, and yellow—offering gifts of ivory, apes, leopards, skins, gold, and other valuables. Some of its illustrations are important

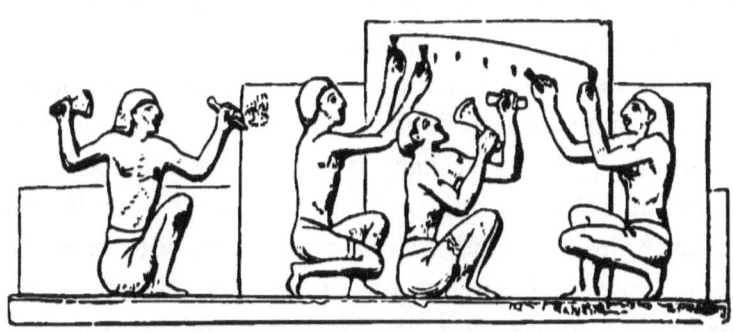

EGYPTIAN MASONS.

from the light they throw on the handicraft and industry of the Egyptians. You may see the masons, for instance, at work upon a monstrous sphinx, and chipping away at the huge granite blocks from which it is to be fashioned.

* Sir G. Wilkinson, "Modern Egypt and Thebes," ii. 201–210

The *Tombs of the Priests* are situated in the rocky gorge known as the Valley of Assasif; and the largest is that of Petumenap, chief priest in the reign of Pharaoh Necho. Its winding galleries are covered with hieroglyphics; but the only figures which it contains are those of the priest and his wife, sitting side by side, with arms entwined around each other's necks.

About three-quarters of a mile north-west of Medinet-Aboo are the *Tombs of the Egyptian Queens*, twenty-four of which have been discovered. Each bears the title of "Wife of Amun," as if the king had borne along with his own name that of the great god of Thebes, or been apotheosized after death. The most perfect sepulchre is that of Taia, wife of Amunophis III.

We now cross the Nile to what has been rightly called the "most magnificent spot in Egypt"—the eastern quarter of Thebes—Thebes proper—now partly occupied by the little Arab village of KARNAK.

When the French army, led by Napoleon Bonaparte, came in sight of the Theban monuments, they suddenly halted, and, in an ecstasy of admiration, clapped their hands and broke out into a loud shout; as if, says Denon,* the end and object of their glorious toils, and the complete possession of Egypt, were achieved and finally secured by their having gained possession of its ancient metropolis. Here, in the silence and the solitude, lie the shattered memorials of an extinct civilization;

---

* Dominique Vivant, Baron Denon, born 1747; died 1825. He accompanied the French expedition to Egypt in the capacity of a *savant;* and in 1802 published a full account of his experiences and discoveries in his "Voyage dans la Basse et la Haute Egypte."

memorials so grandly impressive, so sublimely beautiful, that, like Napoleon's soldiers, we are stirred by the spectacle as by the sound of a trumpet. Here, when the rest

RUINS AT KARNAK.

of the world, perhaps, was buried in darkness, the human intellect had ripened into an extraordinary maturity. Here, where the beetle crawls over the sunny rocks, or in the twilight the bat flits among the ruined columns, the oldest of the world's monarchies placed its royal seat, and surrounded itself with an architectural pomp that is almost inconceivable. Here, too, a mysterious creed —a creed of dark enigmas and subtle symbolism, with a strange weird medley of the sublime and the grotesque —erected such temples as no other creed has ever dreamed of possessing! It is a phantasmagoria, this Karnak; or, rather, it is like a series of visions succeeding one another so closely that their various features become blended to the mind.

Avenues of vast *propyla*, or gateways, whose huge sculptures were painted in glowing colours, concentrated from all points of the compass upon Karnak, while a dromos of andro-sphinxes connected it with the quarter of the city now represented by Luxor. These are mostly in ruins.

The principal structure at Karnak is the *Palace of the Kings*, which was approached by a remarkable avenue of crio-sphinxes, about seventy in number, each having a ram's head and a lion's body, and distant from the other eleven feet. The Palace itself has twelve principal entrances, each composed of several huge propyla and spacious courts. The gateway figured in the text consists wholly of granite, and is literally covered with exquisite hieroglyphics. On both sides of these propyla were formerly planted colossal statues of granite and basalt, from 20 to 30 feet in height, either sitting or standing erect.

In examining the famous Palace, we enter first a spacious court, where two obelisks of Thothmes I. attract the attention; one is in fragments, the other upright and

PROPYLON AT KARNAK.

uninjured. In the second, or Great Court, 275 feet broad by 329 feet long, were also two obelisks: the one remaining is 94 feet in height. Then we pass into the superb "Hall of Columns," which is 80 feet in height, and 329 feet long by 179 feet broad. Its roof is supported by 134 pillars,—12 in the centre, and 122 in the aisles; the central each 66 feet in height, without their pedestals, and 11 feet in diameter, with an intervening space of about 27 feet. The side columns are disposed in seven rows; they are 41 feet high, and 27 feet 6 inches in circumference.

The sanctuary, or adytum, built entirely of red granite,

GREAT COURT AND OBELISK OF KARNAK.

consists of three apartments, of which the central, 20 feet long, 16 feet wide, and 13 feet high, is the principal. Three blocks of granite form the roof, which once shone with clustered golden stars in a sky of azure. In various parts of the Palace the most precious materials were employed for decoration, and cornices have been found inlaid with ivory mouldings or sheathed with beaten gold!

Dean Stanley has justly spoken of Karnak as the grandest building which the world ever raised to the glory and adoration of God, and he styles it the oldest consecrated place of worship in the world. But the reader must remember that it was also dedicated to secular purposes: it was not a temple only, but a palace; and not only a palace, but a *Champ de Mars*, where reviews took place, and ambassadors were publicly received, captives executed or apportioned among their conquerors, and the spoils and honours of victory distributed. Religious festivals were also held there, in which king and priests and people alike participated.

One of the most interesting features of Karnak is the sculptured record, in a narrow corridor, of the conquest of Sheshonk—the *Shishak* of Scripture—first noticed by Champollion. It occurs, says Mr. Fairholt,* in the third line of a row of sixty-three prisoners presented by the agency of the god Amun-Ra to Sheshonk; who thus, as usual with the Egyptian kings, attributes his victories to Divine interposition. Each figure, or rather semi-figure, has his arms tied behind him, a rope round his neck, and is placed upon a turreted oval indicative of a walled city, within which the name is inscribed. In this instance it is *Judah Melek*—the " King of Judah," the Rehoboam of Scripture, who was defeated by Sheshonk: this, we may add, is the only *direct* illustration of Biblical history afforded by the monuments of Egypt, though *indirect* illustrations abound.

In addition to the magnificent group of halls, courts, columns, and gigantic statues at which we have thus cursorily glanced, various propyla and portions of temples are to be seen south of the Great Hall. On either side the pyla of one of the courts lie the remains of four enormous Ramessid statues hewn out of limestone or granite. They all wear sculptured belts, most richly and beauti-

* Fairholt, "Up the Nile," p. 324.

fully wrought. One is armed with the sacred breastplate. Mr. Aveling, a recent traveller, measured the latter figure, and found it to be 6 feet across the chest; the middle figure was 10 feet broad, with arms 8 feet long.

A row of ninety crio-sphinxes, or more, leads southward from the temple to which these colossal statues belong—running parallel to the one which follows the direct road to Luxor, and connected with it by a narrow avenue crossing at right angles. One sphinx, in a group found here, has a woman's head, with features beautifully expressive both of power and gentleness, and wearing that aspect of profound repose with which the old artists loved to represent their deities and kings.*

Further details of the wonders of Karnak—of its obelisks and statues, and pyla and propyla, all involved in mournful ruin, but all attesting the intellectual supremacy of the men who designed them so far back in the world's dim history—would perplex rather than interest the reader. He will already have pictured to himself this scene of splendid desolation, and formed some idea of the majesty of Egyptian achievement. Across the plain —following the grand dromos of andro-sphinxes, 40 feet wide, once traversed by the sumptuous processions of priests, and kings, and worshippers—the solemn avenue, once alive with toiling thousands, and brilliant with the works of a subtle art and an exhaustless industry—we move onward, in thoughtful silence, to EL-UKSOR,† or

---

* Rev. T. W. Aveling, "Voices of Many Waters."

† The distinguished traveller, Mr. W. G. Palgrave, has the following remarks on these interesting localities:—"Luxor, Karnak, Kornah, Rameseum, Medinet-Abou, and the intervening ruins, all belong to one and the same huge city,

RIVER-VIEW OF LUXOR.

Luxor, where the mud hovels and paltry buildings of an Arab village strangely jar with the remains of its ancient grandeur.

Here a vast and splendid temple stands on the rising ground, commanding a fine view of the Nile and the Theban plain. In approaching it from the north—the most convenient route—the first notable object is a superb propylon, 200 feet long, with its summit 57 feet above the present level of the soil. Two of the finest obelisks in the world formerly guarded, as it were, the portal of this noble pile; but one has been removed to the Place de la Concorde at Paris; the other lies deeply

the Thebes of Egypt. Within historical memory the site was yet one, not divided as now; for the Nile, instead of flowing west of Luxor and Karnak, thus separating one half of ancient Thebes from the other, followed a much more easterly course under the mountains by the Red Sea side, leaving the Libyan plain wide and unbroken. Indeed, it is said to have adopted its present direction only two centuries since. Now ploughing up the mid-level, and wandering as at random among the ruins, it undermines some, tilts up others, and will probably sweep not a few clean away—Luxor, for example. A few thousand years more and Herodotus and the Ghizeh Pyramids will probably alone remain to vindicate for Rameses and his brethren the eternity they sought to secure by so much labour and costly forethought.

"The situation of Thebes, as the river formerly ran, was admirably adapted for a capital of that time; a noble plain, nowhere wider or richer in Upper Egypt, constantly refreshed by the free play of the winds from north, east, and west, closing in southwards only; while direct land communications lead on one side to Koseyr, that ancient arbour and deposit of Arab commerce; and on the other to the great oasis of the 'Wah,' once of Jupiter Ammon, and thence right to Central Africa: north and south passes the great liquid and ever open road of the Nile. We should remember that in the days, those ancient days, when Thebes flourished, the staple trade of Egypt lay all with Africa and Arabia; at a much later date, Greek influence and the growing importance of the Mediterranean coast brought down the capital towards the Delta, and ultimately fixed it at Alexandria, on the northern shore. But Greece only entered Egypt to degenerate, and to help Egypt to degenerate in turn; the best days of the Nile Valley were certainly the earliest."—*From "A Visit to Upper Egypt," by William Gifford Palgrave (Macmillan's Magazine, January 1867).*

embedded in the sand, a monolith of red granite, between seven and eight feet square at the base, and upwards of 80 feet in height. The hieroglyphics which embellish it are cut with unusual distinctness to a depth of nearly two inches. In the rear of the obelisks, and immediately in front of the propylon, stand two colossal statues, or Ramessids, also of red granite. Though buried in the ground to the chest, they still measure about 22 feet from thence to the top of their mitres.*

The eastern wing of the northern façade of the propylon is enriched with an animated sculpture of a crowded battle scene. So truthful is it, and so minutely accurate, that as one sees the shock of contending squadrons, and the rush of the furious chariots, one almost hears the clash of swords, the twang of whirring arrows, and the shouts of maddened foemen. The king rises above the mêlée in a car drawn by two horses; behind him waves the royal standard. Here, the empty chariots are swept by the uncontrolled steeds down a precipitous descent, and headlong into a rolling river; there, the charioteers are rushing towards the walls of the town, flying from the arrows of the victorious Egyptians. Others are crowding through the open gates, amid the shrieks and lamentations of the despairing citizens, who have thronged to the battlements to witness the defeat of their fellow-countrymen. Everywhere the scene is instinct with life, energy, and movement. The battle rages before your eyes with all its alternations of hope and despair, the swift charge, the confused retreat. It is a kind of Homeric picture embodied in vivid colour-

* Wilkinson, "Modern Egypt and Thebes," vol. ii., *in locis*.

THE RAMESSIDS AT LUXOR.

ing. And, to close the drama, you see in another compartment the conqueror enthroned, with a sceptre in his left hand, and before him a sad array of captives about to perish under the headsman's sword; while the vanquished monarch, with his arms bound behind him to a car, also approaches to receive his doom.

Passing through this noble portal, we enter a ruined portico of very large dimensions; from which a double row of seven columns, with lotus-wreathed capitals, conducts us to a court 160 feet long by 140 feet wide, terminated on either hand by a similar range of pillars. Beyond lies another court of thirty-two columns; and then comes the *adytum*, or inner sanctuary of the temple. Some antiquaries have been of opinion that here, and not at Karnak, should we look for the "palace of Osymandyas" described by Diodorus; and it is also a point of dispute whether the true Diospolis is Karnak or Luxor.

Before we quit the site of the once-famous city, we think it desirable to add a few words respecting the Theban territory, or the THEBAID, the modern *Sais* or *Pathros*, and one of the three principal divisions of Egypt. On the east it was bounded by the Arabian, on the west by the Libyan hills and desert; north, it extended to Hermopolis Magna, south to Syene (or Assouan). Its vegetation is of a tropical character; the sycamore giving place to the date-palm and the Theban-palm, and the lotus spreading its blue and white cups on the waters. Anciently, it was divided into ten nomes, and ten halls in the Labyrinth were therefore appropriated to their princes.

For the most part the Thebaid, as Mr. Donne remarks, was, and is, a narrow valley, intersected by the river and bounded by a double row of hills; hills, bold, lofty, and precipitous on the Arabian side; on the Libyan, of lower elevation, and intersected by sandy plains and valleys. The desert on either bank produces only a dwarf vegetation of shrubs and herbs, which emit a slight aromatic odour. The cultivable soil is restricted to a narrow belt on each side of the river, whose glowing verdure contrasts agreeably and strikingly with the brown dry hue of the surrounding wilderness. The breadth of the Nile Valley never exceeds eleven, and is frequently reduced to two miles.

Of the present appearance of the Thebaid, however, a recent traveller speaks in more eulogistic terms.* He says that no pleasanter ideal can be imagined of "a summer land." The purple Desert mountains here narrow in the valley, and enclose a landscape of tropical character and extraordinary fertility. Even to the edge of the sandy waste all is growth. You wander through fields of maize and millet, and between bright flanking patches of yellow-blossoming cotton, amid thickets of ricin and meadows of flowering poppy. The heart rejoices in the clustering palm-groves, which whisper of peace and plenty; and from the midst of their lustrous bloom the eye may range over acres of sunny cornfields, whose rich wealth of produce waves in the very neighbourhood of the eternal barrenness. How glorious must have been the landscape when, in the old time, amidst all this bloom of fertility, rose the marble palaces, the " shapely obelisks," and the gigantic statues, in serenely-perfect beauty!

* Howard Hopley, "Under Egyptian Palms," pp. 221, 222.

Book Third.

CHAPTER I.

ESNEH—THE ALMEHS, OR DANCING GIRLS—'EILYTHIA: THE ROCK TOMBS—EDFOO, AND ITS TEMPLE—SILSILEH, AND ITS QUARRIES—KOUM OMBOS.

> Et viridem Aegyptum nigra faecundat arena,
> Et diversa ruens septem discurrit in ora.
> VIRGIL, *Georgics*, iv. 200.

> And where the stream . . .
> Broods o'er green Egypt with dark wave of mud,
> And pours through many a mouth its branching flood.
> SOTHEBY.

BIDDING farewell to Thebes and its Monuments, we resume our voyage up the Nile. The first point of interest above Thebes is *Erment*, the Hermonthis of the Greeks, about six miles from Medinet-Aboo. Here the traveller may profitably devote a few hours to an examination of the ruins of a temple founded by Cleopatra, and to the smaller temple, or "lying-in chamber" of the goddess Leto. Of the former the shattered remains indicate a comparatively debased style of architecture, but no opinion can be formed of its general plan and character. The latter is also in a dilapidated condition; all the columns but one of the outer court have disappeared; only a few are extant of those of the hall; the ancient shrines, consisting of two small chambers, support with their massive walls the residence of the sheikh of the village, while the entire ruin is encumbered by the mud huts of the villagers and a plain mosque.* Near at hand are the remains of a Christian church, belonging to the period of the Lower Empire; and measuring, according to Wilkinson, 190 feet in length by 85 feet in width.

Gebel-Ain, supposed to be the site of the ancient Crocodilopolis, is the next striking object on which the eye of the traveller rests. It starts up from the level plain with a curious resemblance to the Gibraltar Rock. Just beyond, a large island of sand is described as a favourite haunt of crocodiles, which bask here in the hot sun, attended by their little feathered monitor, the *Ziczac,* or *Charadarius spinosus* (Spur-winged plover). This, the *trochilus* or "crocodile bird" of Herodotus, is said to live upon the leeches which adhere to the crocodile's throat, and to give his friend due notice of any hostile intruder.

Mr. Fairholt, whom we have already quoted, states that he has certainly seen the plover busied about sleeping crocodiles, and clamouring at any boat's approach, in a sufficiently loud manner to waken them, and teach them that their only safety was in flight. The real solution of the story, he adds, seems to be very simple. The bird is attracted to the crocodile by the flies and insects

* Fairholt, "Up the Nile," p. 231.

THE TROCHILUS, OR CROCODILE BIRD.

which settle about it; and its own alarm at the presence of man induces the cries which are imagined to be entirely for the benefit of its supposed friend.

We now arrive at *Esneh*, or Isna, on the west bank, in lat. 25° 30′, where our attention is called to the noble ruins of the temple once sacred to the ram-headed deity, " Noum" or " Kneph," who presided over the work of creation. With the exception of the twenty-four columns and roof of its portico, or pronaos, the temple is buried deep in sand and earth. But these columns are well worth studying for the beauty and significance of their sculpture,* which belongs to a late period of Græco-Egyptian or Aegypto-Roman art (A.D. 41–70)—the names of Tiberius, Germanicus, and Vespasian occurring in the dedicatory inscription over the entrance, and those of Trajan, Hadrian, and Antoninus in the interior. The figure of Ptolemy Euergetes is found on the wall, followed by a tame lion, and in the act of striking down an antagonist. It would seem that the present temple was raised on the site of an older sanctuary.

Esneh was the ancient *Latopolis*, or *Lato*, and derived its name from the fish *Lato*, the largest of the Nilotic species, which always appears among the symbols of the goddess Neith (or Pallas).† Its present population exceeds 4000. It is the head-quarters of the *Almehs*,‡ or dancing-girls, who inhabit various squalid huts upon the shore, to which the voyager's curiosity almost invariably attracts him. If he resolves, as we shall do, on paying them a visit, his dragoman acts as guide and interpreter, and introduces him into the interior of some particular hovel, which he has selected as a suitable theatre for the performances. Here, in the middle of the apartment, he finds the dancers assembled; usually young and well-made women, but without any pretensions to personal beauty. They wear a scanty vest, open at the bosom; large silken pantaloons fastened round the waist by an embroidered girdle; and an inner tunic of flesh-coloured gauze or *tulle*. The feet of some are naked; of others,

---

* Denon, "Voyage en Egypte," vol. i., p. 148.
† The triad of Isneh was composed of Neith, Kneph, and Hak their son.
‡ They were banished hither from Cairo in 1834 by the late Mehemet Ali.

thrust into long loose slippers, red or yellow; collars sparkle round their necks, bracelets round their wrists, and a band of medals on their foreheads, while their long hair is frequently adorned with golden coins, and bound up with a silken kerchief.

The dance commences with a series of graceful attitudes, and these are succeeded by a variety of animated gestures and rapid movements, swiftly culminating in the eloquent expression of unbridled passion; the dancer, meanwhile, preserving the bust immovable, while the remainder of her body is agitated almost to frenzy.

After the performance olives and liqueurs are served around, and the spectators prove their satisfaction by a liberal distribution of largess.

A recent French traveller* has observed that these days of profit are not, however, very numerous, and that if the Almehs dance in the winter, they have no motive to sing in the summer. The population among whom they dwell cannot afford to pay them for the exercise of their talents; while they themselves, skilful enough in attitude, gesture, and motion, are wholly unfitted for work, and hence fall into the power of usurious money-lenders.

They pass their time in smoking tobacco, and in drinking *aqua vitae* (a kind of anise-seed), and the everlasting coffee.

Owing to the difficulties of this wretchedly precarious existence, the number is daily decreasing of these Almehs, who, in the days of the Mamelukes, abounded throughout the length and breadth of Egypt. Esneh is now

* Cuminus, "Voyage en Egypte," in *Tour du Monde*, 1863, p. 211.

their last asylum, as, undoubtedly, it was their cradle. The sisters of the bayadères of India, and of the colleges of priestesses consecrated to the service of Mylitta or of Venus, they anciently performed their fantastic dances before the shrine of Neith, the patron goddess of Esneh, the primarchial and prolific divinity, mother, wife, and sister of Amun. There may still be seen, in the centre of the town, at the base of an ascent which is lined with mummies, the beautiful *pronaos* of the Temple of Neith, transformed into a granary. Elevated by the Romans on a foundation of venerable ruins, the different portions of the edifice are covered with ill-wrought sculptures; but the portico is a noble construction, and the columns are tall and shapely, with richly wrought capitals of plants and flowers.

In this neighbourhood the reader will be disposed, perhaps, to obtain a glimpse of the social life of Egypt, and to officiate at an Egyptian marriage in the capacity of spectator. It cannot be said that the ceremonies attending it, at least among the *fellahs*, are of a very complicated description. It is not, as with us, a public act, sanctioned by the church and attested by the law. When the intending bridegroom and the parents of the intended bride have agreed upon the sum which the former is to pay—for the bride brings no dowry—they proceed to celebrate the nuptials before two witnesses. Sometimes notice is given to the cadi, but this formality is by no means indispensable. In such a union, with no ulterior guarantee, there is little happiness or safety for the wife: she is no more, in truth, than a bought slave; nor can she claim a divorce except under very extreme circumstances. The birth of the children is never registered; and consequently, during their earlier years, their condition is sadly precarious. Often, indeed, they fall victims to the envy or vengeance of one of their mother's rivals.

But let us suppose ourselves invited to the marriage of a fellah. A great tent is erected, according to custom, before the house of the betrothed, and for the last two days it has been the rendezvous of her and her future husband's friends, who have passed the time in smoking, and feasting, singing, laughing, gesticulating, and talking. At length the hour of prayer having arrived, the bridegroom repairs to the neighbouring mosque, attended by all the kinsmen and acquaintances who have been honoured with an invitation: on his return a banquet is served. To us, as Europeans, every dish is in turn presented; but anxious though we may be to do honour to our host, an ill-cultivated taste compels us to reject them, and to content ourselves with a few thin wheaten cakes. All the female friends of the bride have had a share in the preparation of this *cuisine*, and it is allowable to conclude that their joy has had an effect upon the sauces. We can hear them laughing and singing within the house.

In the evening the guests march through the town in procession, their ranks swelled *en route* by all the idle of the population, and men with flaring torches stalking by their side. It is a complete illumination; almost everybody seems to carry torch or taper; and a rich neighbour has lent one of those magnificent Oriental lustres, which are perfect trees of iron, embellished with glass tubes reflecting and glowing in the flames. And strange is the scene to European eyes as the light plays over and upon the noisy surging crowd, communicating a dazzling freshness to the vivid colours of their hoods, and vests, and girdles. Meanwhile the bridegroom, unattended, has entered the house where his betrothed with her kith and kin await him: after a brief interval he comes forth, accompanied by the women (who certify the perfect purity of the young girl), and proudly plants himself against the wall. Then, amid loud shouts, and discharges of musketry, the guests defile before him, everybody congratulating him, and placing in his hand a few pieces of money. This agreeable part of the ceremony being concluded, the husband re-enters the house, and again sallies forth bearing his young bride in his arms. Followed by his friends he seeks his own dwelling, and after some further ceremonies the bridal festivity terminates.

At 'Eilythia,* or El-Kab, about twenty miles beyond Esneh, on the eastern bank, we meet with a curious group of rock-tombs of the third period; that is, immediately after the expulsion of the Shepherds. Their decorations furnish some valuable glimpses into that inner life of Old Egypt of which we have already spoken. We see the people at work in the fields, and busy on the river, and merry in their houses.† This is no vision rising from the depths of a conscious imagination. We have it all before us in vivid colours painted on the rock. Under our very eyes, as it were, the ploughman is furrowing the fertile

---

* The *Eiliethyias*, or "City of Lucina," of the ancients.
† Miss Martineau, "Eastern Life: Present and Past."

soil; and the sower, scattering the seed, follows in his footsteps; and then come the labouring oxen which bury the grain by trampling it in; so that afterwards the husbandman has only to await quietly the time of harvest. The driver of the oxen treading out the wheat is singing; and here is his song, written up beside his picture :*—

> "Thresh for yourselves, O oxen!
> Thresh for yourselves.
> Thresh for yourselves, O oxen!
> Thresh for yourselves.
> Measures for yourselves!
> Measures for your masters.
> Measures for yourselves!
> Measures for your masters."

We can imagine this to be the lay which the Egyptian drivers chanted long ago, when Moses was a child. The scribes, meanwhile, are measuring the wheat as it is deposited in the granary; and the owner of the estate is surveying his live stock, his cattle, and his pigs, like a midland county squire. Yonder is a wine-press at work, crushing out the purple grapes which ripened in sunny vineyards far away among the distant hills. And now a boat passes by, with bright-coloured sail and steady oars; while, after his water-excursion, the master betakes himself to a sumptuous banquet—flesh, and fowl, and fruits, and cakes, and wine from his own vineyards—all, as you may note, to the sound of merry music. But like those bright lyrics of the poet Horace, which begin so blithely and end with so sad a strain, these pictures of a full and vigorous career terminate in darkness. You see the wealthy land-owner and noble in the hands of the em-

* Champollion, "Lettres sur l'Egypte," 11me et 12me lettres.

balmers; next, as a mummy, stretched upon the bier which the sacred boat carries across the Silent River; and, lo, now he tarries at the gates of the Eternal Land, where the shadows of the dead, and the judge, awful Osiris, sit in solemn majesty to pass sentence upon the deeds done in the flesh.

JUDGMENT OF SOULS, AND THEIR FUTURE DESTINY.
(From the Sarcophagus of Alexander.)

It should be noted that all the female figures in these frescoes are painted yellow, and all the male red.

The next point of interest for the Nile voyager is *Edfoo*, two miles above El-Kab, on the west bank of the river.

Edfoo is the *Apollinopolis Magna* of the Greeks, which, under the Roman emperors, was a bishop's see, and the head-quarters of the Legio Secunda Trajana. It had formerly been regarded as the capital of the Apollonite nome, and its inhabitants were avowed enemies of the crocodile and crocodile-worshippers.

The ancient city owed its reputation to two temples, remarkable for their extent, massiveness, and grandeur of architecture. The smaller of the two is, however, but a kind of appendage to the larger; its sculptures represent the birth and education of the youthful Horus, to whose parents—Noum (or Kneph) and Athor—the larger temple was dedicated.

Speaking of the larger temple—which was founded by Ptolemy Philometor, about B.C. 171—Mr. Bartlett says: It stands on rising ground not far from the river; and, as the external wall with which it is surrounded is entire, affords an admirable idea of the vast size and solid magnificence of an Egyptian temple in its perfect state, when it served no less as a fortress and a palace for the sacerdotal class than as a place for the solemn rites of religion. The sanctity of the scene, however, is impaired by the wretched village of mud hovels, swarming with ragged fellahs, which has risen among the gigantic ruins.*

The entrance consists of a noble propylon, 50 feet high, flanked by two converging wings, in the form of truncated pyramids, each 107 feet high, 100 feet long, and 30 feet wide. They contain ten stories, and are pierced with loop-holes for the admission of light and air. Their exterior walls are enriched with bold and vigorous sculptures of singularly felicitous design. Hence we proceed into a large court, surrounded by a colon-

* W. H. Bartlett, "The Nile Boat," p. 199.

nade, with a flat roof of squared granite; and on the opposite side stands a *pronaos*, or portico, 53 feet high, and having a triple row of six columns, whose carved capitals belong to the Ptolemaic era. This leads into a vestibule; and through two courts, one roofed and one open, we pass into the *adytum*, or sanctuary. There are also

TEMPLE OF NOUM AND ATHOR, AT EDFOO.

eighteen small lateral chambers. The entire area is surrounded by a solid wall, 20 feet in height.* Recent explorations, conducted by M. Mariette, have revealed the whole of this fine building, including its great hall and sacred shrine of red granite, to the visitor's curious investigation.

* Sir G. Wilkinson, "Modern Egypt and Thebes," pp. 436-438.

Passing the romantic ruins of the Arab town of Booayh, we continue our voyage through a succession of rich, bright, and picturesque landscapes, until we arrive at the pass of Hadjur Silsileh (Gebel Silsilis), or "the Rock of the Chain;"* its banks consisting of lofty and abrupt precipices that descend to the margin of the waters, and shut them up in a very narrow channel. Here the voyager lands to explore the grottoes excavated in the face of the crag, some of which belong to a remote antiquity, and record, in their hieroglyphic inscriptions, the triumphs of the early Pharaohs over their Ethiopian enemies.† Of greater interest, however, are the Silsileh quarries of sandstone, whose vast excavations might lead one to suppose that the whole world had been supplied from this spot with building materials for its nobler edifices. They give one a keen idea of the industry and persistent toil of the Egyptians; for only generation after generation of diligent labourers could have accomplished such enormous works. For an extent of several miles the mountain has been cut, by the hand of man, into yawning chasms and lofty menacing precipices, which, in their dimensions and picturesque variety of outline, seem to mimic the designs of Nature. As the stone nearest the river bank is of a porous character, and not well adapted for architectural purposes, passages were cut through the useless strata into the very heart of the rock. Several of these artificial avenues are nearly half-a-mile

---

* So named from a tradition that an ancient Egyptian sovereign was wont to impede the passage of the river at this point by stretching across it a chain, and laying a toll on every vessel.
† W. H. Bartlett, "The Nile Boat," p. 200.

in length, by 50 or 60 feet wide, and 80 deep. Many large masses remain as the workmen left them, and the marks of their tools—made three or four thousand years ago—are plainly visible. From the crosses painted in different places, it is supposed that the persecuted Christians afterwards sought shelter in these labyrinths; and very suggestive is this juxtaposition of the emblems of Christianity with the memorials of an earlier faith.

The rock-hewn temples on the western bank are less gigantic, but more interesting; and the traveller wanders amazed among a mass of pillars, grottoes, tablets, niches, statues, sculptures, and paintings. Here the victorious Pharaoh—Hor-em-heb, successor of Amunophis IV.—rides down the vanquished Ethiopians, receives the trembling captives, or drags them by the hair, threatening them with instant execution. There we see him borne in a shrine on men's shoulders, with files of soldiers in attendance, and the lion, emblematic of his power, pacing beside the royal chariot. In another place, he receives the symbol of life from the supreme god.

The historian, as Miss Martineau observes,* revels among such memorials as these. The invariable practice here of sculpturing the names and titles of the kings, and often of their chief officers, and the descriptions of the people conquered, and the names of the votaries as well as of their gods, makes research a self-rewarding effort. How would the English archaeologist rejoice if such relics existed of the aborigines of his own country; or the classical antiquary, if equally permanent and accurate information had been graven on the rock to light up the dim

---

* Miss Martineau, " Eastern Life : Past and Present," i. 266.

uncertain annals of Old Rome! But not less interesting is this written—this sculptured history—to the moralist and the poet. It shows how sacred a labour temple-building was considered, when the very quarries were dedicated to the gods. We cannot venture to doubt the sincerity of belief of the ancient Egyptians; and may be pardoned for wishing that religion made as intimate a part of our daily life as it did of theirs. Call it superstition, if you will; yet was it a superstition that inculcated a high morality, and nourished as true and vivid a conception of the Supreme as, perhaps, man ever attained without the help of a revelation from on high. The Egyptians looked upon their children as given by the gods; led them in bands to the temples, that at an early age they might worship and pray; invoked at their banquets the blessing of the Judge of all things; presented their triumphs and achievements as sacrifice to the celestial powers; and hallowed their great work of temple-building—which seems to have been the main purpose of their lives—by "making the very rocks holy which were to furnish the material." Here, at Silsileh, a great assembly of the gods accept the offerings of the kings. Savak is the deity of the place; but the god Nilus holds a higher rank than usual, either because the river here pours through the rocky pass with so much fulness and force, or because much of the stone cut for far-off temples was intrusted to the charge of Nilus for transport.

Some of the tablets are lettered with inscriptions of historical importance, and especially with a record of certain assemblies held in various years of the reign of the great Rameses. The object and nature of these assemblies have not yet been ascertained. They had either a religious or a political character. All we know is, that they were held in the great halls of the temples, and were considered of such high importance, that the title of "President of the Assemblies" was bestowed upon the king alone on earth, and was supposed to be not unworthy of the gods in their own mysterious realm.*

Passing through the Silsileh defile, we emerge upon a broad and open valley, whose gently-ascending slopes are clothed with palm groves. Here is situated the village of *Koum Ombos* (or Kóm Umboo), supposed to represent Ombi, the ancient capital of the Ombite nome, or province, and celebrated in all ages for its magnificent temples.

The façade of the principal one, which crowns the summit of a sandy hill, consists of a portico of fifteen columns, five in front, and three deep, thirteen of which are still standing. It was rebuilt by the Ptolemys on the site of an edifice which dated from an early part of the third period, and dedicated to Arveris (Apollo) and the other gods of the Ombite nome.†

A common architectural device of the Egyptians may here be advantageously studied. They regularly diminished the size of their inner chambers, so as to give, from the entrance, the appearance of a longer perspective than really existed. They built on an ascending ground, disguising the ascent by flights of extremely shallow steps.

---

* Sir Gardner Wilkinson, "Manners and Customs of the Ancient Egyptians," v. *in loc.*

† Hamilton, "Aegyptiaca," p. 35; Champollion, "L'Egypte," i. 167.

The roof was constructed with a still greater inclination, which was concealed by the introduction of deep architraves and large cornices. The sides were made to draw in, so that the appearance which a building exhibits on paper, when represented in perspective, the Egyptian temples had in reality. Thus the adytum, sanctuary or

TEMPLE OF ARVERIS AT KOUM OMBOS.

holy place, was invariably small; but to the worshippers, who looked on from the further chambers, it seemed not small, but remote; and this remoteness invested it with an air of awful solemnity. The effect, indeed, when viewed through a long vista of sculptured columns and painted walls, must have been singularly imposing; must have far exceeded any of the dramatic contrasts which obtain in the Roman Catholic ritual.

The other temple, built on an artificial platform at the north-western angle of the enclosure, was erected in the reign of Ptolemy XII. and Cleopatra (about 50 B.C.),* and dedicated to the goddess Isis or Athor, with whose visage the capitals of the columns are adorned. The sculptures on the walls are very numerous, and even now, after the lapse of nearly twenty centuries, retain their brilliancy of colouring. So extensive are the ruins of Koum Ombos, that it seems difficult to believe they could have been effected by any other agency than an earthquake; or that, at least, Nature began the destruction which human barbarism has completed. The people of Ombos were worshippers of the crocodile, and hence were frequently at war with the men of Denderah, who hunted the monster. Of one of these conflicts a vivid description occurs in the fifteenth chapter of Juvenal.

* Hamilton, "Aegyptiaca," pp. 34-36.

CHAPTER II.

ASSOUAN, OR SYENE—ITS ANCIENT CELEBRITY—ITS QUARRIES—ISLAND OF ELEPHANTINE—TEMPLE OF KNEPH—ISLAND OF PHILAE—TEMPLE OF ISIS—OTHER MEMORIALS—SACRED CHARACTER OF PHILAE—ITS TRIAD: OSIRIS, ISIS, AND HORUS.

> Amid the foaming breakers' silvery light,
> Where yon rough rapids sparkle!
> MOORE.

> It seemed as she was doing sacrifice
> To Isis, deckt with mitre on her head,
> And linnen stole after those priestes guize....
>   For that Osyris whilest he lived here
> The justest man alive and truest did appear.
> SPENSER.

THE approach to Assouan—which lies on the east bank of the river, about thirty miles south of Koum Ombos—is through a scene of romantic beauty. The Nile, bending abruptly, broadens into a kind of bay, which is shut in by the green and lovely island of Elephantine, whence an early dynasty of Egyptian kings derived their name. The high bold rocks which rise on every hand seem like the boundaries of a lake. On the left, nestling under rocky crags, whose summit is crowned with ruins, lies the modern village;

in the distance, the yellow sandy hills are covered with remains of Saracenic architecture. To the right, the shattered walls of a convent mark the crest of a sandstone eminence; and all around, between the desert and the river, the palm-groves cluster in verdurous masses.

The word "Assouan" is the Coptic *souan* or *suan*, an "opening," with the addition of the Arabic *el*, or "the," softened into *es* or *as*.* The town so called lies on the east branch of the Nile, near the frontier of Nubia, 110 miles south of Thebes, in lat. 24° 5′ 23″ north, and long. 32° 55′ east. Of old, this position was strategetically important; was the watch-tower on the frontier between Egypt and the south; the most commanding point near the First Cataract, which, though no very formidable obstacle to modern navigation, must have been a serious obstruction before the great depression of the bed of the Nile. Syene, as it was called by the ancients, was the depôt of the merchandise which passed between the north and the south. Here were the quarries whence much of the Egyptian building-stone—that peculiar kind of marble still known as *syenite*—was drawn. A Nilometer stood here, to record the rise of the great god Nilus. Temples at Elephantine ministered to the religious wants of strangers and natives. There was a garrison in the time of the Persians, and again in the days of the Greeks, and Roman and Saracenic fortifications still lie in ruins on the heights around. Thus, on this frontier spot, the evidence is abundant that successive races prized it as the important "Opening" which its name declares it to be—the "Gate" through

---

* The word is supposed to be derived from *Suan*, an Egyptian goddess, the "Ilithya" or "Opener" of the Greeks.

which the fertilizing floods of the Nile broke into the land of Egypt.

The view from the environing rocks is very striking—a view of hill and water, wood and lowland; and beyond, the confused and blown heaps of the rolling sands of the Desert. The river hurries past in a succession of rapid eddies and foaming whirls. In their midst lie various black-coloured islets, marking the boundary of the Cataract; and nearer at hand, and in a more tranquil reach of the stream, rises the beautiful Elephantine. Ruin, however, is written in gigantic letters on the entire scene. The island of Elephantine looks as if it had been ravaged by an earthquake, scarcely one stone being left upon another of all its once famous edifices. In a hollow of the wilderness lies the great cemetery, each grave with its memorial-tablet inscribed in Cufic letters. The hoary walls of the Saracenic fortress on the one hand, and of the Christian convent on the other, preach the same striking lesson of mutability.

At a short distance from the village, on the opposite bank of the Nile, are situated the celebrated *Quarries* which furnished the colossal structures of Egypt. The excavations, says a modern traveller,[*] are on a scale proportionate to the vast works they were destined to construct, and the solid rocks have been hewn out like so much clay.

The wedge, that most ancient of building tools, was the potent instrument in rending each adamantine mass. The dimensions of the required block were marked out by wedges, which, being wetted, duly expanded, and the

---

[*] G. Melly, "Khartoum, and the Blue and White Niles."

rock, split asunder, yielded up the rough material for a column or a god. And the grooves and notches made by labourers who died thousands of years ago, in preparation for works which were never carried out, may still be seen! So, too, the idle or playful scratches which amused a leisure hour or a joyous mood. So, too, a variety of rude inscriptions, referring to hewn blocks, or commemorating the victories of the kings, as if the glad tidings of triumph awoke a feeling of national enthusiasm from Thebes to Syene. All seems, says Mr. Melly, as if it were the creation of yesterday; as if the artificers, called off by some emergency, had but just left their mighty labour. Yonder lies an unpolished obelisk, ninety or a hundred feet long, and ten feet broad, waiting for those final touches which it shall never receive!* The excavations are said to have been arrested when the Persian Conquest swept, like a destroying simoom, through the Nile Valley. And so the huge columns moulder in the sand, and there is none to provide for their removal or completion. The old creed has vanished, and its shrines are the resort of curious pilgrims from remote lands which the worshippers never knew of.

Here the problem again suggests itself to the observer, How were such stupendous masses removed to so great a distance as Thebes? The appliances employed for their transit remain a mystery. Certain it is, that the task would prove of very great, insuperable difficulty to modern engineers. It would seem that most, if not all, of the blocks were conveyed to their destination by land. But how? Herodotus relates that two thousand men

---

* Hamilton, "Aegyptiaca," p. 105.

were employed for three years in the removal of one block.* Yet the colossal structures of Thebes were mostly erected within a comparatively limited period, and consist of innumerable blocks. How could men be found, in a population generally estimated at four or five millions only, to toil in these quarries, to transport the material to distant sites, to build the temples and palaces, to design and embellish and perfect them, while all the time an advanced civilization made other demands upon labour, and wars were conducted, and extensive conquests made, and agriculture and commerce also claimed their thousands and tens of thousands?

The island of Elephantine is rich in architectural remains, though, unhappily, they are all in a sadly dilapidated condition.† In the midst of a vast field of bricks, and fragments of baked earth, a column or two stand as a memorial of the ancient Temple of Noum, or Kneph, the good genius—he who, of all the Egyptian Pantheon, approaches nearest in his attributes to our ideas of the Supreme Divinity.‡ All the ornaments are accompanied

* Among the Egyptian paintings is the representation of a colossus drawn on a sledge by one hundred and seventy-two men, who are ranged in four rows of forty-three each. In one respect ancient and modern expedients were alike. An individual stands on a leg of the image, and claps his hands for a signal to the team of men to pull together. When the single piece of granite, weighing twelve hundred tons, which forms the pedestal to the equestrian statue of Peter the Great at St. Petersburg, was drawn to its site, a drummer was placed on the top of the huge block to perform the same service.—*Quarterly Review*, No. ccxl., p. 430.

† The temples were destroyed in 1822, by Mohammed Bey, to build a palace at Assouan.

‡ Some authorities contend that this temple was dedicated to Khnum, the god of the waters, and his colleagues, Anouké and Sate. It was founded by Amunophis III., and embellished by Rameses III. See Denon, " Travels in Upper and Lower Egypt," ii. 30–36; Hamilton, " Aegyptiaca," &c.

by the serpent, symbolic of eternal and pre-eminent wisdom. A statue of red granite, with the Ramessid or Osiride emblems, has also escaped destruction; and the lower portion of the Nilometer. There is also a granite gateway of the time of Alexander; and near it lie some slender and broken pillars, which, as one of them bears a sculptured cross, evidently belonged to a Christian church. Other memorials of interest have rewarded the research of travellers: numerous fragments of pottery, bearing receipts in the Greek language for taxes paid by the farmers in the reigns of the Antonines; and part of a calendar recording the rise of the Dog-star in the time of Thothmes III. (1445 B.C.),—that is, three thousand three hundred and sixteen years ago.

Elephantine (or Elephantina) was anciently called *Abu*, or the "Ivory Island," and was the depôt of the large traffic carried on in that costly product. From hence the Greek mercenaries in the pay of Psammetichus I. were despatched in search of Egyptian deserters; and in successive eras it was garrisoned by the Persians, Greeks, Romans, and Saracens. It gave the fifth dynasty of kings to the throne of Egypt.

From Assouan it is customary for the Nile voyager to make a pilgrimage, beyond the First Cataract, to the Holy Island of *Philae* (Φιλαί)—the "Unapproachable" (ἄβατος)—which marks the extreme boundary of Upper Egypt.

> The footprints of an elder race are here,
> And memories of an heroic time,
> And shadows of the old mysterious faith;
> So that the isle seems haunted, and strange sounds
> Float on the wind through all its ruined depths.

"By Him who sleeps in Philae!"—such the oath
Which bound th' Egyptian's soul as with a chain
Imperishable. Ay, by Amun-Ra,—
The great Osiris,—who lies slumbering here,
Lulled by the music of the flowing Nile.

Ages have gone, and creeds, and dynasties,
And a new order reigns o'er all the Earth;
Yet still the mighty Presence keeps the isle—
Awful, serene, and grandly tranquil he,
With Isis watching—restless in her love!

DISTANT VIEW OF THE ISLAND OF PHILAE.

Philae was called by the Egyptians *Menlak*, "the Place of the Cataract;" or *Menuab*, "the Sanctuary." It is a small rock of syenite, about 1250 feet long, and 400 feet broad.*

Philae proper, or the larger island, has always excited

---

* There are really, as the name indicates, *two* islands, but the smaller one is of no importance. They are situated in lat. 24° N., at about six miles from Assouan, and just above the First Cataract.

the admiration of the traveller. Mr. Curzon speaks of it in rapturous terms. Every part of Egypt, he says, is interesting and curious, but the only place to which the epithet "beautiful" can be correctly applied is the island of Philae. Eliot Warburton characterizes it as the most unearthly, wild, strange, and lovely spot he ever beheld. No dreamer of the old mystical times, when beauty, knowledge, and power were realized on Earth, ever pictured to himself a scene of wilder grandeur or more perfect loveliness. For all around the traveller tower up vast masses of gloomy rocks, piled one upon the other in wildest confusion;—some of them, as it were, skeletons of pyramids; others requiring only a few strokes of giant labour to form colossal statues that might have startled the Anakim. Here spreads a deep drift of silvery sand, fringed by rich verdure and purple blossoms; there, a grove of palms, intermingled with the flowering acacia: and there, through vistas of craggy cliffs and gloomy foliage, gleams a calm blue lake, with the Sacred Island in the midst, green to the water's edge, except where the walls of the old temple-city are reflected.

It is true, however, that Dean Stanley speaks of it as more curious than beautiful. From this disparaging statement we should infer that the Dean made but a cursory inspection of it, for a recent traveller, admitting that at first he was somewhat disappointed with the island, acknowledges that on *closer* acquaintance he became one of its most devoted admirers. There is, he says, a grace and loveliness attached to Philae pre-eminently of all Nile views; the chief charm, nevertheless, being in the island itself, as seen from a little distance, lying so picturesquely and calmly in the very midst of the river, which is shut in here by perpendicular black granite rocks: it is the contrast of the fertile, sunny island, with the stern, rugged iron-bound precipices which tower above it; so that in connection with Philae there always rises up in the mind a picture of perfect repose, and of nature in its most smiling aspect.*

To the ancient Egyptian, Philae was simply the sacredest spot upon Earth,—what Mecca is to the Moslem, or Calvary to the Christian. The most solemn oath that he could utter was, "By Him—the Un-named and Un-nameable—that sleeps in Philae." It was the resting-place of his god of gods, of the all-powerful Osiris, of the supreme divinity, whose singular love for Egypt was manifested in the yearly overflow of the great river. Therefore it was considered profane for any but priests to approach it; and men believed that, in awful reverence for its sanctity, no bird flew over it, no fish drew near its shores. These, however, were the traditions of an early age, when the religion of Egypt was a real and living creed. At a later period it became a favourite resort of pilgrims to the tomb of Osiris; and an inscription on an obelisk removed to England by Mr. Bankes shows that the priests petitioned Ptolemy Physcon (B.C. 170–117) to prohibit officials and public personages from visiting the island, and living there at their expense.

It is a curious fact to be noticed, in reference to Philae,

---

* Compare Curzon, "Monasteries in the Levant;" Eliot Warburton, "The Crescent and the Cross;" Dean Stanley, "Sinai and Palestine;" the Rev. A. C. Smith, "The Nile and its Banks;" and Hamilton, "Aegyptiaca."

that peculiar effects of light and shade are produced by its vicinity to the Tropic of Cancer. As the sun approaches the northern boundary of its course, the shade thrown by the cornices, mouldings, and projections of the temples creeps lower and lower down their granite walls, until, when the orb of day attains its highest point of elevation, these walls are invested in deep, dark shadows, which present an almost weird contrast to the intense glow that lights up the surrounding landscape.

The surface of the island may, without exaggeration, be described as strewn with ruins, like the sea-shore after a storm. This wide-spread desolation seems to have been effected by the Persians, who, defied in their destructive efforts by the massive edifices of Karnak and Luxor, found here a more suitable field for their barbarian rage. The most ancient thing on Philae is the shattered Temple of Athor (Aphrodite), built in the reign of Nectanebus (B.C. 381–363). The other remains belong, for the most part, to the reigns of the Ptolemys, Philadelphus, Epiphanes, and Philometor (B.C. 282–145); and numerous inscriptions show that the sacred structures were repaired and restored by the Roman emperors down to the epoch of Claudius (A.D. 54). After the introduction of Christianity, Philae still preserved a reputation for sanctity. Some of the *adyta* bear traces of having been adapted to Christian worship; and among the ruins are those of a Christian church.

The triad to whom Philae was sacred were Osiris, Isis, and Horus.

The principal temple was dedicated to Osiris. From the river-bank it was approached by a double colonnade,

TEMPLE OF ISIS, ISLAND OF PHILAE.

which terminated with two colossal lions of granite, and a couple of obelisks, each 44 feet in height. The columns differed each from the other in the sculptured foliage of their capitals, which represented the indigenous vegetation of the country, — palms and tobacco, water-plants and acacias. Through the colossal propylon, its lofty pyramidal towers graven all over with mysterious allegories, the worshipper passed, and between the solemn sphinxes, into an open court surrounded by columns; and thence, through another pylon, into the pronaos,—an area reminding the modern traveller of a convent cloister. Beneath the shadowy arcades on either side, loaded with hieroglyphic carving, various doors lead down into dim chapels and chambers. The porch, entered by a third pylon, is of a solemn character, spanning the whole breadth of the building, overshadowed by heavy cornices, and bearing the mystic emblem of supreme divinity, a winged globe, blazoned in azure. It is supported by a twofold range of gigantic columns, whose capitals even now are dazzling with their rich bright hues.*

HORUS, ISIS, AND OSIRIS.

A lofty doorway opens from the portico into the *sekos*, or *adytum*, in each corner of which formerly stood a

* Howard Hopley, "Under Egyptian Palms," pp. 290-292.

TEMPLE OF OSIRIS AT PHILAE.

monolithic shrine,* the cage of a sacred hawk, and whose walls are covered with emblems. Here, in the thickness of wall or buttress, secret staircases lead to chambers in the roof; the surface of every passage, however narrow or apparently insignificant, being wrought into devices of genii, and beautiful with the serene, sublime face of Isis.

Mr. Hopley describes in graphic language his exploration of a chapel, small as an attic, situated in the roof of the western corridor. He came upon it, he says, at

---

* One of these is now in the Louvre at Paris, the other in the Museum at Florence.

TEMPLE COURT AT PHILAE.

hazard, after wandering over the whole of the temple, between the massive blocks which, at different heights, roof in transepts, vestibule, and adyta. Egyptologists call it the "resurrection chamber," from the sculptures on its walls representing the death and resurrection of Osiris. It stands in a sunny nook. Seven stairs, flanked by a smooth groove, adapted, apparently, for the descent of a coffin, lead down to its entrance. You bend your head, and pass in. There is no need of torches or tapers, for the light through a loophole breaks on the pictured walls. The subject is treated in successive stages. You see women weeping about the bier of the dead Osiris: anon the scene changes—winged figures, like cherubim, stand at the head and foot, as if on guard, and shelter him with their overspreading pinions; then the soul, symbolized as a bird, hovers and flutters over the motionless body;—hush! life is stealing into the throbbing veins......a leg, an arm moves. Thus, in many gradations, and through a series of impressive pictures, the theme is carried on; until, at length, on the furthest wall, fully robed and mitred, the god stands manifest......Osiris, the living, the supreme, the eternal, bearing, in hands crossed over the breast, the sceptre and the flail, as emblems of power and judgment.*

On the left hand of the entrance into the principal court, we should add, is situated a small temple or chapel, dedicated to Athor. It is profusely embellished with sculptures depicting the birth of Ptolemy Philometor, under the figure of the god Horus, and its inner chambers with symbolic carving illustrative of the mysteries of the Egyptian worship.

Its sculptures, however, have been grievously mutilated; the evil being due, in the first place, to the relig-

* Hopley, "Under Egyptian Palms," p. 296.

ious zeal of the early Christians, and afterwards to the fanaticism of the so-called Iconoclasts.

At the southern extremity of the dromos of the Great Temple stands a smaller temple, supposed, by some authorities, to have been consecrated to Isis, and vulgarly called "Pharaoh's Bed." Its portico consists of twelve columns, crowned with the head of that goddess. The capitals are finely carved with the doum leaf, the flower of the lotus, and the palm branch; and every inch of surface glows with exquisite colouring, which, owing to the dryness of the atmosphere, preserves its original lustre.

A few words, in conclusion, may be offered, perhaps, in explanation of the sacred character and attributes of OSIRIS. He is reputed to have been the son of Seb (or "Saturn") by Nu (or "Rhea"). He was the brother and husband of Isis ("Ceres," or "the Moon") by whom he had Horus ("Apollo"), and in some instances seems identified with the Sun or the Creative Power. The later myths record that he became king of the Egyptians, to whom he taught agriculture and the art of making wine; that he afterwards travelled over the world, everywhere extending the influence of civilization; and that, meanwhile, his kingdom was ruled over by Isis, who repressed the ambitious designs of Typhon ("Satan," "Sin," or the "Evil Principle") the brother of Osiris. Typhon, however, persuaded seventy-two persons to join him in a scheme for the murder of his brother, which, on the return of the latter, was successfully carried out; but in the shadow-world Osiris was restored to life, and the important office was assigned to him of judging the dead and ruling over the spirits of the blessed.

His names were numerous, like his attributes. He was called Onnophris, or "the meek-hearted;" the "Manifester of Good," because he appeared on Earth to benefit mankind; "Lord of Lords;" "Lord of the East;" "King of the Gods;" but in his most sacred and mysterious office, and as superior to every other deity, his name was forbidden to be mentioned. When Herodotus has described the lamentations and self-chastisements which formed part of the sacrificial rites at the feast of Isis, he says that it is not permitted him to tell in whose honour these took place. He invariably speaks of Osiris by allusion, and never by name.* In the earlier and purer days of the Egyptian worship, Osiris represented the Universal Goodness of the Supreme Being, all whose several attributes were afterwards personified as separate deities for or by the common people. It was believed that he quitted his celestial throne and assumed a human form, but without becoming human, for the benefit of mankind; that on Earth he was vanquished by the Power of Evil; that he rose again to conquer Evil by his resurrection; and that he was then appointed Judge of the Dead and Lord of the Celestial Region.

He was adored by all Egypt, not only for his benefits to man, but because he was the only manifestation on Earth of the One Supreme God. For this special reason he was made superior to the eight great gods, *after* whom he ranked on other accounts. It must always remain a mystery how the Egyptians supposed his manifestation to have taken place in the form of humanity without adopting its nature.

* Herodotus, book ii.

But when we speak of Osiris as the only manifestation of the One God upon Earth, we mean the only manifestation made by a supernatural power; for, otherwise, all living beings, in the creed of the Egyptians, as in the philosophy of Pantheism, emanated from the Source and Centre of Life.* The very worm beneath the sod, the insect that sported its little hour on a blade of grass, the mighty hippopotamus, and the huge behemoth, had thus a common origin and a mutual bond. It was from Egypt, in all probability, that Pythagoras derived that doctrine of the metempsychosis, which afterwards spread through the civilized world. It accounts for the peculiar observances with regard to animals which prevailed in Egypt. As Porphyry observes, it was the teaching of the Egyptians that the Divinity entered not only the human body, but that of the beast; and that the soul, while on Earth, dwelt not in man alone, but passed in a measure through all animals.

But if all life was thus linked with its Creative Principle, Osiris, nevertheless, was the only one of the sons of the Supreme who had revealed Him to man, and therefore was justly worshipped above them all. As the highest illustration of his goodness, he was naturally identified with the peculiar blessings of old Egypt—with the annual overflow of the Nile, and the consequent fertility of the land. Hence arose the fable that his body was deposited in the Cataract, whence he arose once every year to enrich the glad Earth with his measureless bounty. Hence, too, he came to be called the

---

* Sir Gardner Wilkinson, "Manners and Customs of the Ancient Egyptians," iv. 187-189.

founder of agriculture; or, more poetically, the eldest-born of Time and cousin to the Day.

As Osiris was cousin to the Day, the "kinsman of Light and Morning," so his murderer, Typhon, was the god of the Eclipse, of "Darkness and the Shadow"—that is, the personification of Evil. He was in hateful league with Antae, or the Desert; a myth which, in the course of ages, suggested that world-wide belief in an eternal struggle between the powers of evil and good, which we trace in the *Ormuzd* and *Ahriman* of the Persians, as well as in other Oriental creeds.

ISIS was the sister and wife of Osiris. The Egyptians called her Hes, daughter of *Seb* (or "Chronos") and *Nu* (or "Rhea"). On the monuments she is variously styled the "Mistress of Heaven," the "Regent of the Gods," the "Eye of the Sun." She would seem to have been the prototype of Ceres or the Moon, though at a later time her attributes, under the name of Athor, somewhat resembled those of the Greek Aphrodite; and her worship was accompanied by certain mysterious rites known only to the initiated. A veil always hung before her shrine, which, said the well-known inscription, "None among mortals have ever lifted up;" typifying, perhaps, the inscrutable course and deep secrets of Nature. Sometimes she represented the land of Egypt, as Osiris did its fertilizing river, the Nile. She was also his colleague in the solemn judgment of the dead, and in this office suggested to the Greeks their Heklé or Hecate. Her infant, HORUS, or Childhood—the emblem of reproduction—was also adopted by the poets and priests of Hellas, who converted him into Harpocrates, the "god of silence," with his finger ever pressed to his lips.*

Such were the deities to whose mysterious worship Philae, the Holy Island, was solemnly dedicated; and it still seems haunted, even in this utilitarian age, by the presence of the mighty triad. The whole island is not above fifty acres in size, but, as Eliot Warburton remarks, it is richer, perhaps, in objects of interest than any spot of similar extent in the world. And just as the great allegorical religion of Egypt has a deeper significance and a broader meaning than the fanciful myths of Greece, so should Philae possess, for the student of philosophy, a higher interest and a stronger charm than the fabled birthplace of the Cyprian goddess or the oak-groves of Dodona.

* Sir Gardner Wilkinson, *ut ante*, iv. 317, 321, 367, 384, *et in loc.*

CHAPTER III.

THE FIRST CATARACT—HOW ITS ASCENT IS ACCOMPLISHED
—THE SHEIKH AND HIS MEN.

> The Nile! the Nile! I hear its gathering roar:
> No vision now, no dream of ancient years—
> Throned on the rocks, amid the watery war,
> The king of floods, old Homer's Nile appears.
> LORD LINDSAY.

WHILE directing the reader's attention to the antiquities of Syene and Elephantine, we considered it convenient to include in the survey those of the island of Philae; but the reader must bear in mind that while the former are *below*, the latter is *above* the First Cataract. To continue our river voyage, therefore, we must return to Assouan, and prepare for our ascent of the rapids.

Just beyond lies Birbé, a sort of river-port for the upper Nile, where it is worth while for the traveller to land and climb the neighbouring heights, if he have any taste for the picturesque. From these he will obtain a view of Philae, which will long live in his memory, and often, in after-times, rise upon him like a vision of the beautiful.

The ascent of the Cataract, when the waters are low, is a matter of difficulty rather than of danger. In fact, as already stated, it is not a cataract, but a *rapid*, caused by the sudden compression of the river into a narrow rocky channel, obstructed by numerous masses of crag and stone, which vex the waters into many a swirling eddy. To drag the boat against the impetuous stream, and to avoid these little islands of rock, the assistance is secured of an important official, known as the Sheikh of the Cataract,* who brings with him from forty to fifty followers—swart, athletic Nubians, all naked but for a white turban on their heads, and a cincture of cotton round their waists. Of these, a portion take possession of the dahabeeyah, while the remainder are posted at those points on the lofty bank where their services will be more immediately required.

The commencement of the Cataract has been expressively described as a complete archipelago of granite rocks, some red, others black, and all shining in the sun, as though highly polished, with various torrents rushing between them in all directions. These rocks are of the most extraordinary forms; now awful, now grotesque; they look as ancient as the Earth itself—the very skeletons of the antediluvian world. On the western bank the sands of the Great Desert, yellow as gold, and broken by the action of the wind into rolling waves, descend to the water's edge, interspersed with great masses of black basalt; on the east, crag rises above crag in such chaotic confusion that one can only suppose the scene to have resulted from some volcanic explosion.†

---

* There are (or were) four of these Sheikhs—Hassan, Ali, Suleiman, and Ibrahim.

† Mrs. Romer, "Temples and Tombs of Egypt," &c., i. 169, 170.

The northerly breeze, which almost always prevails in this part of Egypt, carries our boat through the intricate archipelago to the base of the Cataract, and we moor it to the rocks while preparations are made for our ascent. The scene now commends itself to the artist's eye:— enormous masses of dark stone lie around in every direction; the foaming river whirls and scurries through every fissure and ravine; innumerable swarthy demon-like figures—like those in " Don Giovanni"—hurry to and fro among the rocks, upon the sands, upon the deck of the dahabeeyah, or amid the seething waters; the Sheikh, with his long robes floating in the wind, takes his stand on a vantage-point where he can overlook the whole transaction; a stout English rope is made fast to the main-mast; the Nubians cling to it with a vice-like grasp; " Yallough! Wallah!" a mighty shout, and away we go up the hill of water which forms the first stage of the Cataract.

It is over! and our amphibious attendants take a quiet breathing pause. The Sheikh gesticulates, " Yallough! Wallah!" and again they set to work. Now we hang suspended on the very ridge where the waters seem to hesitate ere they plunge below; another pull; a long pull, and a strong one; " Yallough!" one more pull, and the second fall is safely passed. After a short space we move on, over a quiet reach of the stream, to the third and most difficult stage of the rapid—called *El Bab*, or " the gate"—where the Nile hurls the whole volume of its waters between two towering cliffs.

Now, indeed, the Sheikh appears fully equal to the responsibilities of his position. He flings off his encumbering robes, and stands forth stripped of everything but his drawers; his turban even thrown aside, and the long Mussulman tuft of hair that crowns his shaven head "floating like a horse-tail in the wind." His gestures and his ejaculations are ceaseless and violent. His followers seem animated with Herculean vigour. They shout and they strain; they dart hither and thither; they jump upon the rocks; they leap into the waters: now they

FIRST CATARACT OF THE NILE.

fend off the quivering boat from some dangerous crag; now they tug lustily at the straining rope; the cries of "Yallough! Wallah!" are redoubled, and replied to from the shore by shouts of "Haybe sah!"—"God help you!" —a minute, and another—we are half buried in foam and spray; and now, hurrah! we have surmounted the dreaded Cataract, and ride triumphantly on the tranquil river. We bid adieu to the Sheikh and his trusty men, take our own crew on board, and with swelling sails glide through the portal of gloomy rocks that shuts in Ethiopia from the world. Egypt is left behind us; that strange and mysterious land of Art, Religion, and Literature; the land of Osiris and Isis; the land of the Pyramid and the Sphinx; of Memphis, and Thebes, and Heliopolis; the mother of countless nations; the fountain of Greek philosophy and science; which inspired the lore of Athens and the subtle policy of Crete; which, long before Greece and Rome had a name and a habitation, possessed all the graces of intellectual life, all the secrets of a penetrating wisdom;—Egypt, the cradle of human history and human knowledge, whose solemn memories surround it with an imperishable glory!

> " Whose shrines and palaces and towers,
> (Time-eaten towers that tremble not!)
> Resemble nothing that is ours."

We have passed the First Cataract, and have entered Nubia; the Sacred Island remains with us now only as a dream; the river grows narrower and more rapid; the cliffs, of a dark red, encroach more and more upon its channel; rich leafy glens open up wild glimpses of the Nubian Desert; a tropic sky burns overhead; the hot rays are thrown back from the gleaming waters and the naked rocks like blazing swords; and right glad is the traveller when he comes to an anchor in the cool evening off the large town of Kalabsché! Here, then, we may find it convenient to put together a few geographical notes upon the country we have just entered.

Book Fourth.

CHAPTER I.

NUBIA: ITS BOUNDARIES AND EXTENT—ITS ANNALS—CHARACTER OF ITS INHABITANTS — NATURAL RESOURCES—PRINCIPAL TOWNS.

> Where rippling wave and dashing oar
> The midnight chant attend;
> Or whispering palm-leaves from the shore
> With midnight silence blend.—KEBLE.

HE name "Nubia," or "Nubah," seems to have been derived from the Egyptian and Coptic *noub*, or "gold," which we still find extant in the Wâdy Nouba, a valley on the frontiers of Dongola. It was known to the ancients as Ethiopia, though the exact limits comprised under that appellation cannot now be determined. Generally speaking, it included all the west bank of the Nile from Meroë to the "Great Bend," and was supposed to be a happy and fertile region, peculiarly favoured by the gods. In the "Iliad," Thetis informs Achilleus that

> "Ζεὺς γαρ ἐπ' ὠκεανον μετ' ἀμύμονας Αἰθιοπηας."*
> "Jove is to a solemn banquet gone
> Beyond the sea, on Aethiopia's shore."

* Homer, "Iliad," lib. i, v. 123—Earl of Derby's translation.

The ignorance which prevailed in reference to all the African interior was favourable to the growth of such poetic conceptions; but a closer acquaintance with the Nubian deserts scarcely induces the modern traveller to acquiesce in the ancient fables. The only fertile portions are the great plains in the immediate vicinity of the Nile, which undoubtedly, in former times, inundated, and consequently enriched, a wider extent of country than it does at present.

Modern Nubia may be considered to extend from Philae, above the First Cataract, to Sennaar, in 18° north latitude. It thus comprises a kind of valley or hollow, bounded on the west by the sands of the Great Desert, south by the uplands of Abyssinia, north by Egypt, and east by the Arabian Gulf. Under the Pharaohs it was called Kesh, or Cush, and was ruled by a viceroy entitled Prince of Cush or Ethiopia, until it regained its independence and was governed by its native rulers. These appear to have invaded and subjugated Egypt, and to have extended their sway from Meroë to Syene, which marked the limits of the possessions of the Ptolemys and the Romans. Meroë became the seat of a powerful empire, and the emporium of the commerce of India, Libya, Carthage, Arabia, and Egypt. A severe blow was dealt to its prosperity by the Persian Cambyses, who conquered it about 530 B.C. After the destruction of Thebes, however, numbers of its inhabitants fled to Meroë, which again waxed strong and rich, and assumed a markedly Egyptian character. In the reign of Augustus it was captured by the Romans, and we read of one of its sovereigns, a Queen Candace, as his tributary.

Its decay appears to have been rapid, for even as early as the time of Nero its site was only known by the ruins of its once splendid temples and palaces.

After the Moslem conquest of Egypt, Nubia was invaded by the Arabs, who spread themselves over its valleys and plains, and now consist of five principal tribes: the Djowabere, El-Gharbye, the Kenons, the Koreish, and the Djaafere. Further to the south, in a fertile country, dwell the Berbers or Barabra; then come the Ababde and the warlike Sheygya; while from Dongola and Sennaar, a Negro state, the people, of mixed Arab and Nigritic blood, are called Noubas.

The Nubians, as a whole, are a more athletic and vigorous race than the Egyptians. They are honest, courageous, and independent. The women are more virtuous, while they are also more beautiful; the face being a fine oval, the eyes dark and expressive, the complexion a glowing bronze, the figure light and elegant. They possess, too, the singular charm of a very sweet and plaintive voice. The virgins wear nothing but a leathern girdle round the loins, and a blue or white scarf dependent from the back of their heads. The matrons clothe themselves in a long and loose blue robe. Few of the young men wear any covering except a cincture round the loins. They carry a knife, slung in a sheath over the left shoulder; and a club of ebony, or a long spear, ornamented with the skin of serpents or crocodiles. Their hair glistens in the sun with the castor-oil which they very freely use.

They eat little animal food, and their staple diet is the fruit of the doum-palm, dates, tamarinds, and maize.

They breed large flocks of poultry. The principal products of the country are aloes, musk, many valuable and useful gums, maize, tamarinds, myrrh, frankincense, and senna. The inhabitants trade also in skins, cotton, coffee, tobacco, ostrich feathers, ebony, ivory, gold dust, and salt. They have no currency of their own; glass beads, coral, cotton, tobs or shirts, and samoor or cloth, they receive as money; but the coins of Europe and Egypt are never refused. They sell their grain by the handful, and measure their cloth from the elbow to the fingers. They plait skilfully, but are ignorant of the use of looms. Their houses are low huts of stone or sun-dried clay. Their musical instrument is a kind of five-stringed banjo or guitar; and their music, as with almost all savage nations, is of a melancholy character.

Nubia is traversed by the windings of the Nile, which forms five cataracts within its bounds, and receives its principal tributary, the Atbara or Tacazzé. At Khartûm, the two branches, the Bahr-el-Abiad, or White Nile, and the Bahr-el-Azrek, or Blue Nile, unite to form the great Egyptian river.

The principal towns are *Khartûm*, with a population of 40,000; *El Obeid*, in Kordafan, with 20,000; *Shendy*, above the junction of the Atbara, a large and prosperous market for cattle, senna, cotton, and grain; *New Dongola;* and *Derr*.

Nubia belongs to the kingdom of Egypt. It was conquered by Ismael Pasha, second son of Mehemet Ali, in 1820–22. He swept over the country like a destructive simoom, burning and ravaging the crops and villages, until his terrible career was cut short by a fearful death.

He had insulted a native chief—the Melek of Shendy—who took advantage of his separation from the main

MEHEMET ALI.

body of his army, to surround his hut with piles of straw, and, setting them on fire, burned to death the Pasha and his suite. Mehemet Ali's revenge was signal. He slew all the inhabitants of the village nearest to his son's funeral pyre, and cut off the right hands of five hundred men besides.*

* Malte Brun, "Géographie Universelle;" "Nubia and Abyssinia" (Edin. Cab. Lib.); Mrs. Romer; "Temples and Tombs of Egypt, Nubia," &c.

CHAPTER II.

KALABSCHÉ — DENDOUR — GHIRSCHÉ HOUSSEYN — ITS TEMPLE — DAKKEH — VALLEY OF THE LIONS — IPSAMBÛL.

> Here Desolation keeps unbroken Sabbath,
> 'Mid caves and temples, palaces and sepulchres;
> Ideal images in sculptured forms,
> Thoughts hewn in columns, or in caverned hill,
> In honour of their deities and their dead.
> JAMES MONTGOMERY.

THE first five miles after leaving Philae, the voyager's course is south by east, then it turns towards the west, and finally resumes the former direction. He sees little to invite his attention until he reaches Debodeh, a village situated on the left bank, where the remains of a small temple may be seen.

Here the Nile flows in a steady and copious stream, for the most part washing the base of the eastern and western mountains; but wherever the inundation has deposited a thin stratum of soil upon the rocks, or has accumulated mounds of sand and mud, the Nubian cultivates such spots, and plants them with the universal date-tree. Thus a succession of little hamlets and water-wheels—for the one is never seen without the other—greets the eye on both sides as the traveller ascends the Nile Valley.

At Kalabsché (the *Talmis* of the ancients), lat. 23° 30' N., where we resume our voyage, stands one of the largest and most perfect rock-temples in Nubia. Its remains consist of an abutment of masonry, rising above the bank of the river, at about 180 feet from the front, to which there is a paved approach. On each side of the pavement appears to have stood a row of sphinxes, one of which remains, but is headless; and at its extremity a flight of steps led to a terrace 36 feet broad, crowned by two pyramidal masses, 18 or 20 feet thick, with a gateway between them—the whole forming a façade of not less than 110 feet. Inside, there is a court of about 40 feet, which must originally have had a colonnade linking the portico to the propylon.* The former consists of four massive pillars, attached for half their height to a wall, raised in the centre to form an entrance. Its front is plain, but the well-known emblem of the winged globe surmounts the gateway. It is divided by a lateral wall from a group of nine chambers, three of which are embellished with the usual hieroglyphical and allegorical figures, in colours still fresh and brilliant.

The temple was founded by Amunophis II., dedicated to a god named Mandulis, a son of Isis, rebuilt by one of the Ptolemys, and repaired by Augustus, Caligula, and Trajan. As the largest in Nubia, the Christians afterwards laid hands upon it, and a saint and several halos are strangely conspicuous among the Pagan decorations

---

* Dr. Richardson, " Travels along the Mediterranean," &c.

of one of the inner chambers. For the rest, it is "a heap of magnificent ruin;" magnificent for costliness and vastness, but not conspicuous for simplicity or sublimity of design.

At the rock-temple of *Beyt-el-Wellee*, two miles from Kalabsché, we once more find ourselves face to face with the genuine early art. It is full of the glory of the great Rameses.* It is dedicated to Amun-Ra, the Sungod; and to Kneph, or Knuph, the ram-headed god, who, in conjunction with Ptah, or Artistic Intellect, infuses life into organized beings, animates and inspires the material clay. But this little temple was sacred also to another deity, the virgin goddess Anouké, the goddess of "Home and Purity."

We approach the cave-entrance between quarried rocks covered with remarkable sculptures. On one side sits Rameses enthroned, receiving the costly tribute and servile homage of the conquered Ethiopians, among whom may be recognized, for they are named, the Prince of Cush and his two children. There are oxen and gazelles, lions and antelopes, cameleopards, apes, elephants' teeth, quaint gorgeous fans, bags of gold, and heaps of ostrich eggs; Ethiopia has poured out all her wealth to secure the victor's clemency. Proceed a few steps further, and you see the battle-scene, which was the prelude to this triumph: it glows with rude vigorous life: the foe is fleeing; a wounded chief is borne aloft by his warriors; Rameses bends his bow as he

---

* Harriet Martineau, "Eastern Life," i. 232. See also Dr. Richardson, *ut antè*.

sweeps along in his mighty chariot; a Nubian peasant boy flings dust upon his head, lamenting over his country's downfall. Turn to the other side, and your eye fastens upon other pictures of the storm and the strife—all tending to the glorification of the great sovereign who erected this temple as a thanksgiving for his victories and a monument to his fame.

The temple itself contains two chambers only; the outer court, and the adytum, or holy place. The walls, as usual, are covered with hieroglyphs and pictures. A Mohammedan hermit is said to have made his abode here, and probably he defaced much of the fine Egyptian handiwork.*

At *Dendour* stands a Romano-Egyptian temple, comparatively of little interest. It is sacred to the triad—Osiris, Horus, and Isis; and in the holy place you see nothing but a tablet, with a sculpture of Isis upon it, and a few hieroglyphic signs. In a grotto, excavated in the rock behind, yawns a burial-pit.

Of far greater interest is the next place at which our dahabeeyah comes to an anchor—*Ghirsché Housseyn*, *Guerf Hassan*, or *Gerf Hossayn* (the ancient *Tutzis*).† It is one of the strangest and wildest spots in Nubia. To reach it, the traveller, on landing, crosses a breadth of corn-field, and then a strip of yellow sandy desert. Lo, before him, a tall cliff, and in the face of it the propylon of a superb temple! It looks like the portal to a subterranean palace of the Genii. The shadow of a remote

---

* Sir G. Wilkinson, "Modern Egypt and Thebes," ii. 310–313.
† Belzoni, "Travels," i. 112.

ROMANO-EGYPTIAN TEMPLE AT DENDOUR.

antiquity is upon it. Far back, in the days of Pharaonic Egypt, it was hewn out of the rock—in the reign of the great Rameses; who dedicated it to Ptah, the "Lord of Truth," the "God of creative or artisan Intellect," and the "Maker of the Universe;" and sculptured here his symbols—the scarabaeus, whose ball of earth, the depository of its eggs, affords an apt image of the habitable

SACRED SCARABAEUS OF THE EGYPTIANS.

globe—and the frog, which typifies the embryo of the human species. Ghirsché Housseyn, as well as Memphis, was formerly named after this deity—Pthahei, or Thypthah.*

The whole of the temple, except part of the portico, is within the rock. The portico consists of five square columns on each side, which are hewn out of the live stone, with a row of circular ones in front, constructed of several blocks. Before each of the square pillars stands a colossal statue of sandstone about 18 feet high, holding a flail in one hand, the other hanging down. These are Ramessids, or male figures, with the high sphinx-

* Sir G. Wilkinson, "Manners and Customs of the Ancient Egyptians," iv.

helmet on their heads, and narrow beards under their chins; the shoulders covered with hieroglyphic inscriptions. A large gate opens from the portico into the pronaos, which measures 45 feet square, and contains two rows of three huge columns, and colossal Ramessids. The workmanship is rude, but the whole has a very impressive effect. Burckhardt asserts* that accustomed as he was to the grandeur of Egyptian temples, he was, nevertheless, struck with admiration on entering this gloomy pronaos, and beholding these immense figures standing in triumph before him. On the side walls are four recesses or niches, in each of which are three statues of the natural size, representing the different symbolical male and female figures seen on the walls of the temples of Egypt. The centre figures are generally clothed in a long dress, while the others are naked. All these, as well as the colossi, are covered with a thick coat of stucco, and had once been painted: they must then have had a splendid appearance. A door leads from the pronaos into the cella, in the middle of which are two massy pillars, and on either side a small apartment, which was probably used as a place of sepulture: on the floor of each are high stone benches, which may have served for supporting mummies, or perhaps as tables for embalming the bodies deposited in the temple.

The groups in the recesses consist of Amun-Ra, or the Sun, in the centre; and, perhaps, Anouké and Athor as his supporters. The temple extends 130 feet into the rock. Its general appearance, as Mrs. Romer remarks, when the traveller enters the excavated parts never

---

* Burckhardt, "Travels in Nubia," pp. 99, 100.

visited by the rays of the sun, is singularly solemn and imposing.* The fitful light flung upon the stupendous pillars and colossal statues by the torches which the Nubian attendants bear in their dusky hands, gives a weird and unearthly colouring to the whole scene; and it is still further intensified by the multitude of bats which, scared from their dark retreats by the unwelcome blaze, flit to and fro like malignant demons.

The next place at which we stop is *Dakkeh* (the ancient *Pselcis*), standing in solitary grandeur in the centre of a wild and dreary desert. But in the distance lies a patch of cultivated land, and a small Nubian village stands near the river-bank. This is the furthest point to the south, according to Champollion, where any monuments were built, or, more correctly speaking, reconstructed by the Ptolemys and the Caesars, whose sway, it seems evident, did not extend beyond Ibreem. As long as the Romans held Ethiopia, it was the head-quarters of a body of Germanic cavalry. Its temple was commenced by Eugamenes, the most famous of the Ethiopian kings of Egypt; it was continued by Ptolemy Euergetes and his two immediate successors; the Roman Emperor Augustus contributed to its embellishment; but it was never completed. Eugamenes dedicated it to Thoth, the god of intellect and the arts—the "Trismegistus" of the later magicians—and his emblem, the ibis, with the hawk sacred to Ra, is sculptured on the walls of the ancient *adytum*. Their surface is also covered with figures of gods and kings, the water-plants of the god Nilus, and

---

* Mrs. Romer, "Temples and Tombs of Egypt and Nubia," i. 234.

other decorative devices,—in blue, and green, and red,—still wonderfully clear and vivid. The chambers erected by the Ptolemys have some modern decorations blended with the ancient symbols, such as the Greek caduceus—the serpent-wand of Mercury—the cithara, or harp—and the olive-wreath. Here, too, are the daubs perpetrated by Coptic Christians: saints, with " huge wry faces, and flaring glories over their heads."

The traveller can ascend to the summit of the propylon by a winding flight of sixty-nine steps. The panorama spread out before him is somewhat monotonous, but grand in its monotony; the rolling sands of the Nubian Desert stretching far away into the warm soft haze of a tropical horizon, the blue riband-like course of the Nile, the strip of verdure on either bank, and the groves of palms which serve to relieve the landscape.

These propyla, as Miss Martineau remarks,[*] were the watch-towers and bulwarks of the temples in the old days when the temples of the deities were the fortifications of the country. If the inhabitants had known early enough the advantage of citadels and garrisons, perhaps the Shepherd kings might never have conquered the country; or would at least have found their conquest of it more difficult than, according to Manetho, they did. "It came to pass," says Manetho (as Josephus cites him), " I know not how, that God was displeased with us; and there came up from the east, in a strange manner, men of an ignoble race, who had the confidence to invade our country, and easily subdued it by their power, without a battle. And when they had our rulers in their

---

[*] Harriet Martineau, " Eastern Life," i. 219, 220.

hands, they burned our cities, and demolished the temples of the gods, and inflicted every kind of barbarity upon the inhabitants, slaying some, and reducing the wives and children of others to slavery." It could scarcely have happened, adds Miss Martineau, that these Shepherds "of an ignoble race," would have captured the country "without a battle," and laid hands on the rulers, if there had been such citadels as the later built temples, and such watch-towers and bulwarks as these massive propyla. Whenever you ascend any one of them, and look out through the loop-holes in the thick walls, you cannot but feel that these erections were for military full as much as religious purposes. Indeed, it is clear that the ideas were scarcely separable, after war had once made havoc in the Valley of the Nile. As for the non-military purposes of these propyla, they gave admission, through the portal in the centre, to the visitors to the temple, whether they came in the ordinary way, or in the processions which were so imposing in the ancient times.

But they were also used as observatories, whence the priests watched the starry face of the tropical heavens; and from their summits, on days of festal pomp or religious ceremony, were unfolded the mystic banners blazoned with hieroglyphic symbols. Those priests of old well understood the truth, that, for the mass of mankind, Imagination is the handmaid of Faith, and knew how to stimulate the heart by appealing to the eye. The forms and rites of their worship were not less splendid than mystical. There was the shrine of the deity borne aloft by shaven and white-robed *flamens;* then came flags with emblematic figures of the god or hero embroidered on their folds; and long trains of suppliants followed, with red oxen, fruits and cakes, turtle-doves and incense, as offerings. The king, himself the arch-priest and visible representation of the Supreme, shone conspicuous in all the splendour of Eastern pomp; and crowds of warriors, with their bows and spears, enlivened the scene; and music filled the air with the varied sounds of joy, or grief, or humility, or triumph; while in the dim, dark recesses of the adytum, rested the sacred wings of the god whose manifold attributes were defined by a myriad fanciful allegories. All was adapted to enchain the attention of the "common herd;" and yet in all lay hidden, for the thoughtful, a treasury of suggestive lore.

But while thus musing at Dakkeh, our dahabeeyah waits for us. We must resume our voyage. There is little in the scenery to interest us here, the Desert stretching down to the very margin of the river. We pass the village of *Seegala*—which is surrounded on all sides by the lonely waste, on whose border rises the sand-column, to stride giant-like across leagues of wilderness, and fall devouringly upon the unhappy caravan—and pause a moment at *Wady Sebou*, or *Sabooa*, the "Valley of the Lions;" so named from the broken sphinxes that guard the approach to its rock-hewn temple. There are four on each hand as you go up to the propylon; but one is wholly covered, and five others more or less completely hidden. A couple are unburied, but their features have almost disappeared. The head of the one uncovered is nearly complete, and very impressive in the awful serenity of its countenance. Two rude statues, about ten feet in height, look out upon the river with lack-lustre eyes: they are unbearded males, roughly executed. Opposite to the entrance a colossus lies on the ground, shattered and half-buried in the sand. Within the propylon is the portico, or pronaos, with five columns on its two longer sides. In front of each, and attached to it, stands a Ramessid or colossal figure, 16 feet in height, having the arms crossed upon the breast, with the flail in one hand, and the priest's wand in the other. The whole fabric is very ancient, belonging to the Ramesean period. Burckhardt suggests that it afforded a model for the later Egyptian architects.* The two statues in front of the propylon, he says, are the miniatures of those in front of the Memnonium, and the sphinxes are seen at Karnak. It is certain that this is one of the most venerable of the Nubian sanctuaries.

Yet of a still remoter antiquity must be the temple at *Derr*. Derr, let us note, is the capital of Nubia, a large town of mud-built houses, scattered among gardens of herbs, melons, and cucumbers, and groves of palm-trees, on the eastern bank of the river. The governor's house, or palace, is mostly built of burned brick, and has a magnificent sycamore in front of it.

The temple is partly hewn out of the rock, only its area and portico being in the open air. The area had once eight pillars, of which only the bases remain; and numerous pictures on its walls, of which scarcely a trace is discernible. The corridor, or portico, is faced with four Ramessid pillars—pillars supporting huge figures,

* Burckhardt, "Travels in Nubia," p. 90.

decorated with the usual symbols. The sanctuary is the rock part of the temple—a hall adorned with six square columns. The walls are sculptured in what has been termed "intaglio relevato;"—that is, the outlines are cut in a groove, whose depth affords the requisite relief to the impression. From its design we perceive that the temple was built by Rameses the Great, or, more probably, was commenced before his time, and completed by that most restless and ubiquitous of architect-kings. Here are his lion, his children, his enemies, his gods, his wealth, his triumphs.

The adytum is small, and its images have vanished. There are two lateral chambers of no importance. The entire depth in the rock is about 110 feet.

Once more we are on the Nile, and making our way through the Nubian sands. At times we light upon very pleasant spots of greenery, upon patches covered with the yellow blossoms of the cotton-shrub, upon fields enriched with blooming crops of grain and pulse. At *Tosko* we ascend some dangerous rapids formed by a reef of rocks, and pass under the lofty crag crowned by the castle of *Ibreem*, the *Premnis* of Strabo, and the *Primis* of Pliny, which was defended against Petronius, the lieutenant of Augustus Caesar, by a masculine queen, called in history Candace; though Candace was unquestionably a title, and not a name. It was afterwards occupied by Roman and Saracenic garrisons. Its height above the river, which is at this point about a quarter of a mile broad, has been estimated at 200 feet.*

* Kenrick, "Ancient Egypt," ii. 464.

Our voyage now brings us to one of the most famous spots in Nubia—ABOU-SIMBEL, or IPSAMBÛL, the chief wonder, perhaps, of all the Upper Valley of the Nile; the ancient *Napata*,* and capital of the Ethiopian kingdom.

For generations the drifting sands of the Desert accumulated over its buried sanctuaries, and nothing was visible but the head of a single colossal statue to excite the wonder of the traveller. No one inquired what this solitary ruin *meant*—whether it marked the site of a city, or a palace, or a tomb—until, in the year 1817, the enterprising Belzoni, who possessed a peculiar genius for such achievements, accompanied by Captains Irby and Mangles, undertook an excavation. Their toil was well rewarded, for it brought to light a monument not unjustly attributed by Champollion to the grandest epoch of Pharaonic civilization. Here, exclaims Warburton, the daring Genius of Ethiopian architecture ventured to enter into rivalry with Nature's greatness, and found her material in the very mountains that seemed to bid defiance to her efforts.† You can conceive nothing more singular and impressive, says Mrs. Romer, than the façade of this great temple.‡ From Burckhardt to Miss Martineau, every writer has run riot in eulogium. Ipsambûl, says Sir F. Henniker,§ is the *ne plus ultra* of Egyptian labour, and in itself an ample recompense for the journey.

There are two temples at Ipsambûl, one much larger than the other, but both hewn out of the solid sandstone

---

* Ritter, "Erdkunde," i. 571.
† E. Warburton, "The Crescent and the Cross," chap. xiii.
‡ Mrs. Romer, "Temples and Tombs of Egypt and Nubia," i. 207.
§ Sir F. Henniker, "Notes During a Visit to Egypt," &c., p. 160. See also Champollion, Dr Richardson, and Burckhardt.

rock. Let us first visit the more considerable, the Ammonium, dedicated to Osiris, or Amun-Ra.

Here, an area of about 187 feet in breadth, and 86 feet in height, is hewn out of the mountain, smooth, except for the relievos. The façade is composed of a vast gateway, flanked on either hand by two colossal statues of Rameses II., seated, and each about 65 feet high. There they sit enthroned, as they have sat for ages, and

TEMPLE OF OSIRIS, IPSAMBÛL.

their motionless faces look out upon the desert with a kind of stony calm. From the shoulder to the elbow they measure 15 feet 6 inches; the ears 3 feet 6 inches; the face 7 feet; the beard 5 feet 6 inches; across the shoulders 25 feet 4 inches. The faces are exquisitely moulded. The beauty of the curves is surprising in the stone; the fidelity of the rounding of the muscles, and the grace of the flowing lines of the cheek and jaw.* It is remarkable that the proportions of these colossal

* Harriet Martineau, "Eastern Life," i. 197.

visages, though the artist could have had only a life-size model to guide him, are admirably harmonious.

Between the legs of these gigantic Ramessids are placed smaller statues; mere pigmies compared with their huge neighbours, and yet considerably larger than human size.

The doorway is about 20 feet high. Above it stands a statue of Isis, wearing the moon as a turban—or, as

INTERIOR OF TEMPLE OF OSIRIS, IPSAMBÛL.

some say, of Osiris—of about the same dimensions as the doorway, and on either side are some huge hieroglyphical bas-reliefs; while the whole façade is finished by a cornice and line of hieroglyphs and quaintly-carved figures, surmounted by a frieze of sculptured monkeys, twenty-one in number, and each measuring 8 feet in height, and 6 feet across the shoulders.

On entering the temple you find yourself within "a

vast and gloomy hall, such as Eblis might have given Vathek audience in;" a reception-chamber not unworthy of the most splendid of the Egyptian kings. As soon as the eye becomes accustomed to the gloom, there gradually reveals itself, above and around, "a vast aisle, with pillars formed of eight colossal giants, upon whom the light of heaven has never shone." The tops of their mitre-shaped head-dresses, each bearing in front the serpent, the emblem of royalty, for each is an image of the magnificent Rameses, nearly touch the roof. They are all perfectly alike; all bear the crosier and flagellum; and every face is full of deep and expressive meaning.

A RAMESSID AT IPSAMBÛL.

" Vigilant, serene, benign, here they sit, teaching us to inquire reverentially into the early powers and condition of that human mind which was capable of such conceptions of abstract qualities as are represented in their forms."

These images of the great king are backed by enormous pillars, behind which run two great galleries whose walls are profusely embellished with hieroglyphical representations of battle and victory; of conquering warriors, fleeing foemen, bleeding victims, cities besieged, whole companies of chariots, long trains of soldiers and captives—all painted with a surprising truth and vigour.

The hall measures 57 feet by 52. It opens into a smaller chamber, 22 feet high, 37 broad, and $25\frac{1}{2}$ feet long, which contains four pillars, about 3 feet square; its walls are also enriched with fine hieroglyphs in excellent preservation. Beyond it lies a shorter chamber, but of the same width, leading into the adytum (23 feet long and 12 feet broad), where, in front of four large figures—Amun-Ra, Khem (or Egypt), Kneph, and Osiris—seated on rocky thrones, stands a simple altar of the living rock.

On the right side of the great hall, entering into the temple, may be seen two doors at a short distance from each other, which lead into separate chambers; the first, 39 feet long and $11\frac{1}{2}$ feet wide; the other, $48\frac{1}{2}$ feet by 13 feet 3 inches. At the lateral corners of the entrance from the first into the second apartment are other doors, each conducting into a room hewn out of the solid rock, but with no visible means of ventilation, and each $22\frac{1}{2}$ feet long by 10 feet broad. These rooms open into others, 43 feet in length and 11 feet in width. The six lateral chambers are almost wholly covered with graceful representations of offerings to the gods—lamps, vases, flasks, and piles of cake and fruit. The lotus is painted in every stage of growth. And the boat—a frequent symbol everywhere—is incessantly repeated: the seated figure in the convolution at bow and stern, the central pavilion, and the paddle hanging over the side. One of these boats is borne aloft by a procession of priests, as a shrine, upon poles of palm-trunks lashed together. Many of the hieroglyphics are unfinished; yet, though merely sketched, they give one a very favourable idea of the Egyptian manner of drawing.

The smaller temple, likewise entirely excavated in the sandstone rock, was dedicated to Isis by Nofre-Ari, queen of Rameses the Great, and dates from about

TEMPLE OF ISIS AT IPSAMBÛL.

1320 B.C. Either side of the doorway is ornamented by three statues, 35 feet high, sculptured in relief, and standing erect, with their arms hanging stiffly down. The two central represent Nofre-Ari, the queen, as Athor, whose gentle face is surmounted by the usual crown— the moon contained within the cow's horns. The other images are those of Rameses and his eldest son. Beneath each hand is placed an upright statue, 7 feet in height, which does not, however, rise above the knees of its principal. These are the children of the royal couple.

The part of the rock which has been hewn down for the façade of the temple measures 111 feet in length.*

The devices begin on the north side, with a figure of Rameses brandishing his falchion, as if about to strike. The goddess behind him lifts her hand in suplication for the victim; while Osiris, in front, holds forth the great knife, as if to command the slaughter. He is seated there as the judge, and decides the fate of the nations conquered by the Egyptian king. The next object is a colossal statue of about 30 feet high, wrought in a deep recess of the rock: it is standing, and two tall feathers rise up from the middle of the head-dress, with the globe or moon on each side. Then comes a mass of hieroglyphics, which are also thickly sculptured on each side of the door, and above them are seated Osiris and the hawk-headed deity. On each side of the passage, as you enter the temple, offerings are presented to Isis, who holds in her hand the lotus-headed sceptre, surrounded with numerous emblems and inscriptions. This hall is supported by six square pillars, all bearing the head of Athor on the front face of their capitals; the other three faces being occupied with sculptures, once gaily painted, and still showing blue, red, and yellow colours. The shafts are covered with hieroglyphs, and representations of Osiris, Isis, Kneph, and other gods.

Within the outer or entrance hall is a transverse corridor, ending in two rude chambers. And beyond the corridor lies the sanctuary, or *adytum*, where Isis appears in all her majesty, with the emblematic disk of night's beautiful luminary above her head. In another part she

* Dr. Richardson, " Travels along the Mediterranean," &c., 428, 429.

stands, as a cow, in a boat surrounded by water plants; the king and queen presenting rare gifts to this "Lady of Aboshek, the foreign land."

The temple, which is only a few yards from the river's brink, and about twenty feet above the present level of its water, extends seventy-six feet into the rock. A number of ovals, or *cartouches* as Champollion calls them, containing the name and prænomen of Rameses the Great, are cut in several places of the square border that encloses the façade of the temple like a frame, and on the buttresses between the colossal figures.*

Napata marks the boundary of the Roman Conquest south of Egypt, and was captured and plundered by the Romans in B.C. 22 by Petronius, the lieutenant of Augustus.

---

* The two lions of red granite—one bearing the name of Amunophis III., the other of Amuntuoneh—now at the entrance of the Gallery of Antiquities in the British Museum, were brought from Napata by Lord Purdhoe (the late Duke of Northumberland). They belong to the period of the 18th dynasty of kings.

CHAPTER III.

GEBEL-ADHA—WADY HALFA—THE SECOND CATARACT—THE TEMPLE OF SOLEB—MEROË, AND ITS ANTIQUITIES—RUINS AT NAJA AND EL-MESAOURAT—THE SACRED BOAT.

> ......Wild and desolate
> Those courts, where once the mighty sate;
> Nor longer on those mouldering towers
> Were seen the past of fruits and flowers.....
> Neither priest nor rites were there.
> MOORE.

IN the cliff, nearly opposite Ipsambûl, is excavated another rock-temple, called *Gebel-Adha*, which was used in later times as a Christian church. It was a curious sight, remarks Mr. Warburton, to see images of our Saviour and the Virgin blazoned in glowing colours on these walls and roofs, surrounded by trophies and memorials of the idols whose worship they had swept away. Steps, also hewn in the rock, descended to a certain point towards the river, and then suddenly ceased: a proof, among others, that the level of the Nile was much higher (even so lately as the Christian consecration of this temple) than at present.*

* Eliot Warburton, "The Crescent and the Cross," chap. xii.

The ordinary route of Nile voyagers terminates at the Wady Halfa, where begins a succession of rapids and rocks, stretching up the river for about one hundred miles to the Second Cataract, which is impassable for boats ascending the river. The immediate country is generally beautiful as well as fertile. In some places the river broadens into a channel of four or five miles span, enclosing numerous romantic islands clothed with a luxuriant vegetation.

Near the landing-place at Wady Halfa moulder the ruins of a temple begun, if not wholly erected, by two of the Theban kings soon after the expulsion of the Shepherd race, and long before the grand structures of Thebes had been conceived by the genius of Rameses. "About this time," says Miss Martineau, "Moses was watching the erection of the great obelisk (which we call Cleopatra's Needle) at Heliopolis, where he studied." The remains are few, and only remarkable on account of their extreme antiquity, and because they exhibit the rudiments of the so-called Doric column.

From this spot it is customary to make a pilgrimage to the rock of *Abou-Seir*, or *Abooseer:* a steep and craggy hill of red sandstone, about 200 feet high, which overlooks the whole range of the Cataract, and commands a far view of the Nubian wilderness—of that wide, desolate waste, which was once a fertile and populous kingdom. The only living things are a partridge or two, a gazelle, and a jerboa; though in some remote recesses the hyaenas lurk, and in the shallow waters of the river the crocodiles are basking unseen. The whole scene is composed of desert, river, and black basaltic rocks, except

VIEW OF THE SECOND CATARACT FROM THE ROCK OF ABOU-SEIR.

where, against the dim horizon, may be traced the rounded and softened outlines of the blue Arabian hills.

At a considerable distance above the Second Cataract, and far beyond the usual limits of Nile-travel, is the *Temple of Soleb;* of sufficient interest to justify a brief description.

The remains of two sphinxes guard either side of the

TEMPLE OF AMUN-RA, SOLEB.

approach, which terminated at a flight of stone steps leading to the main building. The front of the portal, now in chaotic ruin, measured 175 feet in length, and the breadth of the steps was not less than 57 feet. The wall is 24 feet thick, and honeycombed with numerous cells, whose object cannot now be determined.

The first chamber, 100 feet broad and 89 feet deep, is embellished on three sides by a row of pillars, making in the whole, when perfect, thirty columns. The diameter of the base of each is 5 feet 7 inches; the height about 40 feet. They are covered with hieroglyphics. Only a few columns are left entire.

The second chamber had twenty-four pillars, all of which have been prostrated and shattered by some sudden subsidence of the ground. A few feet of masonry indicate the site of the adytum, which appears to have contained twelve columns, sculptured with figures about 3 feet high. From these it has been conjectured that the temple was dedicated to Amun-Ra. The general character of its architecture is light and graceful.

Our ascent of the river terminates at *Meroë*, or *Merawe*, a portion of the ancient Ethiopia.* A glance at the map of Nubia will show the reader that at Old Dongola, in latitude 18° N. nearly, the Nile suddenly turns to the north-east, ascending above the 20th parallel, when it retraces its course in a southerly direction to its point of confluence with the Tacazzé. The peninsular tract thus enclosed formed the ancient kingdom of Meroë (Μερόη). The exuberant fertility of its soil, its numerous animals, and its valuable mineral deposits, made it, at a very remote time, the seat of a powerful kingdom, which attracted thither a constant stream of commerce, and exported its treasures to Carthage, Arabia, and India. About 1000 B.C. it was esteemed one of the leading states of the world, though nominally a tributary of the Egyptian Empire. Two centuries and a half later it regained its

---

* That is, the country of the "sun-burned" (Αἰθίοψς).

independence, under King Sabaco, and for eighty years held Egypt in subjection. It was afterwards subdued by Cambyses, who fortified the capital-town, and called it Meroë. Gradually the Egyptians emigrated thither; the country lost its ancient character; and, after being invaded and conquered by the Romans, it sank into a decay as rapid as its former prosperity was surprising. Even in the reign of Nero nothing remained of the past splendour of its capital, but piles of shapeless ruins and fragments of mighty buildings.

There would seem to have been two great Cushite cities: Napata (the present *Gebel-el-Birkel*), and Meroë, which retains its ancient name.

Meroë is situated about 560 miles above Assouan, between the Fifth and Sixth Cataracts, in latitude 17° north. It is chiefly conspicuous for its great necropolis, whose eighty pyramids, though far inferior to those of Egypt in size, surpass them in architectural excellence. An immense plain is literally crowded with them! A modern traveller counted eight different groups of these mysterious piles—temples, tombs, observatories, whatever may have been their real character—one containing twenty-five, one twenty-three, and one thirteen pyramids. The loftiest is 160 feet in height. Each has a portico, invariably facing towards the east. Each is built of granite. The corners are partly ornamented, and the walls of the pyla are decorated with sculpture, in which some of the figures appear to be employed in making offerings for the departed. Isis, Osiris, Horus, and Thoth, also figure conspicuously.

This necropolis is situated near a place now called

Assom. At two neighbouring villages, *Woad Naja* and *El-Mesaourat*, the ruins consist chiefly of temples. Those of the former place lie about twenty miles south-east of Shendy, and nearly the same distance from the Nile. The remains of the principal edifice show that it was dedicated to the god Amun. An avenue of huge rams couched upon massive pedestals leads into an open

TEMPLE AT MEROË.

portico of ten columns; out of which, after threading his way through a similar avenue, the traveller arrives at the pylon. Adjoining is a colonnade of eight pillars, and beyond this a hall opens into the adytum. Columns, walls, and doorways are of hewn stone; the remainder of the structure of bricks, with a coating which still retains traces of the original painting. The sculptures of gods, and kings, and queens; of attendants making oblations; of the insignia of royal power, exhibit a remarkable energy and truthfulness. But from their general character, as well as from the arrangement of the temple, we may reasonably infer that it belongs to a remote antiquity.

The western temple is smaller, but more copiously embellished. War-pictures adorn the pyla; and the king and queen appear with an eagle and a globe over their heads, and the emblem of royal power on their headdress. It is noticeable that here the queens are represented as heroines and conquerors, as the independent wearers of royalty. And it is in reference to this very kingdom Strabo remarks, that among the Ethiopians the women are also armed. From other historical sources we gather that no Salic law prevailed in Meroë. A long succession of queens, with the title Candace, must have reigned here; and even when, in course of time, the seat of the empire was removed from Meroë to Napata, near Gebel-el-Birkel, a female sovereign, so distinguished, exercised the supreme power. It is therefore in consonance with Ethiopian usage to see a queen in warlike array by her consort's side, though the custom is peculiar to that celebrated people.

The colossal figures at Naja are described as of surpassing excellence. , Every traveller praises their boldness of outline and vividness of expression, no less than the general richness and perfection of the workmanship.

Cailliaud, the French traveller, is our principal authority for the antiquities at *El-Mesaourat*, which he describes as an extensive valley in the Desert, eight hours' journey from Shendy towards the south-east, and eighteen miles from the Astayrus. The ruins here are considerable. They consist of eight small temples, all connected by corridors and terraces, and the whole forming an immense edifice, surrounded by a double enclosure. From the main central building radiate, in every direction, connecting passages and galleries, which vary from 185 to 300 feet in length. Each temple has its pylon and sanctuary; and all the buildings are placed in an exact order, consisting of eight temples or sanctuaries, as already stated, forty-one chambers, twenty-four courts, three galleries, and fourteen staircases or flights of steps. The remains cover an area of ground nearly half a mile in circumference.

The different parts, however, are not on the colossal scale to which the Egyptian antiquities have accustomed us. The largest temple, says Cailliaud,* is only 51 feet long; some of the pillars are decorated with figures in the Egyptian style; others in the same portico are fluted like the Grecian: on the base of one seemed discernible the traces of a zodiac. Time and the elements seem to have been willing to spare to us the observatory of Meroë. It excites one's wonder to discover so few hieroglyphics in this mass of ruins; the six columns which form the portico of the central temple alone present a few examples, for all the other walls are free from sculpture. Six hundred paces from the ruins lie the remains of two other small temples, and also of a considerable tank, surrounded by little hills, which must have protected it from the sand. But there are no traces

* Cailliaud, "Voyage à Meroe, au Fleuve Blanc," &c. (Paris, 1826-27).

of any city, no heaps of débris, no tombs. It is the opinion of Cailliaud that a college or seminary of learning was established on this spot: the form of the building and the style of the architecture seem to prove it; but the city itself must have been situated in the vicinity of the sepulchres, where the pyramids are still found.

Heeren, in his "Historical Researches," concludes from the facts recorded by Cailliaud, that El-Mesaourat was the site of the once famous "Oracle of Jupiter-Ammon." He remarks that a mere glance at the ground-plan of the ruins would support this opinion. Such a maze of passages and courts could only be intended as an imposing introduction for the neophyte or votary to the secret sanctuary in the midst. According to Diodorus, he observes, the Temple of Jupiter did not stand in the city of Meroë, but at some distance from it, in the Desert. When, again, a certain sovereign resolved to free himself from the dominion of the priesthood, he marched, with a company of soldiers, to the sequestered spot where the sanctuary with the golden temple stood, and surprising the dismayed priests, put them and their attendants to death. Nor is the smallness of the edifice any objection to this view of the subject, for the same remark might be applied to the Ammonium in the Libyan Desert. It was probably intended only as an asylum for the "sacred ship," which is understood to have been placed between the pillars of the sacred shrine. Its locality in the wilderness appears to be less extraordinary, if you reflect that it was situated on one of the great routes of commercial intercourse between the Mediterranean and the Red Sea.

Here we stand, if we may accept the theory of Heeren,* on that remarkable spot which the ancients regarded as the cradle of the arts and sciences; where hieroglyphic writing was invented; where temples and pyramids had already sprung up, while Egypt remained in ignorance of their existence. Hence flowed the mighty stream of civilization, following the course of the Nile itself, until Greece also drank of its living waters; and gathering in volume as they rolled westward, they overspread in time the limits of the Roman Empire, and extended their beneficial influence to the furthest bounds of Christendom.

In describing the antiquities, both of Egypt and Nubia, we have sometimes had occasion to refer to the "sacred ship," or "boat," which appears among their sculptures. The king called Sesostris is said to have dedicated one of cedar-wood to Amun, or Ammon, the chief deity and tutelary spirit of Thebes; it was 420 feet long, and resplendent with gold on the outside and silver within. The use of this emblem is supposed to have denoted the foreign extraction of their priesthood and religious rites, and to have kept alive in the minds of the worshippers the distant land from whence their creed was originally derived.† Once a year, says Diodorus Siculus, the Greek historian, the sanctuary or shrine of Zeus was borne across the river in solemn pomp to the Libyan bank, and after a few days brought back, as if the god were returning from Ethiopia. This grand procession is

---

* Heeren, "Historical Researches," &c., i. 403-406.
† Dr. Russell, "Nubia and Abyssinia," p. 258; Heeren, "Historical Researches," &c., i. 301.

represented, as we have seen, among the sculptures of the Great Temple at Karnak; the sacred ship of Amun floats on the Nile, with its entire equipment, and is towed along by another boat. It is probable that Homer alludes to this ceremony when he describes Jupiter's twelve days' visit to the Ethiopians: he had heard of it from some traveller's tradition, from some floating legend, or vague recollection, and adapted it to the Greek deity :—

> "The sire of gods, and all th' ethereal train,
> On the warm limits of the furthest main,
> Now mix with mortals, nor disdain to grace
> The feasts of Aethiopia's blameless race;
> Twelve days the Powers indulge the genial rite,
> Returning with the twelfth revolving light."
> HOMER, *Iliad*, bk. i. (*Pope's Transl.*)

CHAPTER IV.

THE LIBYAN OASES—THEIR EXPLORERS—THE GREAT OASIS—THE LITTLE OASIS—SIWAH, THE NORTHERN OASIS—THEIR ANTIQUITIES, AND ORACLES.

......The tufted isles
That verdant rise amid the Libyan wild.
THOMSON.

THOUGH they are not included in the Nile Valley, our view of Ethiopian antiquities would be incomplete if we omitted all reference to the Libyan Oases. These fertile spots lie amidst a dreary level, sunken in the stratum of limestone, like basins of water. The Coptic word *ouahé* literally means "an inhabited place;" and an oasis is the solitary strip of vegetation and verdure where the Libyan tribes are able to pitch their tents.* Elsewhere, all is burning stone—leafless, waterless; no shelter from the fierce rays of the tropical sun, which at noonday, strikes the wanderer with deadly shafts of fire; no springs where he can slake his torturing thirst; no pleasant hill or leafy grove where he can rest his wearied limbs. Nor is the oasis in itself an Armida's garden of enchantment—

---

* Oasis is also said to be derived from the Arabic *wadi*, a ravine, corrupted by the Greeks into οἀσίς.

a Happy Valley, like that of Rasselas: it is attractive chiefly from its contrast with the surrounding desolation, just as a mouldy crust of bread seems an inexpressibly delicious viand to the poor wretch who has hungered through days and nights of famine. By the Greeks and Romans they were used as places of banishment; and many an earnest Christian, in the early days of persecution, was doomed to linger out his life in the oases of the Libyan Desert.* They lie a few days' journey from the Nile, and were known to the Egyptians during the twelfth dynasty under the name of Sutur-Khenu. They are first mentioned by Herodotus in his vivid narration of the destruction of the Persian hosts by the blasts of the simoom. The Persians, after their conquest of Egypt in 525 B.C., seem to have permanently occupied them. Every schoolboy knows that one of them— the Siwah Oasis, and its Temple of Amun or Ammon— was visited by Alexander the Great, and that the priests declared the Greek conqueror the son of the god, and the destined lord of the entire globe. They are also described by Strabo, Pliny, Ptolemy, Olympiodorus; by the Arab travellers Edrissi (1150 A.D.) and Abulfeda (1240 A.D.); by Leo Africanus (1513 A.D.); and, among modern explorers, by Browne (1792), Cailliaud (1819), Minutoli (1824), Sir Archibald Edmonstone (1819), and Mr. Hoskins (1837). The ancients only knew of three oases, but they are really five in number.† These are:—

* The poet Juvenal was banished there by the Emperor Domitian; and Athanasius is supposed to have found in them an asylum during the supremacy of the Arians. See Canon Kingsley's book on "The Hermits."

† See Hoskins, "Visit to the Great Oasis" (London 1837); Sir A. Edmonstone, "Journey to Two of the Oases" (1819); Modern Traveller, "Egypt," vol. ii., &c.

1. The *Great Oasis* (Oasis Magna):—chief town, *El-Khargeh;*
2. The *Little Oasis* (Oasis Minor):—chief town, *El-Dakkel;*
3. The *Northern Oasis,* or *El-Siwah;*
4. The *Oasis of El-Farafreh;* and
5. The *Oasis Trinytheos,* or *El-Bacharieh:*—chief town, Zabou.

1. The *Great Oasis* lies about 90 miles west of the Nile. It consists of an extensive depression of the soil, watered by a stream which rises nearer the village of Genah, on the north-west, and after traversing the oasis disappears in the sand. On its banks flourish groves of palms and acacias; and the ground is clothed with a coarse verdure, which, after the rains, blooms with an attractive freshness. Springs are numerous, though all strongly impregnated with sulphur and iron, and so warm that the water cannot be drunk until it has been cooled in an earthen jar. They continue full, however, all the year; a blessing which can only be appreciated by travellers in the Desert.

This is the first stage of the Darfur caravan, which starts from El-Siout,—about four days' journey. It is nearly the same distance from Farshout, the second stage.

The principal ruins lie about seven miles from El-Khargeh, the metropolis of the oasis. They are situated in the midst of a rich wood of palm, acacia, and other trees, with a bright stream of water in front. The entrance to the great temple (468 feet in length) is through a *dromos*, or avenue, of ten columns on each side, now prostrate in hopeless chaos. The façade of the temple, which was dedicated to Amun-Ra, is profusely embellished with colossal figures and hieroglyphic inscriptions. Through a finely sculptured doorway the traveller passes into a superb hall, 60 feet by 54, with twelve pillars, each 13 feet in circumference. A species of screen separates it from the second chamber, which measures 56 feet by 18, and is traced all over with figures and other carvings on stucco, which have once been painted. The third apartment, 31 feet by 29, is also ornamented; and the carvings in the *adytum* or sanctuary, 20 feet by 8, are of the richest workmanship, though much blackened and defaced by smoke.

To the east of the temple stand three detached propyla, or gateways, of remarkable interest. Among the figures sculptured on the first propylon may be seen a colossal representation of Darius making offerings to Amun-Ra, Osiris, and Isis. On the roof are four eagles or vultures, with outstretched wings, painted red and blue. The carvings on the second are much defaced. On the third remains an inscription, in Greek letters, containing a rescript, in the second year of the Emperor Galba, enjoining certain reforms in the Egyptian administration. An avenue of sphinxes formerly led up to the temple in one direction.

In the vicinity lies a superb necropolis, or cemetery, containing nearly two hundred tombs, each the receptacle of a number of mummies. Most of them are square, and crowned with domes, while the columns placed around, with their Doric and Corinthian capitals, show that they belong to a comparatively recent period. One large sepulchre is divided into aisles like a church; and that it was used as such by the Christian exiles is clearly shown from the traces of saints painted on the walls. All bear the Greek cross, and the famous Egyptian hieroglyph, the *crux ansata,* or cross with a handle, whose original purport cannot be determined, but which the Christians naturally adopted as an emblem of their faith. The origin of these remarkable sepulchres is, to some extent, involved in obscurity. As they were designed for the reception of mummies, they can hardly be later than the first century; for the practice of embalming was discontinued soon after the introduction of Christianity; and if they were constructed by the Romans, they must date from a period posterior to the conquests of Pompey, B.C. 52.

There are several other remains in the vicinity of El-Khargeh, in which the relics of the Egyptian creed appear combined with the symbols of the Christian worship, leading to the inference that these edifices were repaired in the early ages of our faith after being abandoned by their ancient occupants.*

2. The *Little Oasis,* or *El-Dakkel,* is a valley surrounded with rocks, about 12 miles long and 6 miles broad, four or five days' journey to the south-east of Siwah, which appears at one time to have been wholly cultivated, and to have fully repaid the labourer's toil. The remains are those of a Ptolemaic temple, several rock-tombs, a Christian church, a necropolis, and a Roman triumphal arch. There are some hot springs, and especially one, 60 feet

* Dr. Russell. " History of Ancient and Modern Egypt," p. 361

deep, whose temperature varies several times in the twenty-four hours. The natives of this sequestered spot live chiefly upon rice, and their whole wealth consists of a few camels, donkeys, cows, buffaloes, goats, sheep, and the ubiquitous date-palm.

3. *El-Siwah*, the *Ammonium*, or the *Northern Oasis*, which has been repeatedly visited, lies to the west of the Natron Lakes, in lat. 29° 12' north, and long. 26° 6' east, and about 120 miles from the Nile river. It extends three miles in length, and between eight and nine in breadth. A large portion of the soil blooms with the tufted crests of the palm, but in its gardens abound the pomegranate and the fig, the olive, the vine, the apricot, the plum, and even the apple. Tepid springs occur throughout the district, and a salt lake at Arachieh, which is regarded with superstitious veneration. The mythical Fountain of the Sun wells forth in a pleasant grove of date-trees at Siwah Shargieh. It was dedicated of old, as well as a small temple that stood upon its bank, to the great solar god, Amun-Ra. Travellers describe it as a small marsh, rather than a well, about 90 feet long and 60 feet broad. Its waters, which are remarkable for their transparency, undergo a diurnal change: they are warmer in the night than in the day, and every morning throw off a thick vapour or steam. The bubbles constantly rising to the surface reveal the chemical action which they undergo.

The two chief villages in the oasis are Shargieh and Kebir: the population exceeds 8000.

At Ummebeda, about two miles' distance from the rock-built town of Siwah, moulder the ruins of an Egyptian temple, which most antiquaries agree in regarding as the ancient "Temple of Ammon." The vestiges of a triple enclosure, enormous blocks of granite lying prostrate, and portions still standing of the walls and gateway, prove that it must have been a superb and massive pile. The only chamber which can now be distinctly traced was 112 feet in length; the whole area occupies a rectangular space about 360 feet by 300. The decorations are of the later Egyptian character, and embody representations of the ram-headed god, processions of priests, councils of deities, and of other objects common to these sacred structures; but time, and, perhaps, human barbarism have dealt so violently with these interesting ruins that enough remains to stimulate—far too little to gratify—the antiquary's legitimate curiosity.

Minutoli believes this temple to have been erected by Nekt-har-hebi (Nectanebus I., about 387–369 B.C.), in honour of the god Khnum, who was here identified or blended with Amun—Amun Khnumis, or Chembis. He was the great water-deity, and consequently presided over the water to which the formation and conservation of the oasis were due. Here was the celebrated "Oracle of Ammon"—the "Jupiter-Ammon" of the Greeks—which obtained so world-wide a renown that Alexander the Great marched through the Desert to consult its priests (B.C. 331). The response was delivered either by some movement of the statue of the god, or by the appearance of a spirit or phantom. When it first rose into repute is uncertain; it fell into decay after the establishment of Christianity.

The antiquities of the Siwah Oasis are very numerous. Among them may be noted a series of rock-tombs, on a magnificent scale, excavated in a neighbouring mountain. Temple after temple, catacombs, churches, and convents —all in ruins, but all hallowed by sacred associations— spread far away to the westward, and testify to the existence in this region of a large population at some remote period. At a short distance from the sacred lake of Arachieh are situated the remains of a beautiful Doric temple, which, occurring in the heart of the Libyan Desert, cannot fail to excite the traveller's wonder. Other ancient relics are crumbling among the sands of these dreary wastes, whose origin and history will never be known to man ; oblivion has descended upon them.

Of the other oases it seems unnecessary to speak. They resemble the more celebrated in their physical features ; their antiquities are of little interest.

APPENDIX.

THE SUEZ CANAL.

HE Isthmus of Suez, as every reader well knows, is a neck of land, about seventy-two miles wide in its narrowest part, which extends from the Mediterranean on the north to the Gulf of Suez on the south, and connects the continents of Asia and Africa. It is a desert of sand and sandstone, whose dreariness is occasionally relieved by a salt lake, or saline swamp, but which is almost entirely destitute of fresh water. The principal interest, however, which, from a remote antiquity, has attached to the region, lies in the possibility of opening up a communication through it by means of a ship-canal, so as to save the long and often dangerous voyage round the Cape of Good Hope. The route to India, so far as passengers, and to a moderate extent merchandise, are concerned, has of late years been greatly shortened by the construction of a line of rail; but it was obvious to every observer that a ship-canal would be an infinitely more important boon to commerce.

It is a well known fact that, in ancient times, an indirect line of canal *did* connect the two seas, the Mediterranean and the Red Sea. According to Herodotus, it was partially executed by Pharaoh Necho, or Nechao (see p. 55); but by whom it was completed we can only conjecture; some authorities say Darius, others (much more probably) the Ptolemys. It began at about a mile and a half north of Suez, and struck in a north-westerly direction, availing

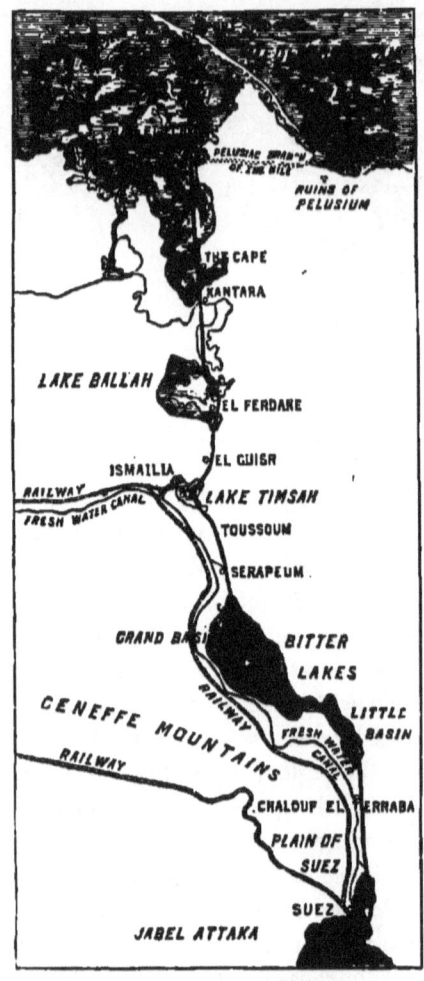

CHART OF SUEZ CANAL.

itself of a series of natural hollows, to Bubastis, on the Pelusiac or eastern branch of the Nile. Its length was 92 miles (60 of which were excavated by human hands), its width from 108 to 165 feet, and its depth 15 feet. After a while it became silted up with sand; was restored by Trajan; was again choked and rendered useless; was re-opened after the Saracenic conquest of Egypt by Amrou the Arab general, and named the "Canal of the Prince of the Faithful;" and finally filled with the never-resting sands in 767 A.D.

Upwards of ten centuries passed before any attempt was made to renew a communication between the two seas. Then the idea occurred to the ingenious mind of Bonaparte; but as his engineers erroneously reported that there was a difference of level between the Mediterranean and the Red Sea to the extent of thirty feet, he suffered it to drop. In 1847 a scientific commission, appointed by England, France, and Austria, ascertained that the two seas had exactly the same mean level. The only noticeable distinction was, that at the one end, there is a tide of 6 feet 6 inches, and 1 foot 6 inches at the other. Mr. Robert Stephenson, the great English engineer, coming to a similar result in 1853, declared that no navigable canal could be constructed, and he then laid down the existing railroad between Cairo and Suez as a substitute.

There arose, however, at this time a Frenchman, with all the *élan* and ingenuity of his countrymen, and an indomitable perseverance peculiarly his own, who came to a different conclusion. Having some influence at the Egyptian Court, he obtained a concession in 1854 from Said Pasha, then Viceroy of Egypt, for the making of a canal across the Isthmus of Suez. The Sultan's assent was less easily procured, owing to the jealousy which had arisen between English and French political interests. It was not until 1858 that M. Ferdinand de Lesseps found himself in a position to appeal to the public for support. A company was then formed with a capital of £8,000,000. In 1859 the work was begun, and by December 1864 the fresh-water canal, required for the supply of the labourers on the ship-canal, was completed. All, however, did not go on smoothly. Difficulties arose between Ismail Pasha, Said Pasha's successor, respecting the concessions originally granted to the company. The dispute was referred to the Emperor of the French as arbitrator, who decided that the company should give up some important privilege, and receive in lieu thereof a total sum of £4,000,000, with a strip of land, about forty-eight yards wide, on each side of the canal. The ship-canal was then proceeded with; a variety of ingenious machinery being invented by the French engineers to meet the exigencies of their novel and magnificent enterprise. In 1867 an additional capital of £4,000,000 was raised; and on the 17th of November 1869 it was formally opened for navigation in the presence of a host of illustrious personages, representing every European State.

The rapid growth of the tonnage carried by the canal is shown in the following table:—

Year.	No. of Ships.	Tonnage.	Dues paid.
1870	486	654,915	£206,373
1875	1,264	2,423,672	£994,375
1880	2,026	4,344,519	£1,629,577
1885	3,624	8,985,411	£2,488,297
1891	4,207	12,217,986	£2,196,673

Both in respect of tonnage and of the number of vessels Great Britain far exceeds all other nations put together.

The following table shows the number and gross tonnage of vessels of the principal European nations that passed through the canal in 1891 :—

Countries.	No.	Tons.	Countries.	No.	Tons.
Great Britain...	3,217	9,484,608	Austria........	51	169,399
Germany........	318	870,548	Turkey........	40	60,619
France..........	171	616,964	Portugal.......	29	74,798
Holland........	147	369,347	Spain..........	28	98,627
Italy............	116	275,861	Russia.........	21	64,554
Norway........	55	114,016	Greece	5	4,571

The cost of the canal was about 20 million pounds. The total length is 100 miles. The width of the water surface was at first 150 to 300 feet, the width of the bottom 72 feet, and the minimum depth 26 feet. It begins at Port Said, on the Mediterranean, where an artificial harbour has been constructed; proceeds to Kantara; traverses the Abu Ballah Lake; at Ismailia enters Lake Timseh; thence to Serapeum; passes through the Bitter Lakes; and terminates at Suez.

At the end of a dozen years the traffic had increased so enormously that a second canal began to be talked about, and in 1886 the task of widening and also deepening the existing canal was commenced. By 1890 the canal had been deepened to 28 feet, and widened between Port Said and the Bitter Lakes to 144 feet, and from the Bitter Lakes to Suez to 213 feet.

Since 1886 the time of making the transit through the canal has been greatly accelerated. In that year a vessel took on an average thirty-six hours to get through; but in 1890 the average time of passage did not much exceed twenty-four hours. Moreover, since March 1887, the electric light has been used to light the way during the night. The first year that this adjunct was in operation it was used by 395 vessels out of 3,137; in the year 1890, 2,836 out of 3,389 used it. The cost of getting through by electric light amounts to about £10 for each vessel.

The construction of the Suez Canal has called into existence two new towns—Port Said, which has now a population of 19,600 inhabitants; and Ismailia, which, from its central position, has become the principal town of the Isthmus. It is described as "one of the prettiest and most charming spots imaginable. Its trim houses, well-kept streets, and beautiful little gardens form a characteristic picture of French taste and neatness." Suez has largely increased its population, which now numbers 13,000.

ON THE EGYPTIAN HIEROGLYPHICS.

"And the learned walls with hieroglyphics graced."—POPE.

So many allusions are made in the preceding pages to the Egyptian hieroglyphics, that it seems desirable to afford the youthful reader some explanation of their character and meaning.

The term "hieroglyphics"—from the Greek ἱερος and γλυφω—simply means "sacred sculptures;" but it is now applied to those representations of real or imaginary objects by which the Egyptians expressed language. It is supposed that they employed in all about one thousand of these; and by their means they were enabled to convey their ideas to others with extraordinary fulness and accuracy. Their variety is very great. All kinds of quaint ideal forms—the celestial spheres, animals, fishes, reptiles, the different parts of the human body, costume, works of art and science,—all these were made vehicles of thought and sentiment. They were engraved in relief, or sunk below the surface, on walls and public monuments, and similar permanent materials; or they were traced in outline with a pen of reed on wood, papyri, and slabs of stone. The former class of hieroglyphics are sometimes embellished with colours and used as ornamentation; sometimes they are shaded, as it were, of one uniform hue; and sometimes they are sculptured and plain. When variously coloured, they are called polychrome; when shaded, monochrome; when traced in outline on the papyri, linear. They are either arranged in columns perpendicularly, or in horizontal rows, or scattered about the picture they are intended to describe. But it should be remembered that they almost invariably face all in the same direction; and when attached to figures, in the direction of those figures. They form a curious and even fantastic written language, and represent in their various uses the earliest processes in the invention of writing.

Hieroglyphics, according to their prevailing applications, are arranged in three great classes: (1.) Symbolic; (2.) Hieratic; (3.) Demotic (or popular). They are also divided into Ideographs, or those which represent "ideas;" and Phonetics, or those which represent "sounds."

1. *Symbolic.* These may be classified in three groups. First, the "iconographic," or "ideographic," where symbols are used in direct imitation of natural objects—the course which would suggest itself to men in the earliest stage of written thought. Thus, ◯ a circle, would naturally represent the sun; ☾ a crescent, the moon; a male figure, man; a dog, canine animals, and the like. A female figure stands for woman. Put a man and a woman together, and you convey the idea of "human kind." After a while men would begin to make use of these natural objects to convey some figurative meaning, and thus create a second group of symbolic hieroglyphics — namely, the "anaglyphic," or "tropical." For instance: the dog is faithful, and the symbol "dog" was accordingly employed to represent fidelity; the jackal is cunning, and therefore conveyed the idea of craft. Similarly, *a leg caught in a trap* means deceit; *a youth with a finger in his mouth*, an infant; *a woman beating a tambourine*, joy. In time, to prevent the accumulation of symbols to an inconvenient extent, one hieroglyph was made to represent a number of collateral ideas. A *seated male figure*, which originally signified man, now indicated all the functions and relationships of man—as brother, father, priest, governor, labourer—the exact meaning being ascertained by its connection with the phonetic symbols preceding it. The circle ◯ thus came to represent all precious stones; and two legs walking, all locomotive actions. It is said that this class of symbols amounts to about 175; but further research will probably increase the number. The third group, "allegorical," or "enigmatic," includes those objects employed conventionally as emblems of other objects. In this way, *two water-plants, of slightly different form*, stand for Upper and Lower Egypt; *a hawk*, for the god Anubis.

Another class of hieroglyphics is the "phonetic," in which the sign represents, not an object, but a sound. The Egyptian syllabarium consisted of about one hundred and thirty of these signs, and was constructed, according to Champollion, on the following principle:—The figure representing a letter was the likeness of some animal or other object whose name began with that letter. For instance: our word *eagle* begins with E. If we drew an eagle, and always used that figure instead of the letter, we should employ a phonetic hieroglyph. The initial letter of the Egyptian word for *eagle* (*ahom*) is A; in the Egyptian alphabet the figure of an eagle, therefore, stands for A. But each figure represented, not only a letter, but a syllable. Twenty-nine letters constituted the Egyptian alphabet at the best period of the language, or from the fourth to the twenty-first dynasty; and twenty-nine familiar objects represented these letters and their corresponding monosyllables :—

Symbol.	Represented by	Symbol.	Represented by
Aá	an eagle.	*Ma*	a weight.
Aa	an arm.	*Má*	a hole.
Aa	a reed.	*Mu*	an owl.
Ba	a heron.	*Mu*	a vulture.
Ba	a leg.	*Na*	a water-line.
Fi	a cerastes.	*Na*	a red crown.
Ga	an eaglet.	*Nu*	a vase.
Ga	a vase.	*Pa*	a flying goose.
Gi	a viper.	*Pu*	a shutter.
Ha	a leg of a stool.	*Qa*	a knee.
Ha	a house.	*Qa*	a stand.
Ha	a papyrus plant.	*Sa*	top of a quiver.
Há	fore-part of a lion.	*Sa*	a goose.
Hi	twisted cord.	*Sa*	a woof.
Hu	a tusk.	*Su*	a reed.
Hu	a club.	*Su*	a bolt.
Iu	two reeds.	*S(eu)* or *S(et)*	back of seat or chair
Iu	two oblique strokes.	*SHa*	a garden.
Ká	a bowl.	*SHa*	part of dress.
KHa	water-lily leaf.	*SHi*	a pool.
KHa	a mormorus fish.	*Ta*	a spindle.
KHa	a mace.	*Ti*	a hand.
KHi	a sieve.	*Ti*	{ a twisted cord with two loops.
KHu, or *Au*	a calf.	*Tu*	a muller.
K'Hu, or *Au*	a garment.	*Ui*	a duckling.
Lu, or *Ru*	a lion.	*Ui*	{ a cord curved or twisted.
Lu, or *Ru*	a mouth.		
Ma	a pen.		

About ninety additional signs were added to the preceding after the twenty-first dynasty.

It should be added that very often the syllable was written in full — that is, both the initial letter and the vowel were given; as *ha* by *ha* and *ahom* (a papyrus plant, and an eagle).

This explanation is necessarily imperfect; but it will enable the reader to form some idea of the mode in which the written language of the Egyptians was originated and developed.

2. The *Hieratic* character may be described as abridged hieroglyphs, reduced into a kind of cursive or running hand, with no very exact resemblance to their original form. As its name implies, it was confined to the priests, and was employed for state papers, religious treatises, rituals, and legal documents; but also at a later period for all records and memoranda of a public and private character. The Hieratic language prevailed from the era of the fourth dynasty to the third century after Christ.

3. The third class is the *Demotic*, or "popular" — also called the Enchorial ("of the country") — and was that which embodied the language of the common people. It was a still more cursive modification of the hieroglyphics, and, being simple in form, was universally employed for contracts, public documents, and, as the knowledge of hieroglyphics decreased, even for religious matters. It prevailed from the beginning of the sixth century before Christ to the third century of the Christian era, when the early Christians introduced the Greek alphabet.

The clew by which Dr. Young and Champollion were guided independently to the supposed principles of hieroglyphic interpretation was the famous Rosetta Stone. This monument was discovered in 1799. It bore a trilingual inscription on its surface, — an inscription in Hieroglyphical, Demotic, and Greek characters, purporting to be a decree of the priests of Egypt in council at Memphis in honour of Ptolemy V. (about B.C. 196). A close investigation of these characters — first by Dr. Young in 1818, and afterwards by Champollion in 1822 — led to the adoption of certain rules of interpretation, which, though their accuracy was seriously impugned by the late Sir George Cornewall Lewis, have been laboriously illustrated by Lepsius, Bunsen, Jablonski, Hincks, Birch, Goodwin, Heath, Chabus, and others.

The invention of hieroglyphics, called *Neter Kharu*, or "divine words," was ascribed to the god Thoth, the Egyptian Logos, "lord of the hieroglyphs." Pliny attributes it to Menes. Hieroglyphics were not understood by the lower classes, to whom they were as great a mystery as our printed characters are to the peasant who can neither read nor write.

For fuller particulars on this interesting subject I refer the reader to the article "Hieroglyphics" in the "Encyclopædia Britannica;" Champollion, "Grammaire Egyptienne" (Paris, 1841-61); Sir G. Cornewall Lewis, "Astronomy of the Ancients," chap. vi.; Birch, "Introduction to the Study of Hieroglyphics;" "Edinburgh Review" for July 1862; D. I. Heath, M.A., "The Exodus Papyri;" and Bunsen, "Egypt's Place in the World's History" (translated by C. J. Cotterell, M.A.).

THE RAMESSIDS.

ACCORDING to some authorities, the chronology of the Ramessids is given as follows:—Ramesses, or Rameses I., chief of the 19th dynasty; Rameses II., the Great, who reigned sixty-eight years; Rameses III. (the Rhampsinitus of Herodotus), chief of the 20th dynasty, and the Rameses of Medinet-Aboo; Rameses IV.; Rameses V.; Rameses VI., who lived, it is supposed, about 1240 B.C.; and so on, down to Rameses XIII.

TELL-EL-AMARNA TABLETS.

OF recent discoveries one of the most remarkable is a number of clay tablets found accidentally in 1887, by a peasant woman, at Tell-el-Amarna in Upper Egypt, the site of the ancient Arsinoe, about 180 miles south of Cairo. The inscriptions are cuneiform, and in the Aramaic language, resembling Assyrian. The writers are Phœnicians, Amorites, and Philistines, but in no instance Hittites, though Hittites are mentioned. The tablets consist of official despatches and letters, dating from B.C. 1480, addressed to the two Pharaohs, Amenôphis III. and IV., the last of this dynasty, from the kings and governors of Phœnicia and Palestine. There occur the names of three kings killed by Joshua—Adoni-zedek, king of Jerusalem, Japhia, king of Lachish (Josh. x. 3), and Jabin, king of Hazor (xi. 1); also the Hebrews (*Abiri*) are said to have come from the desert. The clay from different parts of Palestine differs, so that it has been found possible by the clay alone to decide where the tablets come from, when the name of the writer is lost. "These letters are the most important historical records ever found in connection with the Bible. They most fully confirm the historical statements of the Book of Joshua, and prove the antiquity of civilization in Syria and Palestine" (Conder's "Tell Amarna Tablets," page 6).

DISCOVERIES AT DEIR-EL-BAHARÎ.

PROFESSOR MASPERO, keeper of the museum at Bûlâk, near Cairo, had his attention in 1870 directed to the fact that scarabs—that is, stone and metal imitations of the beetle (symbols of immortality), originally worn as amulets by royal personages—which were evidently genuine relics of the time of the ancient Pharaohs, were being sold at Thebes and different places along the Nile. This led him to suspect that some hitherto undiscovered burial-place of the Pharaohs had been opened, and that these and other relics, now secretly sold, were a part of the treasure found there. For a long time he failed, with all his ingenuity, to find the source of these rare treasures. At length one of those in the secret volunteered to give information regarding this burial-place. The result was that a party was conducted in 1881 to Deir-el-Baharî, near Thebes, when the wonderful discovery was made of thirty-six mummies of kings, queens, princes, and high priests hidden away in a cavern prepared for them, where they had lain undisturbed for thirty centuries. "The temple of Deir-el-Baharî stands in the middle of a natural amphitheatre of cliffs, which is only one of a number of smaller amphitheatres into which the limestone mountains of the tombs are broken up. In the wall of rock separating this basin from the one next to it some ancient Egyptian engineers had constructed the hiding-place, whose secret had been kept for nearly three thousand years." The exploring party being guided to the place, found behind a great rock a shaft 6 feet square and about 40 feet deep, sunk into the limestone. At the bottom of this a passage led westward for 25 feet, and then turned sharply northward into the very heart of the mountain, where in a chamber 23 feet by 13, and 6 feet in height, they came upon the wonderful treasures of antiquity. The mummies were all carefully secured and brought down to Bûlâk, where they were deposited in the royal museum, which has now been removed to Ghizeh.

Among the most notable of the ancient kings of Egypt thus discovered were Thothmes III., Seti I., and Rameses II. Thothmes III. was the most distinguished monarch of the brilliant eighteenth dynasty. When this mummy was unwound "once more, after an interval of thirty-six centuries, human eyes gazed on the features of the man who had conquered Syria and Cyprus and Ethiopia, and had raised Egypt to the highest pinnacle of her power. The spectacle, however, was of brief duration. The remains proved to be in so fragile a state that there was only time to take a hasty photograph, and then the features crumbled to pieces and vanished like an apparition, and so passed away from human view for ever." "It seems strange that though the body of this man," who overran Palestine with his armies two hundred years before the birth of Moses, "mouldered to dust, the flowers with which it had been wreathed were so wonderfully preserved that even their colour could be distinguished" (Manning's "Land of the Pharaohs").

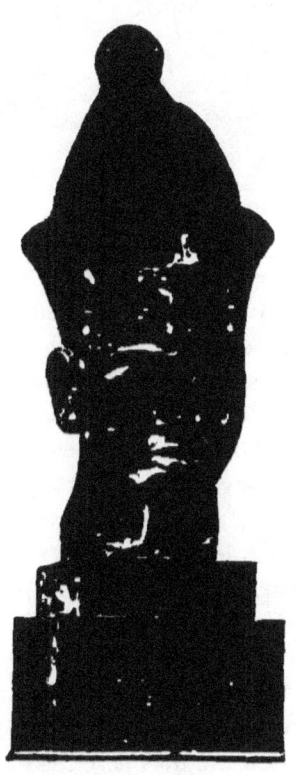

THOTHMES III.

Seti I. (his throne name Merenptah), the father of Rameses II., was a great and successful warrior, also a great builder. The mummy of this Pharaoh, when unrolled, brought to view "the most beautiful mummy-head ever seen within the walls of the museum. The sculptors of Thebes and Abydos did not flatter this Pharaoh when they gave him that delicate, sweet, and smiling profile which is the admiration of travellers.

MUMMY HEAD OF SETI I.

After a lapse of thirty-two centuries, the mummy retains the same expression which characterized the features of the living man. Most remarkable of all, when compared with the mummy of Rameses II., is the striking resemblance between the father and the son. Seti I. is, as it were, the idealized type of Rameses II. He must have died at an advanced age. The head is shaven, the eyebrows are white, the condition of the body points to considerably more than threescore years of life, thus confirming the opinions of the learned, who have attributed a long reign to this king."

Rameses II., the son of Seti I., is probably the Pharaoh of the oppression. During his forty years' residence at the court of Egypt, Moses must have known this ruler well. During his sojourn in Midian, however, Rameses died, after a reign of sixty-seven years, and his body was embalmed and laid in the royal sepulchre in the Valley of the Tombs of Kings beside that of his father. Like the other mummies found hidden in the cave of Deir-el-Baharî, it had been for some reason removed from its original tomb, and probably carried from place to place till finally deposited in the cave where it was so recently discovered.

In 1886, the mummy of this king, the "great Rameses," the "Sesostris" of the Greeks, was unwound, and showed the body of what must have been a robust old man. The features revealed to view are thus described by Maspero: "The head is long and small in proportion to the body. The top of the skull is quite bare. On the temple there are a few sparse hairs, but at the poll the hair is quite thick, forming smooth, straight locks about two inches in length. White at the time of death, they have been dyed a light yellow by the spices used in embalmment. The forehead is low and narrow; the brow-ridge prominent; the eyebrows are thick and white; the eyes are small and close together; the nose is long, thin, arched like the noses of the Bourbons; the temples are sunken; the cheek-bones very prominent; the ears round, standing far out from the head, and pierced, like those of a woman, for the wearing of ear-rings; the jaw-bone is massive and strong; the chin very prominent; the mouth small but thick-lipped; the teeth worn and very brittle, but white and well preserved. The moustache and beard are thin. They seem to have been kept shaven during life, but were probably allowed to grow during the king's last illness, or they may have grown after death. The hairs are white, like those of the head and eyebrows, but are harsh and bristly, and a tenth of an inch in length. The skin is of an earthy-brown, streaked with black. Finally, it may be said the face of the mummy gives a fair idea of the face of the living king. The expression is unintellectual, perhaps slightly animal; but even under the somewhat grotesque disguise of mummification there is plainly to be seen an air of sovereign majesty, of resolve, and of pride."

Both on his father's and mother's side it has been pretty clearly shown that Rameses had Chaldean or Mesopotamian blood in his veins to such a degree that he might be called an Assyrian. This fact is thought to throw light on Isa. lii. 4.

MUMMY HEAD OF RAMESES II.

The Pharaoh of the Exodus was probably Menephtah I., the fourteenth and eldest surviving son of Rameses II. He resided at Zoan, where he had the various interviews with Moses and Aaron recorded in the book of Exodus. His mummy was not among those found at Deir-el-Bahari. It is still a question, however, whether Seti II. or his father Menephtah was the Pharaoh of the Exodus. Some think the balance of evidence to be in favour of the former, whose reign it is known began peacefully, but came to a sudden and disastrous end. The "Harris papyrus," found at Medinet-Abou in Upper Egypt in 1856, a state document written by Rameses III., the second king of the twentieth dynasty, gives at length an account of a great exodus from Egypt, followed by widespread confusion and anarchy. This, there is great reason to believe, was the Hebrew exodus, with which the nineteenth dynasty of the Pharaohs came to an end. This period of anarchy was brought to a close by Setnekht, the founder of the twentieth dynasty.—From Easton's "Illustrated Bible Dictionary," article *Pharaoh*.

Index.

AAH-MES II., his prosperous reign in Egypt, 56; his reason for breaking his alliance with Polycrates of Samos, 56.
Abbas Pasha, administration of Egypt under, 76, 79.
Abou-Seir, pyramids at, erected by kings of the Elephantine dynasty, 47; the rock of, 344, 345.
Abou-Simbel, Belzoni's excavations at, 335; temples at, 335–342.
Abu-Tlea, battle of, 107.
Abydus, ruins at, 218.
Acacia, or sont tree of the Arabs, 33, 34.
Albert N'yanza, the, one of the reservoirs of the Nile, 123.
Alexander the Great, his conquest of Egypt, 59, 60; his plans for developing its resources, 61.
Alexandria founded by Alexander the Great, 61; destruction of the Serapeum at, 71; bombardment of, 93; wealth and population of, 134; its architectural ornaments, 135, 136; picture of its present aspect, 136; its Oriental features, 139–141; a scene at its railway station, 141; its ancient condition, its associations, 142; its religious feuds, 143; its decay, 145; its remarkable ruins, 146; the so-called Pompey's Pillar, 146–148; Cleopatra's Needles, 149, 150; site of the modern city described, 151.
Ali, Mehemet, his massacre of the Mamelukes, 75, 76; incidents of his pashalik, 76.
Almehs, or Almées, the, Egyptian dancing-girls, their costume described, 276, 277; their manners and customs, 277.
Amenemha I., king of Egypt, rebuilds Heliopolis, 47.
Amenemha III., his great erections pointed out, 48; his famous Labyrinth described, 48, 49.
Amunophis II., his capture of Nineveh, 50.
Amyrtaeus, of Sais, the only king of his dynasty, 58.
Animal life of Egypt described, 34–38.
Animal-worship in Egypt, its origin and influence, 26–29, 43, 44.
Annos, or Ormos, king of Egypt, his pyramid at the Mastabat-el-Faroun, 47.
Antinoöpolis, city of, founded by the Emperor Hadrian, 69.
Apis, the Egyptian bull-god, worship of, 196.
Apries, king of Egypt, his prosperous rule, 55, 56.
Arabi Pasha, rebellion of, 93, 94.
Arachieh, the sacred lake, and its temple, 361.
Arians and Athanasians, disputes of, at Alexandria, 143.
Arrian, Greek pentameter by, quoted, 189.
Art in Egypt, influence of the Nile upon, 130.
Assouan, or Syene, in ancient times, 292; view from the cliffs around it, 293; its celebrated quarries, 293, 294.
Athor, the goddess, worship and symbolical representations of, 225.
Aurelian, the Emperor, his defeat of Zenobia, 69.

BAB-EL-MELOOK, or Valley of the Tombs of the Kings, near Thebes, 251–257.
Bahr el-Abiad, the, or White Nile, its course described, 123.
Bahr el-Azrek, the, or Blue Nile, its course described, 123, 124.
Baker, Sir Samuel, discoveries of, 119, 120.
Bartlett, *The Nile-Boat* of, quoted, 285.
Belzoni, quoted, 178, 181, 182; his exploration of the Pyramids, 178, 181, 182.
Beni-hassan, peculiar situation of the Tombs at, 209, 210; their antiquity, 210; their interior described, 210; wall-painting representing a remarkable procession at, 210, 213; Egyptian history depicted by Egyptian artists, 214; the interior of the Tombs regarded as an illustration of ancient Egyptian life, 214–217.
Beyt-el-Wellee, rock-temple at, 324, 325.
Boats in use on the Nile, described, 128, 129.
Boulak, or Old Cairo, view from, 155.

British occupation of Egypt, 94.
Bubastis, great feast of the goddess, described, 129.
Bubastite dynasty of Egypt, 53.
Bull, the sacred, Egyptian worship of, 27, 28.
Burckhardt, the Nubian traveller, quoted, 328, 333.

CAESAR, *de Bello Civili*, quoted, 64.
Cailliaud, *Voyage au Meroe*, quoted, 352.
Cairo, city of, picturesque character of its streets, 155, 156; their purely Oriental aspect described, 156; situation of the city, 156, 157; its history summarized, 157; the citadel, and the prospect from it, 157, 158; the Cairene minarets, 161, 162; life in the streets portrayed, 162; the dancing dervishes, 163, 164, 167; the Cairene donkeys, 167, 168; interior of an Oriental harem, 168, 169.
Cambyses, king of Persia, his invasion and conquest of Egypt, 56; his madness and death, 57, *note;* his treatment of the sacred Apis, 196; plunders Thebes, 233.
Cape of Good Hope, discovery of the passage round the, 72.
Cassius, Avidius, subdues a revolt in Egypt, 69.
Cataract of the Nile, the first, 312, 313; ascent of, described, 314, 315.
Champollion, on the Typhoneion, 226; his *Lettres sur l'Egypte*, quoted, 240, 281, 288.
Christianity, rise of, in Egypt, 70, 143; its struggle with and conquest over Paganism, 144, 145.
Cleopatra, her marriage to Ptolemy XII., 65; fascinates Julius Caesar, who declares her Queen of Egypt, 65; her connection with Antony, and her death, narrated, 66, 67.
Cleopatra's Needles, description of, 149, 150.
Climate of Egypt, its peculiarities, 38.
Colossi, the two, of Thebes, described, 242-245.
Constitution, Egyptian, the, 95, 96.
Crocodile Bird (*Trochilus*) of the Nile, the, 37.
Cuminus, in the *Tour du Monde*, quoted, 277.
Curzon, *Monasteries in the Levant*, quoted, 299.

DAHABEEVAH, a, or Nile-boat, a voyage in, 205, 206.
Dakkeh, temple of Thoth at, 329, 330.
Date palm in Egypt, the, 33.
Death, Egyptian ideas concerning, 252.

Debodeh, the scenery of the Nile near, 322, 323.
Delta, the, landscape of, 152.
Dendera, the temple of, described, 218, 221; its great portico, 222; its dimensions, 225; account of other remains at, 225, 226; the Typhoneion, 226.
Dendour, Romano-Egyptian temple at, 325.
Denon, Baron, his *Voyage en Egypte*, quoted, 276.
Derr, the Temple at, 333, 334.
Dervishes, the dancing, their peculiar ceremony described, 162-164, 167.
Desert, the struggle of the Nile with the, 117, 118.
Diodorus, the historian, his account of Rameses III., 232.
Divisions, administrative, of Egypt, 96.
Djebel Aboufodde, the caverns of, 218.
Dodekarchy, the, or Twelve Kings, their rule in Egypt, 54.
Donkeys of Cairo, the, their characteristics, 167, 168.
Donne, W. B., quoted, 271, 272.
Drumann, on the worship of the bull in Egypt, 28.
Dual Control, the, 91, 92, 94.

EDFOO, the ancient city of, 282, 283; its two temples, 283, 284.
Edmonstone, Sir A., quoted, 357.
Egypt, its attractiveness for the student and traveller, 17, 18; its remote antiquity, 18, 19; its monotonous natural features, 19; its position in regard to other countries, 19, 20; its physical geography, 20; etymology of its name, 23; its *nomes*, or districts, in the olden time, 23-26; its worship of animals, 26-29; Roman divisions of, 29; its general aspect, 29, 30, 33; its soil and vegetation, 33, 34; its animal life, 34-38; its climate, 38; the khamsin in, 39; its present population, 39, 40, 113; its money, weights, and measures, 40; its history under the Pharaohs, 42-56; its history under the Persians, 57-59; under its Greek kings, 59-67; under the Romans, 68-72; annals of modern Egypt, 72-113; its divisions, 96, 113; its commerce, 113; its railways and telegraphs, 113.
Egyptians, manners and customs of the ancient, described by Herodotus, 27, 28, 57, 58.
Egyptian Queens, tombs of the, near Medinet-Aboo, 258.
'Eilythia, or El-Kab, rock-tombs of, 280-282.
Elephantine, island of, its architectural ruins, 295, 296; its ancient history, 296.

INDEX.

El Ghizeh, pyramids of, 174-182.
El Mesaourat, ruined temples at, 351, 354.
Epistrategiae, the, of Egypt, under the Romans, 68.
Erment, the ancient *Hermonthis*, ruins of, 273, 274.
Esneh, ruined temple at, 275, 276; rendezvous and residence of the Almehs, 276-278.
Ethiopia, origin of the name, 348.

FAIOUM, the valley of, multitude of its roses, 30.
Fairholt, *Up the Nile*, quoted, 263, 274.
Fergusson, *History of Architecture*, quoted, 176, 184, 210.
Financial condition of Egypt, 108, 111-113.
Firmus, his assumption of Egyptian sovereignty, 70.

GEBEL-ADHA, the rock-temple at, 343.
Gebel-Ain, site of ancient Crocodilopolis, 274.
Germanicus, his visit to Thebes, 52; his consultation with the bull Apis, 68, 69.
Ghirsché Housseyn, ruins of a temple at, 325-329.
Gibbon, *Decline and Fall*, quoted, 70.
Gordon, General, appointed Governor-General of the Soudan, 88; his administration, 88, 89; letter from, 89, 90; commissioned to withdraw the Egyptian garrisons from the Soudan, 104; his defence of Khartûm, 105, 106; expedition to relieve, 106-108; his death, 108.
Gordon, Lady Duff, *Letters from Egypt*, quoted, 162.
Great Oasis, the, description of, 358; its great temple, 358, 359; its necropolis, 359, 360; its remaining monuments, 360.
Greek era of Egyptian history, 59-67.
Greek influence in Egypt, rise and spread of, 59, 60.
Grote, *History of Greece*, quoted, 56.
Gubat, battle of, 107.

HADJUR SILSILEH, the pass of, 285.
Hadrian, the Emperor, founds the city of Antinoöpolis, 69.
Hamilton, *Aegyptiaca*, quoted, 221, 288, 290, 294.
Harem, scene in an Oriental, 168, 169.
Harpers' Tomb, the, in the "Valley of the Tombs of the Kings," 256, 257.
Hecataeus, visit of, to Thebes, 233, 234.
Heeren, *Historical Researches*, quoted, 50, 248, 353, 354.

Heliopolis, rebuilt by Amenemha I., 47; road from Cairo to, 198; its remains described, 198; its historical associations, 198, 199; its sacredness in the olden time, 199; its scanty relics, 199-201.
Herodotus, the historian, on the worship of the sacred bull, 27, 28; his visit to Egypt, 57, 58; quoted, 177, 183, 190, 308.
Hieroglyphics, their origin, meaning, and interpretation, 370-374.
Homer, quoted, 227, 317, 355.
Hopley, Howard, *Under Egyptian Palms*, quoted, 30, 33; on the birds of Egypt, 35-37; description of the railway-station at Alexandria, 141; on the donkeys and donkey-drivers of Cairo, 167, 168; on the ruins of Thebes, 228; on the temples of Philae, 303, 304-306.
Hor-em-heb, his history told by the monuments, 286.

IBREEM, history of the castle of, 334.
Iseion, the, at Memphis, reference to, 196.
Isis, worship of the goddess, introduced into the Roman cities, 69; her name and attributes explained, 310, 311; her temple at Abou-Simbel, 340-342.
Ismail Pasha, his administration of Egypt, 79, 80; adopts the title of Khedive, 79, 80; his deposition, 91.
Ismail, son of Mehemet Ali, conquest of Nubia by, 84, 320, 321.
Ismailia, on the Suez Canal, 369.

JOSEPHUS, *Antiquities*, quoted, 199.
Jupiter Ammon, oracle of, referred to by Diodorus, 353; visited by Alexander the Great, 60, 362.
Juvenal, the Roman poet, banished to the Libyan Oases, 357.

KALABSCHE, rock-temples at, described, 323, 324.
Karnak, the modern village of, 258; Palace of the Kings at, 260-263; sculpture representing Sheshonk at, 263; general description of the ruins, 263, 264.
Keble, *The Christian Year*, quoted, 244, 317.
Keneh, scenery of the plain of, 218.
Kennard, *Travels in Egypt*, quoted, 139.
Kenrick, *Ancient Egypt*, quoted, 213, 234, 334.
Kerbekan, battle of, 108.
Khamsin, the, effects of, described, 39.
Khartûm, description of, 83; defence of, by Gordon, 105-108.
Khnum, the divinity of the waters, 362.

Kinglake, A. W., *Eothen*, quoted, 186, 187.
Kingsley, Canon, *Hypatia*, quoted, 144.
Kings of Egypt, the, why they erected their mausoleums or pyramids, 172.
Koum-Ombos, ruined temples of, 288-290.
Kurschid Pasha, Governor of the Soudan, 87.

LABYRINTH, the, of Amenemha, described by Herodotus, 48, 49.
Lepsius, *Reise Egypten*, quoted, 197.
Lindsay, Lord, *Letters from Holy Lands*, quoted, 312.
Little Oasis, the, or El-Dakkel, description of, 360, 361.
Longfellow, quoted, 41, 205.
Lucan, *Pharsalia*, quoted, 114.
Luxor, modern village of, described, 264, 267; temple and monuments at, 267-271.

MADOX, *Excursions in Egypt*, quoted, 149.
Mahdi, the, his early history, 97, 98; proclaims a religious war, 98, 99; captures Obeid, 99; destroys an Egyptian army under Colonel Hicks, 100; besieges and takes Khartûm, 105, 108.
Mamelukes, the, Egypt under the sway of, 72, 75; their massacre by Mehemet Ali, 75, 76.
Manetho, the Egyptian annalist, on the birth-place of Moses, 197.
Mariette, his discoveries in connection with the sphinx, 189.
Marriage, an Egyptian, description of, 273-280.
Martineau, Harriet, *Eastern Life*, quoted, 117, 118, 148, 172, 239, 240, 243, 244, 280, 286, 287, 330, 331, 336.
Mastabat-el-Faroun, pyramid at, erected by Annos, 47.
Mausoleums, the royal, of Egypt, how and why erected, 172, 173.
Medinet-Aboo, temple at, 246.
Melly, G., *Khartoum, or the Two Niles*, quoted, 293.
Memphis, site of, 190; foundation and early history, 190; its decay, 191; its Triad, 191; its Serapeion described, 191-196; its Iseion, 196; its statue of Rameses, 197; Biblical associations of Memphis, 197.
Memphite dynasty of Egypt, 44-46.
Men, or Menes, existence of, doubtful, 42, 43.
Menzaleh, Lake, the papyrus of, 30.
Merien-ptah, the Biblical Pharaoh, introduces the worship of Seth or Satan, 52.

Meroë, ancient kingdom of, 348, 349.
Meroë, city of, its position and ruins, 349.
Milman, Dean, *History of Latin Christianity*, quoted, 143.
Milton, *Paradise Lost*, quoted, 114, 190.
Mimosa Nilotica, the, 33, 34.
Mnevis, the sacred ox of Heliopolis, worshipped by the Egyptians, 28, 29.
Modern history of Egypt, 72-113.
Mohammed Tewfik, Khedive of Egypt, 91.
Moore, Thomas, the poet, quoted, 291, 343.
Mosques of Cairo, described by Lady Duff Gordon, 162.
Mud of the Nile, the, described by St. Hilaire, 33.

NECHAO, King of Egypt, his victories in Judah and Assyria, 55; his engineering and naval operations, 55.
Nectanebus II., the last of the Pharaohs, defeated by the Persians, 59.
Niger, Pescennius, declares himself Emperor of Egypt, 69.
Nile, the river, its great struggle against the forces of the Desert, 117, 118; discovery of its sources accomplished, 118-120; the course of the White Nile described, 123; course of the Blue Nile, 123, 124; progress of the united stream traced to the Mediterranean, 124, 125; its average fall and velocity, 125; to what its rise is due, 125; height of the inundation, 126; processes of irrigation, 126; worshipped as a god, 127, 128; the river-boats described, 128, 129; festivals and pageants held on the Nile, 129; its animal and vegetable life, 129, 130; origin of the word *Nilus*, 130; influence of the Nile on Egyptian and Greek art, 130, 133; scenery of its banks, 205, 206.
Nile Valley, the, its dimensions, and general character of its scenery, 20, 23.
Nilometer, the, of Memphis, for gauging the ebb and flow of the river, 196, 197; at Rhoda, 206.
Nilus, the god, origin and festival of, 127; a statue of, described, 127, 128.
Nomes, the, or ancient districts of Egypt, enumerated, 23-26.
Northern Oasis, the, or El Siwah, its situation and warm springs, 361; its numerous antiquities, 361-363.
Nubia, origin of the name, 317; extent and history of the country, 318, 319; manners and customs of its inhabitants, 319, 320; principal towns, 83, 84, 320; its conquest by Ismail Pasha, 84, 320, 321.

INDEX.

OASES, their general characteristics described, 356, 357; their literary and historical associations, 357; the five chief oases enumerated, 358; the Great Oasis, 358-360; the Little Oasis, 360, 361; the Northern, 361-363.
Obelisk, the, of Osirtesen I., 200, 201; some celebrated obelisks enumerated, 202.
Osirei, the sarcophagus of, in the Soane Museum, 255.
Osiris, the god, legendary history of, 307; his various names and attributes, 308; his mythic history, 308-310; his temple at Abou-Simbel, 336-340.
Osirtesen I., his sovereignty over Egypt, 47, 48.
Osirtesen II. and III., their achievements in Ethiopia, 48.
Osman Digna, insurrection of, 100; military operations against, 103.

PAGANISM, decline of, in Egypt, 71, 143, 144.
Palgrave, W. G., description of Luxor and Karnak quoted, 264, 267.
Pasht, the goddess, festival of, 28.
Persian era of Egypt, 57-59.
Pharaonic era of Egypt, 42-56.
Pharos at Alexandria, and origin of the word, 61.
Polycrates, King of Samos, his alliance with Aahmes, King of Egypt, 56.
Pompey's Pillar, described, 146; its history, 147; a relic of a former temple, 147, 148; sketch of the surrounding landscape, 148.
Population, present, of Egypt, 39, 40, 113.
Port Said, 369.
Priests, tombs of the, 258.
Propertius, quoted, 67.
Psammetichus I., his reign over Egypt, 54, 55.
Psammetichus II. completes the subjugation of Ethiopia, 55.
Ptolemy Epiphanes, 64; P. Euergetes, 63; P. Philadelphus, 62, 63; P. Philometor, 64; P. Philopater, 63; P. Soter, 62; Ptolemy XII., 64, 65.
Ptolemys, kings of Egypt, chronological table of, 67.
Pyramids, their eternal freshness of attraction, 169, 170; their associations, 170, 171; their probable origin, 171-173; their massive construction, 173, 174; description of the Great Pyramid, 174-177; of the Second, 177-182; of the Third, 182; groups of pyramids, 182, 183; legends connected with them, 183, 184; mechanical skill displayed in their erection, 184.

RAMESSIDS, the, Egypt under, 51-53, 374.
Rameses II., capture of Salem by, 51; his legendary fame, 51, 52; extent of his empire, 52.
Rameses III., subdues an insurrection in Ethiopia, 53; his reign in Thebes, 232, 233.
Rameseion, the, of Thebes, 235; its admirable position, 236; the Grand Hall, 239, 240; its sculptures and frescoes, 240-242; its dimensions, 242.
Rameseion, the, Southern, of Thebes, particulars of, 246-248.
Rapids, or Cataracts of the Nile, 124, 125, 312-315.
Religious creed of the Egyptians, 171, 172, 287.
Renan, Ernest, quoted, 188.
Richardson, Dr., *Travels along the Mediterranean Coast*, quoted, 248, 323, 341.
Ritter, Carl, *Erdkunde*, quoted, 335.
Roman era in Egyptian history, 68-72.
Roman Senate, admittance of Egyptians into the, 69.
Romer, Mrs., *Tombs of Egypt*, quoted, 313, 329, 335.
Russell, Dr., *Nubia and Abyssinia*, 354.

SABACO, King of Egypt, his alliance with Hoshea, King of Israel, 53, 54.
Said Pasha, administration of, 79.
Sebaste Caesareum, or Temple of Caesar, at Alexandria, remains of, 149.
Seethee I., or Sethos, his conquests enumerated, 51.
Senefern, King of Egypt, 44, 45.
Serapéion, the, at Alexandria, destruction of, 71.
Serapéion, the, of Memphis, described, 192; temple of Osiris-Apis, 195.
Sethos, his arbitrary rule in Egypt, 54.
Severus, the Roman Emperor, visit of to Egypt, 69.
Shakspeare, quoted, 114, 129.
Sheikh-Abadeh, village of, 218.
Shepherd Kings of Egypt, their conquest of the land, 50; expelled by Aahmes I., 50.
Sheshonk, or Shishak, plunders Jerusalem, 233.
Ship, the Sacred, description and allegorical meaning of, 354, 355.
Shufu, King of Egypt, founder of the Great Pyramid, 46.
Silsileh, the sandstone quarries of, 285, 286.
Siout, the capital of Upper Egypt, described, 218.
Smith, Alexander, quoted, 152.
Smith, Rev. A. C., *The Nile and its*

INDEX.

Banks, quoted, 34, 43, 44, 139, 167, 198, 206.
Smyth, Professor Piazzi, *The Great Pyramid*, quoted, 171.
Soil of Egypt, properties of the, 33.
Soleb, temple of Amun-Ra at, 347, 348.
Soudan, the, its area and population, 80, 83; its chief towns, 83, 84, 320; slave-trade in, 84, 88–90; its conquest by Ismail Pasha, 84, 320, 321; Gordon's administration of, 88–91; insurrection in, under the Mahdi, 97–108.
Soul, belief of the Egyptians in the immortality of the, 309.
Sozomen, the historian, quoted, 71.
Spenser, quoted, 291.
Sphinx, the, described by W. H. Bartlett, 185; by Harriet Martineau, 186; by Dean Stanley, 186; by A. W. Kinglake, 186–188; its dimensions, 188; its antiquity, 188; discoveries connected with it, 188, 189; supposed erection of, by Thothmes IV., 50, 51.
Stanley, Dean, on the Sphinx, 186; on the ruins of Thebes, 228; on the scenery around Thebes, 229, 230; on the "Tombs of the Kings," at Thebes, 253.
St. Hilaire, on the Nilotic mud, quoted, 33.
St. Jean d'Acre, besieged by Stopford and Napier, 76.
St. John, J. A., quoted, 221.
Suakim, 84, 100, 103.
Suez Canal, history and construction of, 365–369.

Tacitus, quoted, 52.
Tamai, battle of, 103.
Tarkus, King of Egypt, the Tirhakah of Ethiopia, 54.
Tel-el-Kebir, battle of, 94.
Temple at Dendera, 218–225; at Medinet-Aboo, 246; of Rameses, 246–248; at Karnak, 260; at Luxor, 267; at Erment, 273; at Esneh, 275; at Edfoo, 283; at Hadjur Silsileh, 286; at Koum Ombos, 288–290; at Elephantine, 295; at Philae, 300–307; at Debodeh, 322; at Kalabsché, 323; at Beyt-el-Wellee, 324; at Dendour, 325; at Girsché-Housseyn, 325; at Dakkeh, 329; at Derr, 333; at Abou-Simbel, 336–342; at Gebel-Adha, 343; at Wady Halfa, 344; at Soleb, 347; at Meroë, 349; at Woad Naja, 350; at El-Mesaourat, 352; at El-Khargeh, 359; at El-Dakkel, 360; at El-Siwah, 361; at Ummebeda, 361.
Tennyson, Alfred, quoted, 17, 65, 134, 244.
Thackeray, *From Cornhill to Cairo*, quoted, 169.

Thebaid, the, its boundaries, 271; general features of, 271, 272.
Thebes, city of, 227; origin of the name, 228, 229; its admirable situation, 229, 230; records of its annals, 230–235; the Rameseion, described, 235–242; the two Colossi, 242–245; the Thothmeseion, 246; the palace-temple of Rameses, 246–248; a labyrinth of tombs, 248–258.
Theodosius I., prohibits idol-worship, 71.
Thinite dynasty of Egypt, 43.
Thomson, James, quoted, 356.
Thothmes I. and II., their various achievements, 50; Thothmes III., his conquests in Syria and Mesopotamia, 50; Thothmes IV., erects the Sphinx, 50, 51.
Thothmeseion, the, of Thebes, 246.
Tombs at Thebes—*See* "Priests, tombs, of;" "Egyptian Queens, tombs of;" "Bab-el-Melook, or Tomb of the Kings."
Typhon, the Egyptian personification of Evil, 310.
Typhoneion, the, at Dendera, 226.

Ummebeda, Temple of Amun at, 362.
Upper Egypt, its general aspect as described by Mr. Howard Hopley, 30, 33.

Vegetation, the, of Egypt, 33, 34.
Victoria N'yanza, the, a source of the Nile, 119, 120.
Vopiscus, the historian, quoted, 70.
Vulture, the, or "Pharaoh's Hen," 37.
Vyse, General Howard, *On the Pyramids*, quoted, 175.

Wady Halfa, cataract and temple near, 344.
Wady Sebou, ruins at, described, 332, 333.
Warburton, Eliot, *The Crescent and the Cross*, quoted, 75, 126, 183, 184, 199, 298, 335.
Wilkinson, Sir Gardner, *multa opera*, quoted, 28, 47, 52, 54, 127, 173, 190, 234, 257, 268, 284, 288, 309, 311, 325, 327.
Woad-Naja, architectural ruins at, 350, 351.
Wolseley, Lord, expedition under, to rescue General Gordon, 106–108.
Wordsworth, William, quoted, 205.

Xerxes, King of Persia, crushes an insurrection in Egypt, 57.

Zebehr Pasha, 89, 105.
Zenobia, Queen of Palmyra, conquers Egypt, 69; is herself defeated by Aurelian, 69.
Ziczac, or "crocodile bird" of Herodotus, 274, 275.

www.ingramcontent.com/pod-product-compliance
Lightning Source LLC
Chambersburg PA
CBHW030350230426
43664CB00007BB/601